# Cooking for Today

# Margo Oliver's
# Cooking for Today

**A Today Magazine Cookbook**

First published in 1982 by
Today Magazine Inc.
2180 Yonge Street, Suite 1702
Toronto, Ontario M4S 3A2

**Canadian Cataloguing in Publication Data**

Oliver, Margo, 1923–
  Cooking for today

Includes index.
ISBN 0-88923-000-5

1. Cookery,   I. Title.

TX715.044        641.5        C82-094247-2

Design & Illustrations: Marg Round
Cover Photography: Doug Lingard


Printed and bound in Canada

# Contents

## Salads 49

Carrot-Sprout Salad, Far East Salad, Bean and Chick Pea Salad, Swiss Radish Salad, Potato-Cheese Salad in Tomato Cups, Ham and Egg Salad, Mushroom-Cheese Salad, Left-over Lamb Salad, Mint Dressing, Wiener and Potato Salad, Macaroni and Cheese Salad, Bean and Ham Salad, Spanish Chicken Salad, Chicken and Melon Salad, Grapefruit and Turkey Salad, Fish Salad, Rice and Tuna Salad, Piquant Cauliflower-Salmon Salad, Smoky Caesar Salad, Salad Croutons, Cheese Crab and Potato Salad, Seafood Salad, Thousand Island Mold with Shrimp, Cooked Shrimp, Tomato Aspic with Vegetables, Boiled Dressing, Jellied Potato Salad, Jellied Avocado Salad with Strawberries, Honey Dressing, Confetti Salad, Poppy Seed Dressing.

## Sandwiches and Breads 59

Favorite Whole Wheat Bread, Oat-Bran Bread, Wheat Germ Hamburger Buns, Pita Bread, Chicken Pockets, Italian-Style Pockets, Curried Beef Pockets, Spinach Pasties, Whole Wheat Biscuit Dough, Meat and Potato Pasties, Soybean Turnovers, Carrot and Egg Turnovers, Deviled Western Sandwiches, French-Toasted Ham Sandwiches, Broiled Bacon and Onion Sandwiches, Swiss Broiled Sandwiches, Grilled Peanut Butter Sandwiches, Grilled Tofu Sandwiches, Club House Wieners, Corn Burgers, Butterfly Burgers, Hashed Brown Burgers, Fish Burgers, Salmon French Toast Sandwiches, Puffy Tuna Sandwiches, Lobster Sandwiches.

## Main Dishes 70

Ground Beef and Noodles, Leftover Beef and Macaroni, Swiss Spaghetti, New Zealand Macaroni and Cheese Loaf, Mince and Barley, Stuffed Zucchini with Tomato Sauce, Chili-Stuffed Tomatoes, Beef and Vegetables, Bulgarian Moussaka, Broccoli and Ham Casserole, Corned Beef Hash Cakes, Scalloped Potatoes and Wieners, Chicken with Almonds, Turkey Cakes, Mushroom Sauce, Turkey-Stuffed Avocados, Chicken Liver Spaghetti Sauce, Quick Pasta Sauce, Ham and Eggs à la King, Corn Bread, Deviled Eggs on Toast, Scalloped Eggs and Cheese, Zucchini Omelet Italian Style, Crab Crêpes, Shrimp and Cucumbers, Scallops and Asparagus, Salmon Supper, Egg-Tuna Bake, Creamed Tuna on Toast, Cheese and Noodles, Cheese Pie, Vegetarian Pizza, Beans Italiano, Stir-Fried Vegetables, Vegetable Sukiyaki.

## Desserts 85

Strawberries Cardinal, Yogurt Topping, Strawberries with Raspberry Sherbet, Spiced Pineapple and Blueberries, Fresh Apricots and Peaches, Honey Cream, Peach Crumble, Banana Whip, Orange Fluff, Cheese Layers, Ginger Ice Cream, Apple Snow, Spanish Cream, Chocolate Sauce, Lime Parfaits, Jellied Strawberries and Pineapple, Peach Crisp, Prune Puff, Honey Apples, Johnny Cake with Maple Syrup.

# 3 Dinner

## Appetizers 92

Ham Pâté, Quick Chicken Liver Pâté, Shrimp Pâté, Potted Salmon, Eggplant Appetizer, Herbed Tomato Juice, Peach Appetizer, Melon Frappé, Melon Ambrosia, Fruit Cocktail.

## Soups 96

Asparagus-Potato Soup, Avocado Soup, Tortilla Bits, Lettuce Soup, Pumpkin Soup, Tomato-Onion Soup, Creamy Herb Soup, Spinach Soup, Celery Consommé, Consommé Madrilène, Consommé à l'Alsacienne, Blender Vegetable Soup, Quick Curried Beef Soup, Cream of Green Onion Soup, Green Pepper and Tomato Soup, Jellied Gazpacho.

## Main Dishes    101

Savory Sirloin Tip, Wine Gravy, German-Style Pot Roast, Pot Roast with Kidney Beans, Beef in Beer, Home Corned Beef, Corned Beef Dinner, Sweet-Hot Mustard, Freezer Meatballs, Curried Meatballs, Meatballs Stroganoff, Creole Meatballs, Meatballs Polynesian Style, Hamburger Pie, Porcupine Beef Loaf, Beef Strips in Onion Sauce, Steak and Kidney Pudding, Suet Pastry, Groundnut Stew, Short Ribs and Dumplings, Dumplings, Ranch Ribs, Jellied Tongue, Liver and Bacon Patties, Blanquette of Veal, Jellied Veal and Pork, Veal and Mushrooms, Veal Piccate, Old-Fashioned Veal and Pork Loaf, Veal and Pork Pie, Cheese Biscuit Dough, Loin of Pork with Peach Glaze, Pot-Roasted Pork Shoulder, Sweet and Sour Pork Tenderloin Bits, Pork Chops in Cider, Pork Chops with Onion Sauce, Pork Hocks and Bean Stew, Pork Loaf Oriental, Vegetable Sauce, Chilied Pork Balls, English-Style Boiled Lamb, Mock Venison, Minty Deviled Lamb Chops, Lamb Chops with Potatoes, Lamb Pie, Lamb and Rice Indian Style, Lamb Loaf with Onion Sauce, Onion Sauce, Persian Meat Loaf, Rabbit à l'Orange, Almond-Stuffed Capon, Wine Gravy, Cornish Game Hens Bonne Femme, Scandinavian Roast Goose, Coq au Vin, Old-Fashioned Pressed Chicken, Chicken Cutlets, Stuffed Chicken Breast, Chicken in a Chemise, Spicy Chicken Wings, Honey-Garlic Wings, Hawaiian Wings, Salmon and Cucumber Sauce, Salmon Steaks with Vermouth Sauce, Broiled Ocean Perch, Broiled Mackerel, Mustard Sauce, Herbed Fillets, Fillets of Sole Jeannine, Mediterranean Fish Pie, Cod in Milk, Indian Ocean Fish Curry, Coconut Milk, Cod Cakes, Shrimp and Scallop Curry, Scampi in Creamy Wine Sauce, Baked Vegetable Loaf, Mushroom Sauce, Soybean-Nut Loaf, Tomato Sauce, Split Pea Loaf, Stuffed Cabbage Leaves, Lentil and Barley Stew.

## Salads    137

Mimosa Salad, Red Cabbage Slaw, Lettuce-Pickle Slaw, Turnip Salad, Cheesy Waldorf Salad, Tomato-Yogurt Salad, Cucumber and Yogurt, Hot Spinach-Macaroni Salad, Blender Gazpacho Salad, Eggs in Jelly, Jellied Slaw, Cranberry Salad Mold, Tomato Mayonnaise, Sesame Dressing, Soy Dressing, Lime-Honey Dressing.

## Breads    142

Whole Wheat Rolls, Cheese Buns, Freeze and Bake Rolls, Seeded Batter Buns, Butter Biscuits, Herbed Biscuits, Herb Popovers, Savory French Bread, Crusty French Stick.

## Vegetables    146

Asparagus Indian Style, Yellow Beans Spanish Style, Sesame Green Beans, Herbed Lima Beans, Ginger Beets, Stir-Fried Broccoli, Scalloped Cabbage, Fried Chinese Cabbage, Savory Carrots, Creamed Cauliflower and Peas, Celery Amandine, Celery Victor, Curried Creamed Corn, Indian Corn, Cucumbers in Cream, Butter-Steamed Leeks, Creamed Radishes, Peas in Brown Butter Sauce, Scalloped Peas and Onions, Puffy Baked Potatoes, Potato Cakes, Kugley, Potatoes with Dill, Pumpkin and Corn, Baked Tomatoes with Herbed Corn, Turnip and Apples, Turnip Pudding, Zucchini Fritters, Savory Noodles, Green Noodles and Mushrooms, Fettucine, Nutty Brown Rice, Barley and Peas, Barley and Celery.

## Desserts    157

Pineapple and Strawberries, Grapefruit à la Mode, Peaches with Citrus Freeze, Pears and Blueberries, Pears with Sabayon, Strawberry Shortcakes, Rich Shortcake Biscuits, Lemon Baked Apples, Apple Cream, Frozen Eggnog with Rum-Fruit Sauce, Rum-Fruit Sauce, Raspberry Parfait, Coconut Bavarian Cream with Melon, Rich Chocolate Custard, Ginger-Orange Bavarian Cream, Praline Fromage, Café au Lait Cheesecake, Egg White Custard, Rum-Raspberry Sauce, Queen of Puddings, Raisin Rice Pudding, Honey-Apple Crisp, Rhubarb Pudding, Cherry Cups, Cherry Sauce, Colonial Pudding, Cranberry Pudding, Cinnamon-Orange Sauce, Pineapple Upside-Down Cake, Marmalade Pudding, Caramel Sauce, Cheese and Pear Dumplings, English Apple Pie, Custard Sauce, Deep Plum Pie, Plum Sauce, Rhubarb-Raisin Pie, Presidential Pumpkin Pie, Pumpkin-Pecan Pie, Whipped Orange Pie, Chocolate Wafer Crumb Crust, Pink Grapefruit Chiffon Pie, Standard Pastry.

## 4  Specials

# Preface

Cooking should be one of the great pleasures of living. Our travels and the new people who have come to live in our country have given us a certain sophistication about food. And the variety of food items available from all over the world add to the fascination of cooking. Yet there's an inclination to think that today's cooks are interested only in recipes that are quick and cheap. I just don't believe that's so. Certainly in this busy world, when so often all adults in a household go to work each day, there are times when speedy dishes are needed. But most people who really like to cook are interested first in goodness. They want both good taste and good nutrition, and for this combination they are willing to spend the time and the money when they can.

This book, then, is concerned with today's cooks — those who love to cook. I've considered nutrition, using plenty of whole wheat flour and other good-for-you ingredients, cutting down on sugar where possible and including some vegetarian dishes. Because we all seem to be constantly short of time, I've added do-ahead tips to make some of the more complicated dishes possible for even the busiest cook.

Of course, there are occasions when time, money and nutrition are all forgotten for the joys of some sinfully rich or expensive dish. There are some recipes here for times like that, too.

To help in recipe selection, I've divided the book in a unique way, with sections for each meal — Breakfast/Brunch, Lunch/Supper, Dinner and a final section for Specials such as after-school snacks and what to serve with tea or coffee.

If cooking is your pleasure, I hope this book will add to it each day. Even if it's not, I hope you'll find recipes here that you'll want to try and that they will give you pleasure when you see and taste the results.

# 1
# Breakfast & Brunch

By now everyone has heard how important breakfast is for a general feeling of well-being all day. In fact, it's so important that as much thought should be given to it as to any of the other meals. Of course, that's difficult in many homes, what with everyone dashing off in all directions at different times, but when possible, a few special things will make the first meal of the day not only nutritionally right but more appealing, even to those who have a hard time eating in the morning.

The very North American brunch is a nice meal and one of my favorite ways to entertain. Even after a busy week it's a weekend pleasure to have friends in around noon on Saturday or Sunday for some good food and a visit. Since brunch is usually an entertaining meal, most of the suitable recipes here are planned for larger numbers of servings and are less economical than many of the family breakfast ideas.

# Starters and Drinks

Nearly all of us start the day with a glass of orange juice or half a grapefruit. But who doesn't enjoy a complete change now and then? Here are fruit mixtures and juice treats to tempt even the most tired appetites, as well as some special hot drinks. All fruit dishes that are chilled can, of course, be prepared well in advance.

## Coddled Apples

*1/2 cup sugar*
*2 cups water*
*4 large cooking apples*
*1 tsp. grated lemon rind*
*cream*

Combine sugar and 2 cups water in a large saucepan. Set over high heat and stir until sugar dissolves, then boil 5 minutes.

While syrup is cooking, cut apples into quarters and remove cores. Do not peel. Drop apple quarters into boiling liquid. Add lemon rind. Bring back to a boil, turn down heat and simmer until apples are just tender but not breaking up, about 10 minutes. Turn apple pieces once during cooking.

Lift apple pieces out of syrup with a slotted spoon and put into a bowl. Boil syrup hard until it thickens slightly, about 5 minutes. Pour over apples. Cool.

Serve 2 sections per person and pass the cream. (Serves 8.)

## Apple Flowers

*6 cooking apples*
*1/4 cup red currant jelly*
*six 1/2-inch cubes process or cream cheese*
*butter or margarine*
*1/4 cup water*

Heat oven to 350°F.

Core apples from stem end, leaving blossom end intact to hold filling. Do not peel. Cut each apple into 6 wedges from top to about halfway down toward the bottom. Put 2 tsp. jelly in each apple and add a cube of cheese, pushing it well down into the cavity. Add 1/2 tsp. butter or margarine to each cavity.

Set apples in a baking dish just large enough to hold them. Add 1/4 cup water to baking dish.

Bake until apples are just tender, about 30 minutes. Serve warm. (Serves 6.)

## Grapefruit with Strawberries

*3 large pink grapefruit*
*1 pt. strawberries*
*2 tbsp. sugar*
*mint sprigs*

Peel and section grapefruit and divide sections among 6 sherbet glasses. Chill.

Wash and hull strawberries. Set 6 perfect berries aside for garnish and mash the rest with a fork and press them through a sieve (or buzz in glass of blender) to make a purée. Add sugar and let stand, stirring often, until sugar is dissolved.

Spoon strawberry mixture over grapefruit at serving time and garnish with a whole strawberry and a sprig of mint. (Serves 6.)

## Gingery Pears

6 large pears
$1/3$ cup sugar
3 tbsp. chopped preserved ginger
3 tbsp. ginger syrup (from preserved ginger)
3 tbsp. water

Heat oven to 350°F.

Peel pears and cut into halves. Remove cores and put pear halves, cut side up, in a shallow baking dish large enough to hold them in a single layer. Spoon some of the sugar into the hollowed-out place in each pear half and add some of the chopped ginger to each.

Combine ginger syrup and 3 tbsp. water and pour into bottom of dish. Cover with aluminum foil. Bake until pears are tender, about 20 minutes. Serve warm or cold. (Serves 6.)

## Pear and Grape Compote

2 pears
$1/2$ cup sugar
2 cups water
1 tbsp. fresh lime juice
pinch salt
$1/2$ cup seedless green grapes
$1/2$ cup red grapes, halved and seeded
lemon or orange sherbet (optional)

Wash pears but do not peel. Cut into halves lengthwise and core.

Heat sugar, 2 cups water, lime juice and salt in a medium saucepan. Boil gently 5 minutes. Add pear halves, cover and simmer 15 minutes. Add grapes and simmer, uncovered, until pears are just tender, about 5 minutes. Lift out fruit with a slotted spoon and put into a bowl.

Boil syrup remaining in pan hard, uncovered, until reduced to about half the volume. Pour over fruit. Chill.

Spoon fruit and syrup into sherbet glasses at serving time. Top each serving with a small scoop of sherbet, if desired, and serve immediately. (Serves 4.)

## Peach-Blueberry Compote

$1/4$ cup packed brown sugar
$1/4$ cup water
2 tbsp. lemon juice
$1/3$ cup orange juice
$1/8$ tsp. ground mace
1 tsp. vanilla extract
2 cups sliced fresh peaches
2 cups fresh blueberries

Combine sugar, $1/4$ cup water, lemon juice, orange juice and mace in a small saucepan. Bring to a boil, turn down heat and simmer 5 minutes. Remove from heat and stir in vanilla.

Put peaches and blueberries in a bowl. Pour syrup over. Chill. (Serves 6.)

## Spicy Prunes

12-oz. pkg. pitted prunes
3 slices lemon, quartered
3 slices orange, quartered
$1/4$ cup raisins
1 stick cinnamon, broken
$1/4$ tsp. ground nutmeg

Combine prunes, lemon and orange pieces, raisins, cinnamon and nutmeg in a quart sealer. Cover with cold water. Cover jar and store in the refrigerator 5 days to 1 week before serving. (Serves 6.)

## Prune Tidbits

24 pitted prunes (see note)
1/2 cup crunchy-style peanut butter
6 slices bacon, cut in half
3 slices bacon, fried crisp and crumbled
3 tbsp. finely chopped salted peanuts

Fill 12 of the prunes with half the peanut butter and wrap each with half a strip of bacon. Fasten with toothpicks. Chill until shortly before serving time.

Add crumbled bacon to remaining peanut butter and use this mixture to fill remaining prunes. Shape with fingers so some of filling shows on slit side and dip this side in chopped peanuts to coat the peanut butter. Chill.

Put bacon-wrapped prunes on broiler rack shortly before serving time and slip low under hot broiler. Broil until bacon is cooked, turning as needed. Arrange hot and cold Prune Tidbits on a tray and serve immediately. (Makes 24.)

*Note:* I like to make these tidbits with the prunes that come in a 12-oz. pkg. already pitted. They are soft and do not need plumping. If you are using prunes with pits, you will need to cover them with boiling water and simmer them until they are plumped, about 15 minutes, then remove pits and cool before using.

## Banana-Topped Raspberries

1 pt. raspberries
2/3 cup plain yogurt (one 175 g carton)
1 medium banana

Put rinsed berries in 4 fruit dishes. Put yogurt in glass of blender, add broken-up banana and buzz until smooth. Pour over berries. (Serves 4.)

## Fresh Fruit Bowl

1/2 small watermelon
1 cup fresh pineapple cubes
1 cup fresh blueberries
1 cup fresh raspberries
1 cup halved pitted sweet cherries
1/4 cup sugar
1/4 cup kirsch (optional)
mint sprigs

If you are buying a half melon, have it cut lengthwise. It will make the bowl to hold the fruit. Cut 2 to 3 cups of balls from the watermelon and put in a large bowl. Cut remaining flesh from melon and store for other uses. Chill melon shell.

Add remaining fruit, sugar and kirsch to melon balls. Cover and chill, stirring occasionally.

Pile into chilled melon shell at serving time and garnish with mint sprigs. (Serves 6 to 8.)

## Citrus Compote

2 medium grapefruit
2 medium oranges
1/4 cup liquid honey
2 tbsp. finely chopped preserved ginger
1 tsp. grated lemon rind

Cut each grapefruit into halves and scoop sections out into a bowl. Squeeze any juice left in fruit into bowl. Peel and section oranges and combine with grapefruit sections.

Add honey, ginger and lemon rind and mix well. Cover and let stand at room temperature 30 minutes. Stir again. Chill. (Serves 6.)

### Cantaloupe Ambrosia

2 medium oranges
1 medium cantaloupe
1/3 cup flaked coconut

Peel and section oranges, working over a bowl to catch any juice. Cut cantaloupe into halves and discard seeds.

Scoop out melon in balls using a ball cutter or a 1/2 tsp. measuring spoon. Combine with orange sections. Sprinkle with coconut and chill very well. Serve in sherbet glasses. (Serves 3 or 4.)

### Maple Fruit

2 cups fresh peach slices
2 cups fresh blueberries
3/4 cup light cream
3/4 cup maple syrup

Combine peach slices and blueberries and divide among 6 serving dishes. Combine cream and maple syrup and pour about 1/4 cup of mixture over each serving of fruit. (Serves 6.)

### Ginger Fruit

1 large ripe pineapple, peeled, cored and cut in bite-size pieces
4 large oranges
3 grapefruit
4 large tangerines
2 tbsp. liquid honey
2 tbsp. finely chopped preserved ginger

Put pineapple in a large bowl. Peel and section oranges and grapefruit, working over a bowl to catch any juice. Peel and section tangerines, strip off connective membranes and remove seeds. Add all sections to bowl. Add honey and stir well. Let stand about 30 minutes, stirring often.

Drain all juice from fruit into a saucepan. Add ginger to juice, bring to a boil and boil hard until there is only about 1 cup of juice left. Cool.

Pour ginger-fruit juice syrup over fruit, cover and chill. (Serves 8 to 12.)

### Brunch Fruit Salad

1 1/2 cups cut-up orange sections
1 1/2 cups cubed pineapple
1 cup halved and seeded red grapes
1/2 cup West Indies Dressing (recipe follows)
1 small head lettuce
1 cup diced banana

Combine orange, pineapple and grapes in a bowl. Add 1/2 cup of the West Indies Dressing and toss lightly. Chill.

Tear lettuce into bite-size pieces at serving time and add to fruit along with banana. Toss lightly and serve immediately. (Serves 6.)

### West Indies Dressing

1/4 cup salad oil
1/4 cup lemon juice
1/4 cup lime juice
1/4 cup white rum
1/2 tsp. grated lemon rind
1/8 tsp. salt
3 tbsp. brown sugar

Shake all ingredients together in a small jar with a tight lid. (Makes about 1 cup.)

### Rhubarb-Pineapple Sauce

2 cups cut-up rhubarb
2 cups cut-up fresh pineapple
1 cup sugar
1/2 tsp. ground ginger

Combine all ingredients in the top of a double boiler and let stand at room temperature 1 hour. Stir.

Set over boiling water in bottom of double boiler and cover. Cook, without stirring, until rhubarb is tender, about 30 minutes. Chill. (Serves 4.)

### Sunny Cooler

1 1/2 cups fresh orange juice
1 1/2 cups bottled prune juice
3 tbsp. lemon juice

Combine all ingredients in a large pitcher and chill well. Stir before serving. (Makes 3 cups.)

### Pineapple-Orange Shrub

19-oz. can pineapple juice
orange sherbet
mint sprigs

Combine pineapple juice and 1 cup of the orange sherbet in glass of blender. Buzz until blended and frothy. Pour into juice glasses and top each serving with a small spoonful of sherbet and a sprig of mint. (Serves 6.)

### Orange Eggnog

1 egg
1 tsp. liquid honey
3 tbsp. frozen orange juice
   concentrate, thawed
1/4 tsp. vanilla extract
1 cup milk

Put egg, honey, orange juice concentrate and vanilla in glass of blender. Buzz 15 seconds. Add milk and buzz until smooth and foamy. Pour into a large glass and serve. (Serves 1.)

### Maple Shake

4 graham wafers, crumbled
1 cup milk
2 tbsp. maple syrup

Combine ingredients in glass of blender and buzz until smooth. Pour into a large glass. (Serves 1.)

### Golden Flip

Combine ingredients in glass of blender and buzz until smooth. Pour into a large glass. (Serves 1.)

1 egg
1 tbsp. liquid honey
3/4 cup apricot nectar
1/4 cup pineapple juice

### Tangy Apple Cocktail

Combine all ingredients in a cocktail shaker or blender glass and shake or blend until foamy. Strain into chilled cocktail glasses. (Serves 4.)

1 cup apple juice
1 cup lemon juice
1/2 cup liquid honey
1 egg white
1/2 cup cracked ice

### Orange Juice Flip

Beat all ingredients except ice cubes and mint together with a rotary beater or in glass of blender. Serve in tall glasses over ice cubes and garnish with fresh mint. (Serves 4.)

6-oz. can frozen orange juice
2 cups cold water
2 eggs
1 tbsp. sherry (optional)
ice cubes
fresh mint

### Bloody Marys by the Pitcher

Put ice cubes in a large pitcher. Add all remaining ingredients. Stir briskly until very cold. Strain into short glasses. (Serves 6.)

Advance preparation: Mix, cover and refrigerate everything except ice and vodka.

10 ice cubes
9 oz. vodka
2 cups bottled clam and tomato cocktail
10-oz. can tomato juice
2 tbsp. lemon juice
1 1/2 tsp. Worcestershire sauce
1 tsp. celery salt
3 drops Tabasco

### Lemon Consommé

Heat consommé, 2 1/2 cups water, lemon juice and lemon rind and simmer 5 minutes. Ladle into mugs and float a slice of lemon on each. (Serves 6.)

two 10-oz. cans beef consommé
2 1/2 cups water
1 tbsp. lemon juice
2 tsp. grated lemon rind
paper thin slices lemon

### Instant Mocha

Combine chocolate drink mix, instant coffee and 4 1/2 cups boiling water in a heatproof pitcher, mixing well to blend.

Stir in cream. Serve at once in mugs or cups, topped with whipped cream if desired. (Serves 8.)

3/4 cup instant chocolate drink mix
3 tbsp. instant coffee
4 1/2 cups boiling water
1 cup light cream
whipped cream (optional)

## Hot Tomato Juice

Combine all ingredients down to and including Tabasco in a saucepan. Heat to boiling, turn down heat and simmer 5 minutes. Strain.

Stir in parsley and lemon juice. Serve hot in mugs and top each serving with a lemon slice. (Serves 4.)

Advance preparation: Simmer and strain first 9 ingredients. Chill, then reheat with parsley and lemon juice at serving time.

19-oz. can tomato juice
1 large bunch celery leaves
1 beef bouillon cube
1 small bay leaf
1 tsp. grated onion
$1/2$ tsp. salt
$1/4$ tsp. celery salt
$1/2$ tsp. sugar
dash Tabasco
2 tbsp. minced parsley
1 tbsp. lemon juice
thin slices lemon

## Mexican Coffee-Chocolate

Put chocolate and $3/4$ cup hot water in the top of a double boiler and set over simmering water. Heat until chocolate is melted. Stir in coffee, sugar and salt and stir 5 minutes.

Heat milk, cream and vanilla bean to scalding in a large saucepan. Discard vanilla bean. Combine with coffee-chocolate mixture and beat until foamy with a rotary beater. Serve in mugs. (Serves 6.)

3 squares (3 oz.) unsweetened chocolate
$3/4$ cup hot water
2 cups freshly brewed, hot, strong coffee
$1/3$ cup sugar
pinch salt
3 cups hot milk
$2/3$ cup heavy cream
1-inch piece vanilla bean, split lengthwise

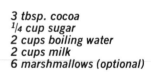

## Hot Honey Tea

Pour 5 cups boiling water over tea and cloves. Steep 5 minutes. Strain.

Add orange juice, lemon juice, honey and 3 cups boiling water. Stir well. Serve hot in teacups, topped with slices of lemon. (Makes 16 teacupfuls.)

5 cups boiling water
4 tbsp. tea or 6 tea bags
2 tbsp. whole cloves
1 cup strained orange juice
$1/2$ cup lemon juice
$2/3$ cup liquid honey
3 cups boiling water
thin slices lemon

## Cocoa

Mix cocoa and sugar together in a medium saucepan. Add $1/2$ cup of the boiling water gradually and blend until smooth. Add remaining boiling water and boil 2 minutes, stirring constantly.

Stir in milk and beat with a hand or electric mixer until foamy. Heat but do not boil. Drop a marshmallow in each of 6 cups or small mugs and pour in the hot cocoa. (Serves 6.)

3 tbsp. cocoa
$1/4$ cup sugar
2 cups boiling water
2 cups milk
6 marshmallows (optional)

# Main Dishes

Hot cereals flavored with apple, or sausage and mushrooms? Quiche, omelet or custard? Hash, steak or fish? For breakfast? Why not? These, plus interesting variations on pancakes and waffles, help make the first meal the best meal.

### Apple-Flavored Hot Cereal

Heat apple juice to a full rolling boil. Sprinkle in cereal gradually, stirring constantly. Add salt and cinnamon and continue cooking over low heat, stirring constantly, until mixture thickens, about 5 minutes. Stir in dates.

Serve immediately, sprinkled lightly with brown sugar (the apple juice makes the cereal sweet, so you may prefer not to use the sugar) and with milk or cream poured over. (Serves 4 to 6.)

*3$^1$/$_4$ cups apple juice*
*$^1$/$_2$ cup quick Cream of Wheat*
*1 tsp. salt*
*1 tsp. ground cinnamon*
*$^1$/$_2$ cup chopped dates*
*brown sugar (optional)*
*milk or cream*

### Brunch Pilaf

Cook rice according to package directions. (Cooking time is about 35 minutes for brown rice. Water should be cooked away at end of cooking. If it is not, continue cooking, uncovered, for a few minutes more.)

Put sausages in a large heavy skillet, add $^1$/$_4$ cup water, cover and simmer 5 minutes. Do not prick sausages. Remove cover, drain and cook over moderate heat until browned, about 20 minutes. Remove from pan and keep hot in low oven.

Drain all but about 1 tbsp. sausage fat from pan. Add 1 tbsp. butter or margarine. Add onion and mushrooms and stir over moderate heat 5 minutes. Add salt and pepper. Add to rice and toss with a fork. Serve immediately with sausages. (Serves 6.)

*1 cup brown rice*
*1 lb. sausages*
*$^1$/$_4$ cup water*
*1 tbsp. butter or margarine*
*1 tbsp. grated onion*
*1 lb. (2 pt.) fresh mushrooms, sliced*
*$^1$/$_2$ tsp. salt*
*$^1$/$_8$ tsp. black pepper*

### Creamy Barley

Combine 1$^1$/$_4$ cups water, barley flakes and $^1$/$_8$ tsp. salt in a small saucepan. Bring to a boil, then reduce heat and cook gently, covered, 10 minutes. Uncover and stir 5 minutes. Remove from heat.

With a spoon, beat eggs, brown sugar, milk and pinch of salt in the top of a double boiler. Add prunes and cook over simmering water until mixture coats a metal spoon like a thin custard, about 10 minutes. Stir in vanilla and cooked barley and heat well. Serve with more milk. (Serves 2.)

*Note:* Barley flakes are available in health food stores.

*1$^1$/$_4$ cups water*
*$^1$/$_2$ cup barley flakes*
*$^1$/$_8$ tsp. salt*
*2 eggs*
*2 tbsp. brown sugar*
*$^3$/$_4$ cup milk*
*pinch salt*
*$^1$/$_4$ cup chopped uncooked prunes*
*$^1$/$_4$ tsp. vanilla extract (optional)*
*milk*

## Baked Apple-Oat Cereal

4 medium cooking apples
2 tbsp. brown sugar
2 tsp. grated lemon rind
1/4 cup seedless raisins
1/2 cup light cream
1 cup quick-cooking rolled oats
1/4 tsp. salt
2 1/2 cups boiling water
2 tbsp. butter or margarine
1 tbsp. sugar
1/4 tsp. ground cinnamon
sugar
pouring cream

Heat oven to 375°F. Butter a 2-qt. casserole.

Peel and slice apples into casserole. Sprinkle with brown sugar, lemon rind and raisins. Pour 1/2 cup cream over all. Bake, uncovered, until apples are just getting soft, about 15 minutes.

Add rolled oats and salt to 2 1/2 cups boiling water in a saucepan. Cook gently, stirring, 5 minutes. Spread over apples. Dot with butter or margarine. Combine 1 tbsp. sugar and cinnamon and sprinkle over all. Return to oven and bake 10 minutes more.

Serve hot. Pass the sugar and cream. (Serves 6.)

## Triticale Treat

2/3 cup plain yogurt
(one 175 g carton)
1 medium banana, peeled
and chopped
1 medium orange, sectioned,
chopped and drained
1 cup triticale flakes
2 cups water
1/4 tsp. salt

Combine yogurt, banana and orange and refrigerate until serving time.

Bring triticale flakes, 2 cups water and salt to a boil in a medium saucepan. Lower heat and stir until like cereal in texture, about 10 minutes. Serve hot, topped with yogurt mixture. (Serves 2.)

*Note:* Protein-rich triticale flakes are sold in health food stores.

## Bacon and Leek Quiche

pastry for 2-crust 9-inch pie
(recipe p. 172)
1 lb. bacon
3 medium leeks (white and
pale green parts only)
1/2 cup thin strips cooked ham
2 1/2 cups grated Swiss cheese
10 eggs
2 cups milk
1/2 tsp. salt
1/4 tsp. black pepper
1/8 tsp. ground nutmeg

Heat oven to 475°F. Divide pastry into halves and line two 9-inch pie pans with it, building up a high fluted edge. Do not prick pastry. Bake 3 minutes. Remove from oven. (Don't worry if pastry puffs a little. It will go down once it comes out of oven.) Turn oven temperature to 350°F.

Cut bacon into 1-inch pieces. Put in a large heavy skillet and fry until crisp. Lift out with a slotted spoon and drain on paper toweling. Drain all but 3 tbsp. bacon fat from skillet.

Cut leeks into halves lengthwise and wash between leaves. Slice thinly crosswise. (You should have 4 to 5 cups.)

Add leeks to drippings in skillet and cook gently, stirring, until beginning to get limp but not brown. Add ham and continue stirring until leeks are tender.

Keep 1/2 cup cheese aside for tops of pies. Sprinkle remaining cheese into partially baked crusts. Keep 1/4 cup bacon bits aside and sprinkle remaining bacon into crusts.

Beat eggs lightly. Stir in milk, salt, pepper and nutmeg. Blend in leek mixture. Ladle egg mixture into pie pans evenly. Sprinkle each pie with some remaining cheese and bacon bits. Put a narrow strip of foil around edge of each pie to keep from browning too much.

Bake until crust is browned and filling is set, about 45 minutes. Serve hot. (Makes 2, serves 12.)

Advance preparation: Complete pies and refrigerate or freeze. If frozen, thaw in refrigerator. Reheat at 400°F 20 to 30 minutes.

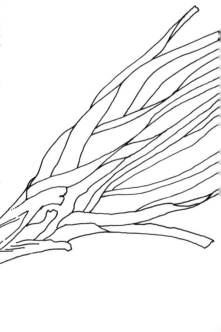

## Mushroom Quiche

Heat oven to 475°F. Line a 9-inch pie pan with pastry, building up a high fluted edge. Do not prick pastry. Bake 3 minutes. Remove from oven and cool. (Don't worry if pastry puffs a little. It will go down once it comes out of oven.) Turn oven temperature to 375°F.

Heat butter or margarine in a large heavy skillet. Add green pepper and onion and stir 2 minutes. Add mushrooms and cook quickly until lightly browned, about 2 minutes. Cool.

Beat cottage cheese, eggs, cream, salt and pepper together to blend. Stir in mushroom mixture and parsley. Pour into prepared pie shell.

Bake until crust is browned and filling is set, about 40 minutes. Serve hot. (Serves 6.)

Advance preparation: Prepare filling up to a day in advance and refrigerate until ready to complete pie.

*pastry for 1-crust 9-inch pie (recipe p. 172)*
*1/4 cup butter or margarine*
*1/4 cup finely chopped green pepper*
*1 tbsp. finely chopped onion*
*1 lb. (2 pt.) fresh mushrooms, sliced*
*1 1/2 cups cream-style cottage cheese*
*4 eggs*
*1/3 cup light cream*
*1 1/2 tsp. salt*
*1/4 tsp. black pepper*
*2 tbsp. chopped parsley*

## Country Scramble

Fry bacon in a large heavy skillet until crisp. Remove from skillet, drain on paper toweling and crumble.

Add oil to bacon drippings in pan. Add potatoes, onion, parsley and savory. Cover and cook gently until potatoes are tender, stirring often, about 20 minutes. Stir in butter or margarine and bacon bits.

Beat eggs, 2 tbsp. water, salt and pepper together with a fork. Pour over potato mixture, cover and cook over low heat until set and lightly browned on the bottom, about 10 minutes. Turn mixture with an egg turner, part at a time. Spread evenly and sprinkle with cheese. Cover again and cook over low heat until cheese is melted, about 3 minutes. Serve immediately. (Serves 6 to 8.)

*6 slices bacon*
*2 tbsp. cooking oil*
*4 cups 1/4-inch cubes raw potatoes*
*1/2 cup finely chopped onion*
*2 tsp. dried parsley*
*1/2 tsp. dried leaf savory*
*2 tbsp. butter or margarine*
*6 large eggs*
*2 tbsp. water*
*2 tsp. salt*
*1/4 tsp. black pepper*
*1/2 cup 1/4-inch cubes old Cheddar cheese*

## Creamy Scrambled Eggs

Melt butter or margarine in a heavy skillet. Beat remaining ingredients together with a fork. Pour into pan when butter or margarine is hot enough to sizzle a little when a drop of egg is added.

Cook over low heat until mixture begins to set on the bottom. Lift edge with a fork and tip pan to let uncooked part run underneath (do not stir) and repeat this until egg is cooked but mixture is still very moist. Remove from heat, stir gently with fork and serve immediately. (Serves 6.)

*1/4 cup butter or margarine*
*12 eggs*
*1/4 cup light cream*
*1 tsp. salt*
*1/2 tsp. black pepper*
*1 cup cream-style cottage cheese*
*2 tbsp. chopped parsley*
*2 tsp. chopped chives*

11

### French Omelet

2 eggs
1 tbsp. water
1/8 tsp. salt
grating fresh black pepper
1 tbsp. butter or margarine
1 tbsp. chopped parsley
(optional)

Beat eggs, 1 tbsp. water, salt and pepper together with a fork just until blended.

Heat an omelet pan over high heat until it is very hot (a drop of water spatters). Add butter or margarine and heat until it foams then subsides but is not browned. Lift pan off heat if butter or margarine begins to brown around edges.

Swish butter or margarine around to coat bottom and partway up sides of pan. Working quickly, add parsley then egg mixture to pan. Hold handle of pan firmly with one hand and a fork, flat side down, in the other hand. As soon as eggs start to set, which is almost instantly, stir right around pan with the fork, shaking pan back and forth to keep omelet free. Continue this stirring and shaking until egg is almost set but still moist on top, about 30 seconds. Smooth egg out with back of fork and let it cook about 2 seconds without stirring to brown lightly.

Starting at side of pan next to handle, slip fork under edge of omelet and, tilting pan so omelet rolls down toward side opposite handle, push it with the fork so it rolls up neatly out onto a hot serving plate. (Serves 1.)

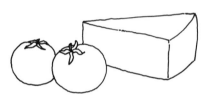

### Baked Eggs and Tomatoes

6 eggs
black pepper
1 cup ground cooked ham
3/4 cup grated old Cheddar
  cheese
6 thick slices tomato
salt
3 English muffins
Easy Hollandaise Sauce
  (recipe follows)

Heat oven to 350°F. Butter six 6-oz. custard cups.

Break an egg into each custard cup. Sprinkle lightly with pepper.

Combine ham and cheese and divide mixture evenly among cups, covering eggs completely. Bake 5 minutes.

Top ham and cheese mixture in each cup with a slice of tomato. Sprinkle with salt. Return to oven and bake until eggs are cooked the way you like them, 10 to 15 minutes more.

Split and toast English muffins toward end of baking time. Put half on each of 6 serving plates. Run a knife around each custard cup and loosen baked eggs gently. Invert on muffins. Serve immediately, topped with Easy Hollandaise Sauce. (Serves 6.)

### Easy Hollandaise Sauce

2 egg yolks, slightly beaten
2 tbsp. lemon juice
1/2 cup ice-cold butter

Combine all ingredients in a small saucepan over very low heat. Stir constantly until butter is melted and mixture is slightly thickened. Serve immediately. (Makes 1 cup.)

### Crisp-Topped Poached Eggs

1 tbsp. butter or margarine
1 cup light cream
4 eggs
2 tbsp. coarse corn or wheat flake crumbs
4 slices hot buttered whole wheat toast
salt and pepper

Melt butter or margarine in a medium skillet. Add cream and heat to boiling. Turn down heat.

Break eggs into skillet one at a time as for poaching. Sprinkle each egg with some cereal crumbs. Turn heat to low, cover and simmer until eggs are done, about 3 minutes.

Put toast on serving plates. Lift eggs out and set on toast. Pour a little of the cream left in pan over each egg and sprinkle with salt and pepper. Serve immediately. (Serves 4.)

### Shirred Eggs and Spinach

1/3 cup finely chopped cooked spinach
salt and pepper
Parmesan cheese
4 eggs
light cream
butter or margarine

Heat oven to 350°F. Butter four 6-oz. custard cups.

Put a generous 1 tbsp. of the spinach in each custard cup. Sprinkle each lightly with salt and pepper, then with 1 tsp. of the Parmesan.

Make a small hollow in each mound of spinach and break an egg into each cup. Add 1 tbsp. cream to each cup, then sprinkle with about 1 tsp. Parmesan. Top each cup with a tiny dot of butter or margarine.

Bake until eggs are done the way you like them, 12 to 15 minutes. (Serves 4.)

### Mushroom Custards

6 strips bacon
1/2 cup sliced fresh mushrooms
4 eggs
1 cup light cream
1 cup milk
1/4 tsp. salt
dash black pepper
1/4 tsp. dried leaf chervil

Heat oven to 350°F. Butter six 6-oz. custard cups. Put a pan of hot water (have water about 3/4 inch deep) in oven.

Fry bacon in a skillet until crisp. Drain, cool and crumble. Drain all but 1 tbsp. bacon fat from skillet. Add mushrooms and cook quickly 3 minutes, stirring. Remove from heat.

Beat eggs lightly with remaining ingredients. Divide bacon and mushrooms evenly among prepared custard cups. Pour egg mixture over bacon and mushrooms. Set in pan of hot water in oven. Bake until custard is set, about 30 minutes. (Serves 6.)

### Ham Hash

3 cups finely chopped cooked ham
3 cups finely chopped cooked potatoes
1/2 cup chopped green pepper
1/2 tsp. salt
1/4 tsp. black pepper
1 tbsp. butter or margarine
2 cups milk
6 eggs

Combine ham, potatoes, green pepper, salt and pepper. Heat butter or margarine in a large heavy skillet and add ham mixture. Pack firmly. Pour milk over all.

Cook gently, stirring occasionally, until mixture thickens, about 30 minutes. Raise heat a little and cook, without stirring, until bottom of mixture browns lightly.

Poach eggs when hash is just about ready. Spoon hash onto serving plates, make a hollow in the centre of each serving and slip an egg into each hollow. Serve immediately. (Serves 6.)

## Corned Beef Hash

12-oz. can corned beef, diced
2 cups diced cold cooked
   potatoes
1 tsp. prepared hot mustard
1 tsp. salt
$1/4$ tsp. black pepper
$1/4$ cup butter or margarine
1 medium onion, very thinly
   sliced
$1/4$ cup milk
1 tsp. Worcestershire sauce

Combine corned beef, potatoes, mustard, salt and pepper, blending very well.

Heat butter or margarine in a large heavy skillet (a black iron one is good) over moderate heat. Add onion and stir until onion is transparent. Add corned beef mixture, milk and Worcestershire. Mix all ingredients well with a fork, then pack down.

Turn heat to moderately low and cook hash until golden brown on bottom, about 25 minutes. Divide mixture into quarters, lift out of pan with an egg turner and invert onto hot serving plates. (Serves 4.)

For a change: For Corned Beef Hash with eggs, prepare hash mixture to point where milk and Worcestershire have been added. Turn into a well-buttered $12 \times 7 \times 1^1/2$-inch baking dish. Make 4 deep holes in mixture with the back of a large spoon. Add 1 tbsp. butter or margarine to each hole and break an egg into each. Sprinkle eggs with salt and pepper and add 1 tbsp. of light cream to each.

Bake at 400°F until eggs are done the way you like them, 15 to 20 minutes. Serve immediately with ketchup or chili sauce. (Serves 4.)

## Turkey Hash

$1/2$ lb. bulk sausage meat
$1/4$ cup chopped onion
$1/4$ cup chopped green pepper
2 tbsp. flour
1 tsp. salt
$1/4$ tsp. black pepper
$1/2$ tsp. poultry seasoning
1 cup milk
2 cups $1/4$-inch cubes cooked
   turkey
2 tbsp. chopped parsley
$1/2$ cup toasted bread cubes
2 tbsp. butter or margarine

Put sausage meat in a cold 10-inch iron skillet, set over moderate heat and cook thoroughly, breaking it apart as it browns. Lift out meat with a slotted spoon and put on paper toweling to drain well.

Drain all but 3 tbsp. fat from pan (add a little oil if there isn't enough fat). Add onion and green pepper and cook gently 3 minutes.

Sprinkle in flour, salt, pepper and poultry seasoning and stir to blend. Remove from heat and stir in milk all at once. Return to moderate heat and stir until thick and smooth.

Add sausage meat, turkey, parsley and bread cubes and blend lightly.

Push mixture to one side of pan and add butter or margarine to other side. Let it melt, then spread the hash evenly in the pan. Cook very slowly until a golden brown crust forms on the bottom, 30 to 45 minutes. (Serves 4.)

Advance preparation: Follow recipe to point where sausage meat, turkey, parsley and bread cubes are blended in. Refrigerate until needed, then brown in butter or margarine as directed.

## Minute Steak Turnovers

6 tbsp. grated old Cheddar
   cheese
6 minute steaks (cube steaks)
bottled steak sauce

Put 1 tbsp. cheese in centre of each minute steak and fold meat over, pressing around edges to seal and enclose cheese. Put on a lightly oiled broiler pan. Brush with steak sauce.

Broil about 4 inches from heat 3 to 5 minutes, turn, brush with steak sauce and broil until browned, about 3 minutes. (Serves 6.)

## Ham and Mushroom Roulades

Melt $1/3$ cup butter or margarine in a large heavy skillet over moderate heat. Add bread crumbs and stir until lightly browned. Cool.

Heat oven to 425°F. Have rack at centre of oven. Grease two $15 \times 10 \times 1$-inch jelly roll pans. Line with waxed paper, leaving a 2-inch overhang at one end. Grease and flour paper well. Sprinkle with $1/2$ cup of the buttered bread crumbs, spreading them evenly.

Melt $1/2$ cup butter or margarine in a large saucepan over moderate heat. Mix in flour and stir 1 minute (mixture will be lumpy). Remove from heat and stir in milk. Return to heat and beat constantly with a wire whip or wooden spoon until boiling, thickened and smooth.

Mix yogurt, salt, pepper, mustard and egg yolks together. Gradually stir in a little of the hot mixture, then stir all of mixture into saucepan. Bring just to a boil, stirring constantly. Remove from heat.

Beat egg whites and cream of tartar until stiff but moist peaks form. Stir about $1/4$ of the egg whites into egg yolk mixture. Carefully fold that mixture into remaining whites. Divide between prepared pans (about 5 cups each) and spread as evenly as possible. Bake, one pan at a time, until puffed and springy to touch, 12 to 15 minutes.

Remove each from oven as it is done and sprinkle top with $1/4$ cup of the buttered bread crumbs. Loosen roulade from edges of pan. Cover a large cookie sheet with a sheet of waxed paper, put it over the roulade and invert quickly. Lift jelly roll pan slightly at end where waxed paper lining shows and pull paper slightly to loosen roulade from pan. Peel off bottom paper.

Spread each roulade with a scant 2 cups of Ham and Mushroom Filling. Roll up from one end, using waxed paper to help with rolling and finally rolling onto a hot serving plate. Cut in thick slices. Top each serving with some of Roulade Sauce. (Serves 12.)

Advance preparation: Roulades can be baked and filled, then covered and refrigerated until needed. To reheat, cover with foil and put in a 350°F oven until hot, about 20 minutes. In a microwave, cover with waxed paper or transparent wrap and heat 5 to 7 minutes.

$1/3$ cup butter or margarine
$1 1/2$ cups fine dry bread
  crumbs
$1/2$ cup butter or margarine
1 cup all-purpose flour
4 cups milk
2 tbsp. plain yogurt
2 tsp. salt
$1/4$ tsp. black pepper
$1/2$ tsp. dry mustard
8 egg yolks
8 egg whites
$1/4$ tsp. cream of tartar
Ham and Mushroom Filling
  (recipe follows)
Roulade Sauce (recipe follows)

## Ham and Mushroom Filling

Melt butter or margarine in a large heavy skillet over high heat and fry mushrooms quickly 3 minutes. Remove from heat. Sprinkle with lemon juice and lightly with salt and pepper. Stir in ham.

Measure out $1 1/2$ cups of the ham mixture and set aside for sauce. Put remaining ham mixture in the top of a double boiler. Beat cheese and yogurt together and stir into ham mixture. Keep hot over simmering water until needed.

$1/4$ cup butter or margarine
1 lb. (2 pt.) fresh mushrooms,
  sliced
1 tbsp. lemon juice
salt and pepper
3 cups finely ground cooked
  ham
250 g pkg. cream cheese
  (room temperature)
2 tbsp. plain yogurt

### Roulade Sauce

2 tbsp. butter or margarine
2 tbsp. flour
1¼ cups milk
1 cup heavy cream
2 tbsp. Madeira or sherry
1½ cups ham and mushroom
mixture (from filling recipe)
salt and pepper

Melt butter or margarine in a medium saucepan. Add flour and stir until bubbling. Remove from heat and stir in milk and cream all at once. Return to heat and stir until boiling, thickened and smooth. Remove from heat and stir in Madeira or sherry, ham and mushroom mixture and salt and pepper to taste. Keep hot to serve as sauce over slices of roulade.

### Creamy Ham and Mushrooms

¼ cup butter or margarine
½ lb. (1 pt.) fresh mushrooms,
sliced
2 stalks celery, thinly sliced
on the diagonal
¼ cup flour
½ tsp. salt
⅛ tsp. black pepper
2 cups milk
4 cups small cubes cooked
ham (about 1½ lb.)
Hot Biscuits (recipe follows)
soft butter
2 tbsp. finely chopped green
onions

Heat butter or margarine in a large heavy skillet. Add mushrooms and celery and cook quickly 5 minutes, stirring constantly. Sprinkle in flour, salt and pepper and stir to blend.

Remove from heat and add milk all at once. Stir to blend, return to moderate heat and stir until boiling, thickened and smooth. Add ham and heat well.

Split six 3-inch Hot Biscuits and put on serving plates. Butter lightly. Sprinkle ham mixture with green onions and spoon over biscuits. Serve immediately. Pass rest of Hot Biscuits as bread. (Serves 6.)

Advance preparation: Ham mixture can be prepared, refrigerated, then reheated in a double boiler.

### Hot Biscuits

3 cups sifted all-purpose flour
6 tsp. baking powder
1½ tsp. salt
⅓ cup shortening
1½ cups milk (approx.)

Heat oven to 450°F. Have an ungreased cookie sheet ready.

Sift flour, baking powder and salt together into a bowl. Add shortening and cut in finely. Stir in enough of the milk with a fork to make a soft dough that is easy to handle. Turn out onto a floured board and knead lightly about 20 times. Round up dough.

Roll or pat to ½ inch thick and cut 6 biscuits about 3 inches in diameter. Cut remaining dough into biscuits about 2 inches in diameter. (You should have about twelve 2-inch biscuits.) Put on cookie sheet with about 1 inch between.

Bake until well browned, 10 to 12 minutes. (Makes about 1½ dozen biscuits.)

### Baked Bacon

Heat oven to 400°F.

Lay 2 or 3 slices of side bacon per serving on a rack in a large shallow pan. Bake 10 to 15 minutes. Do not turn. This is especially useful when cooking a large amount of bacon.

### Ham with Milk Gravy

2 centre-cut slices ready-to-eat
  ham, 1 inch thick
4 tsp. flour
1/2 cup strong coffee
1 cup milk
black pepper

Trim ham slices and slash any fat left around edges to keep ham from curling. Heat fat trimmings in a large heavy skillet until skillet is well greased. Discard fat pieces. Fry ham slices quickly until well browned on both sides. Put on a hot platter and keep hot in low oven.

Stir flour into drippings left in pan and let brown slightly. Stir in coffee gradually, stirring up any browned bits in the bottom of the pan. Bring to a boil. Stir in milk and a good grating or shake of pepper. Heat but do not boil. Pour over ham slices. (Serves 6.)

### English Sausage

1 lb. ground pork
1 lb. ground veal
1 lb. ground beef suet
1 1/2 cups fine dry bread
  crumbs
2 tsp. grated lemon rind
2 tsp. dried leaf savory
1 tsp. dried leaf marjoram
1 tsp. rubbed sage
1/2 tsp. ground nutmeg
1 tsp. salt
1/2 tsp. black pepper

Combine all ingredients, mixing well. Shape into 3 rolls about 2 inches in diameter, wrap them in transparent wrap and refrigerate. When ready to serve, cut off thick slices as needed and fry or broil. (Makes 10 servings.)

Advance preparation: Flavor improves if you let them stand in the refrigerator for a day or so. They should be used within a week if refrigerated but can be frozen up to a month.

### Alsatian Sausage

1 medium green pepper
1 lb. bulk sausage meat
1/4 lb. lean ground beef
2 tbsp. grated onion
1 small clove garlic, minced
1 tbsp. finely chopped green
  onion
1 tbsp. finely chopped parsley
1 tbsp. finely chopped chives
1/2 tsp. poultry seasoning
1/2 tsp. dried leaf thyme
1/4 tsp. ground nutmeg
3/4 tsp. salt
1/4 tsp. black pepper

Put green pepper through the fine blade of the food chopper or chop very finely. Combine all ingredients, mixing well.

Shape into 2 rolls 1 1/2 to 2 inches in diameter. Wrap them in transparent wrap and refrigerate. When ready to serve, cut off thick slices as needed and fry or broil. (Makes 4 servings.)

Advance preparation: Flavor improves if you let them stand in the refrigerator for a day or so. They should be used within a week if refrigerated but can be frozen up to a month.

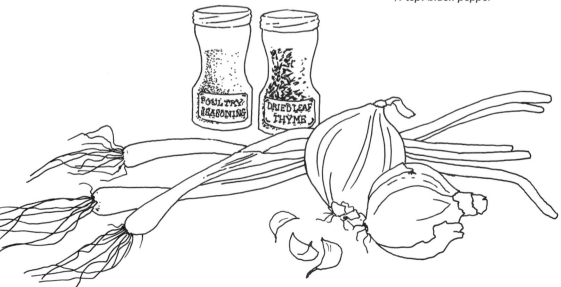

## Chicken Livers and Mushrooms

Fry bacon in a skillet until crisp. Drain on paper toweling and crumble. Set aside.

Drain all but 1 tbsp. bacon fat from skillet. Add chicken livers and mushrooms and sprinkle with salt, pepper and marjoram. Cook over moderate heat until livers are cooked through, 3 to 4 minutes.

Combine cream and flour until smooth. Blend into chicken liver mixture gradually. Cook gently until slightly thickened and smooth, stirring constantly.

Stir in bacon bits and serve immediately over hot buttered toast. (Serves 3.)

4 strips bacon
1/2 lb. chicken livers, cut
  in half
10-oz. can mushroom pieces,
  drained
1 tsp. salt
1/8 tsp. black pepper
pinch dried leaf marjoram
1/2 cup light cream
2 tsp. flour
3 slices hot buttered toast

## Creamed Mushrooms

Heat butter or margarine in a heavy skillet. Add onion and garlic and cook gently 2 minutes. Add mushrooms and lemon juice, cover and cook gently, stirring occasionally, until mushrooms are tender, about 3 minutes.

Sprinkle in flour, salt, pepper and celery seeds. Stir to blend and let bubble up. Remove from heat and add chicken stock and cream all at once. Stir to blend and return to moderate heat. Cook gently, stirring constantly, until thickened and smooth.

Serve immediately over hot buttered toast. (Serves 4.)

3 tbsp. butter or margarine
1 tbsp. grated onion
1/2 small clove garlic, minced
1 lb. (2 pt.) fresh mushrooms,
  sliced
2 tsp. lemon juice
2 tbsp. flour
1 tsp. salt
1/4 tsp. black pepper
1 tsp. celery seeds
1 cup chicken stock
  (recipe p. 48)
1/2 cup light cream
4 slices hot buttered toast

## Fried Tomatoes on Toast

Cut thin slices from tops of tomatoes and discard. Cut each tomato into 2 thick slices. Combine flour, salt and pepper and dip tomato slices in this mixture to coat both sides.

Heat butter or margarine in a large heavy skillet. Add tomato slices. Sprinkle top of each slice with a pinch of tarragon and a pinch of basil.

Cook over moderate heat until bottom side is golden brown. Turn carefully with an egg turner and brown second side.

Put toast on serving plates and top each slice of toast with 2 slices tomato. Add cream to skillet, stir well and pour some of the cream over each serving. Serve immediately with strips of crisp bacon. (Serves 4.)

4 large ripe tomatoes
1/4 cup flour
1/2 tsp. salt
1/4 tsp. black pepper
1/4 cup butter or margarine
dried leaf tarragon
dried leaf basil
4 slices hot buttered toast
1/2 cup light cream
crisp bacon

## Creamed Kippers with Eggs

4 kippers
1 tbsp. butter or margarine
1 tbsp. flour
1 1/2 cups milk
1/4 tsp. salt
dash black pepper
2 hard-cooked eggs, chopped
1 medium boiled potato, diced
2 1/2 tbsp. drained sweet
pickle relish
4 slices hot buttered toast

Put kippers in a large skillet. Cover with boiling water. Heat to boiling, turn down heat, cover and simmer until meat can easily be pulled away from bones, about 5 minutes. Drain. Remove skin and bones from fish and break flesh into bite-size pieces.

Heat butter or margarine in a saucepan. Sprinkle in flour and stir to blend. Remove from heat and add milk all at once. Stir in salt and pepper. Return to moderate heat and cook, stirring constantly, until boiling, thickened and smooth. Stir in eggs, potato, relish and fish pieces. Heat well.

Serve immediately over hot buttered toast. (Serves 4.)

Advance preparation: Poach fish and break up. Prepare sauce, cook eggs and potato and refrigerate separately until near serving time. Heat sauce in the top of a double boiler, add other ingredients and heat well.

## Finnan Haddie with Egg Sauce

1 small onion, sliced paper thin
1 tsp. peppercorns
2 lb. finnan haddie, cut in 6
3 cups milk
1/4 cup butter or margarine
3 tbsp. flour
1 tsp. lemon juice
1 tbsp. butter or margarine
2 hard-cooked eggs, chopped

Separate onion slices into rings and sprinkle them over the bottom of a large heavy skillet or saucepan. Add peppercorns and lay fish on top. Add milk (fish should be covered). Bring to a boil, turn down heat, cover and simmer until fish flakes easily with a fork, about 10 minutes.

Lift fish out with a slotted spoon and put onto a hot platter. Strain cooking liquid and measure out 2 cups. Discard remaining liquid.

Heat cooking liquid in a saucepan. Cream 1/4 cup butter or margarine and flour together and add to hot liquid bit by bit, stirring well after each addition. Cook over moderate heat, stirring constantly, until boiling, thickened and smooth. Turn down heat and continue stirring 3 minutes. Stir in lemon juice, 1 tbsp. butter or margarine and eggs.

Serve the finnan haddie and pass the sauce. (Serves 6.)

## Fish à la King

1 lb. frozen haddock fillets
2 tbsp. butter or margarine
2 tbsp. flour
1/2 tsp. salt
1/8 tsp. cayenne
1 cup milk
1 tbsp. chopped pimento
1 cup cooked peas
hot cooked rice, riced potatoes
or baked potatoes

Cut block of fish into 3 pieces. Boil water 1 1/2 inches deep in a large skillet. Add pieces of fish and simmer until fish flakes easily with a fork, about 10 minutes. Lift out of water with an egg turner and flake it into a bowl.

Heat butter or margarine in a medium saucepan. Sprinkle in flour, salt and cayenne. Stir to blend. Remove from heat and add milk all at once. Return to moderate heat and stir until thickened and smooth. Add pimento, peas and flaked fish and heat gently about 4 minutes, stirring occasionally.

Serve over cooked rice, riced potatoes or baked potatoes. (Serves 4.)

Advance preparation: Cook and flake fish. Refrigerate.

## Kedgeree

1 lb. finnan haddie
1 cup milk
1 cup water
4 1/2 cups cold water
large pinch saffron (optional)
1 1/2 tsp. salt
1 tsp. lemon juice
1 1/2 cups regular long-grain rice
3 hard-cooked eggs
1 1/2 cups frozen green peas,
  cooked
1/2 cup butter or margarine
1/2 cup light cream
salt and pepper
chopped parsley
hard-cooked egg wedges
parsley sprigs

Put finnan haddie in a glass or pottery baking dish. Pour milk and 1 cup water over. Let stand 2 hours, turning occasionally.

Put 4 1/2 cups cold water in a large saucepan. Add saffron, 1 1/2 tsp. salt and lemon juice and bring to a full boil.

Add rice to boiling liquid gradually, stirring with a fork. Add it slowly enough so water keeps boiling. Turn heat to low, cover pan tightly and simmer until rice is tender and water is absorbed, about 25 minutes. (Cook uncovered for a few minutes if rice is ready but there is still some water in the pan.)

Put finnan haddie and soaking liquid in a large skillet (stainless steel if possible). Bring to simmering, turn down heat, cover tightly and simmer until fish flakes easily with a fork, about 10 minutes. Drain fish, discarding liquid. Flake fish, discarding any skin and bones.

Cut hard-cooked eggs into halves and lift out yolks. Put yolks in a sieve. Chop whites coarsely.

Toss rice lightly with fish, egg whites and peas. Add butter or margarine and toss again with a fork. Set over low heat, cover and heat slowly, tossing occasionally and adding cream a little at a time to keep mixture moist. Add salt and pepper to taste when hot.

Turn Kedgeree out onto a large platter and shape into a pyramid with a fork. Press egg yolks through a sieve all over top of pyramid and sprinkle with chopped parsley. Garnish plate with wedges of hard-cooked eggs and parsley sprigs. Serve immediately. (Serves 6 to 8.)

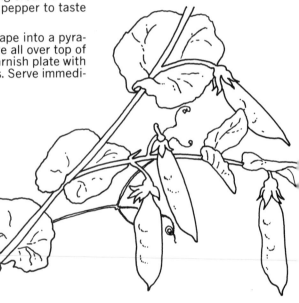

## Baked Fish Scandinavian Style

1 lb. cod fillets
1/2 cup buttermilk
1 small bay leaf, crumbled
4 peppercorns, coarsely
  crushed
1 whole clove, coarsely crushed
1 tsp. grated onion
salt and pepper
garlic powder
1/2 tsp. dried dill weed
paprika (optional)

Thaw fish if necessary until it can be separated. Heat oven to 375°F. Lightly oil a 12 × 7 × 2-inch baking dish.

Combine buttermilk, bay leaf, peppercorns, clove and onion. Put fish in a single layer in prepared dish. Sprinkle lightly with salt, pepper and garlic powder, then with dill weed. Pour buttermilk mixture over. Sprinkle with paprika.

Bake until fish flakes easily with a fork, about 15 minutes. (Serves 2 or 3.)

## Sizzling Twin Crêpes

16 crêpes (recipe follows)
2 lb. (4 pt.) fresh mushrooms
1/2 cup butter or margarine
1/3 cup flour
4 cups chicken stock
   (recipe p. 48)
1 large stalk celery, coarsely
   chopped
3 large sprigs parsley
1/4 tsp. dried leaf thyme
1/4 tsp. salt
1/4 tsp. black pepper
1/8 tsp. ground nutmeg
3 egg yolks
1/3 cup heavy cream
1 cup lightly salted water
2 tbsp. lemon juice
3 tbsp. butter or margarine
1 cup or 5-oz. can flaked crab
1 lb. scallops, cooked and
   quartered (see note)
1 small cooked lobster, shelled
   and cut small (about 1 cup
   meat) or 5-oz. can
1/2 tsp. salt
1/4 tsp. black pepper
2 tbsp. dry sherry
2 hard-cooked eggs,
   finely chopped
2 tbsp. grated Parmesan
   cheese
grated Parmesan cheese

Make crêpes and set aside.

Remove stems from mushrooms and set caps aside to use later for mushroom filling. Chop stems finely.

Melt 1/2 cup butter or margarine in a large saucepan. Sprinkle in flour and stir to blend. Remove from heat and stir in chicken stock all at once. Return to moderate heat and stir until boiling. Add celery, parsley, thyme, 1/4 tsp. salt, 1/4 tsp. pepper, nutmeg and mushroom stems. Bring to boil, turn down heat and simmer, uncovered, 20 minutes, stirring often.

Strain mushroom mixture and return sauce to saucepan. Beat egg yolks and cream together with a fork. Add about 1 cup of hot sauce a little at a time, beating well after each addition. Pour egg mixture gradually into hot sauce, stirring constantly, and bring just to a boil. Remove from heat.

Slice mushroom caps. Bring salted water to a boil in a large saucepan. Add lemon juice and sliced mushroom caps. Simmer 3 minutes. Drain. Add 1/4 cup of the sauce to the mushrooms and blend lightly. Set aside.

Heat 3 tbsp. butter or margarine in a large skillet. Add crab, scallops, lobster, 1/2 tsp. salt and 1/4 tsp. pepper. Cook gently 2 minutes, stirring. Remove from heat. Stir in sherry, eggs and 1/4 cup sauce.

Heat oven to 450°F. Lightly grease 8 shallow individual baking dishes at least 6 inches long (see note).

With well-browned side down, top each of 8 crêpes with 1/3 cup of the mushroom filling. Roll up. Top each remaining crêpe with 1/3 cup of the seafood filling. Roll up. Put one of each crêpe in each baking dish.

Stir 2 tbsp. Parmesan into remaining sauce. Divide sauce evenly among baking dishes (about 6 tbsp. each), spooning it over the crêpes. Sprinkle lightly with more Parmesan.

Bake until bubbling well, about 10 minutes. Turn on broiler and lightly brown tops. Serve immediately. (Serves 8.)

*Note:* To cook scallops, add them to 1 cup boiling water. Add 1 tbsp. lemon juice, 2 sprigs parsley and a small slice onion. Turn down heat and simmer just until scallops lose their transparent look, about 5 minutes. Drain. Choose individual baking dishes that will hold 2 rolled-up crêpes flat and side by side. If you don't have small baking dishes, put the crêpes in two 13 x 9 x 2-inch baking dishes and divide the sauce evenly between them. Heat as for small baking dishes.

Advance preparation: Crêpes can be made far ahead and frozen until needed. They can be frozen flat on trays, then stacked, wrapped and frozen. The eggs can be hard cooked and the sauce made a day ahead. Shortly before guests arrive, the crêpes can be filled and put into baking dishes. Spoon on the sauce just before baking.

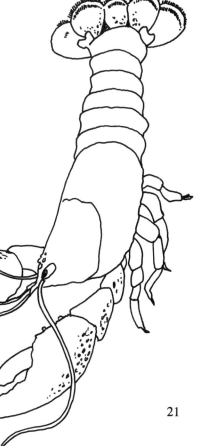

21

## Crêpes

4 eggs
$1/2$ tsp. salt
$1\,1/4$ cups sifted all-purpose
 flour
$1\,3/4$ cups milk
$1/4$ cup melted butter or
 margarine, cooled
 to lukewarm

Beat eggs and salt together. Add remaining ingredients and beat until smooth. Let stand 1 hour. Stir.

Put about 2 tbsp. batter on a lightly greased hot griddle and immediately spread as thinly as possible to make a pancake 5 to 6 inches in diameter. Or put batter in a lightly greased 6-inch skillet or crêpe pan and tip the pan immediately so the batter runs and covers the bottom of the pan completely. Brown first side well, loosen cake and turn. Cook just long enough to set second side (it will be very lightly browned and spotty).

Fill as directed in recipe, putting well-browned side on outside of rolls. Freeze any left over with waxed paper between to fill another day. (Makes about 20.)

## Wheat Germ Pancakes

2 eggs
2 cups milk
1 tbsp. cooking oil
$1\,2/3$ cups whole wheat flour
$2/3$ cup toasted wheat germ
1 tbsp. sugar
3 tsp. baking powder
1 tsp. salt

Heat a griddle or a large heavy skillet and grease if necessary.

Beat eggs, milk and oil together with a rotary beater. Combine whole wheat flour, wheat germ, sugar, baking powder and salt, mixing well with a fork. Add to egg mixture and stir just to blend.

Bake as usual for pancakes, turning to brown second sides when bubbles form on tops. (Makes 18 large.)

## Plain Raised Waffles

$1/4$ cup warm water
1 tsp. sugar
1 pkg. dry yeast
$1\,3/4$ cups lukewarm milk
2 tbsp. sugar
1 tsp. salt
3 eggs
$1/4$ cup soft butter or margarine
$1\,3/4$ cups sifted all-purpose
 flour

Measure water into a medium bowl. Add 1 tsp. sugar and stir to dissolve. Sprinkle yeast over water and let stand 10 minutes. Stir well.

Add remaining ingredients to yeast mixture and beat with a rotary beater until smooth. Cover and let rise in a warm place $1\,1/2$ hours.

Stir batter down and cover again. Refrigerate until needed, then bake in a hot waffle iron. (Makes 3 large.)

Advance preparation: Prepare batter and refrigerate overnight.

## Health Raised Waffles

$1/4$ cup warm water
1 tsp. sugar
1 pkg. dry yeast
1 tbsp. liquid honey
1 tsp. salt
3 eggs
$1/4$ cup cooking oil
$1\,3/4$ cups whole wheat flour
$1/2$ cup wheat germ
$1/4$ cup sunflower seeds
 (optional)
honey

Measure water into a medium bowl. Add sugar and stir to dissolve. Sprinkle yeast over water and let stand 10 minutes. Stir well.

Add remaining ingredients except sunflower seeds and honey to yeast mixture and beat with a rotary beater until smooth. Stir in sunflower seeds. Cover and let rise in a warm place $1\,1/2$ hours.

Stir batter down and cover again. Refrigerate until needed, then bake in a hot waffle iron. Serve topped with honey. (Makes 3 large.)

## Oatmeal Pancakes

3 cups milk
2 cups quick-cooking rolled oats
$1/2$ cup sifted all-purpose flour
3 tsp. baking powder
1 tsp. salt
2 eggs, separated
$1/3$ cup cooking oil
Raisin Sauce (recipe follows)

Scald milk. Pour over rolled oats in a bowl. Stir to blend, then cool.

Sift flour, baking powder and salt together into rolled oats mixture. Beat egg whites until stiff. Beat egg yolks with same beater. Add egg yolks and oil to rolled oats mixture. Fold in egg whites.

Bake on a hot griddle as for regular pancakes, using about $1/4$ cup batter for each pancake and spreading batter slightly. Serve hot with Raisin Sauce. (Makes 12 to 16.)

## Raisin Sauce

1 tbsp. flour
$1/4$ cup packed brown sugar
$1/2$ cup liquid honey
$1^1/2$ cups water
1 cup seedless raisins
2 tbsp. butter or margarine
1 tbsp. lemon juice
$1/8$ tsp. ground nutmeg

Blend flour and sugar thoroughly in a saucepan. Add honey and $1^1/2$ cups water. Bring to a boil. Add raisins and boil gently, uncovered, until mixture thickens slightly, about 20 minutes. Stir in butter or margarine, lemon juice and nutmeg. Serve warm. (Makes about $2^1/2$ cups.)

## Buckwheat Cakes

$1/2$ cup warm water
1 tsp. sugar
1 pkg. dry yeast
2 cups cold water
$1/4$ cup sugar
$1^1/2$ tsp. salt
1 cup sifted all-purpose flour
2 cups buckwheat flour
   (do not sift)
1 tsp. baking soda
$1/2$ cup heavy cream
maple syrup

Measure warm water into a large bowl. Add 1 tsp. sugar and stir to dissolve. Sprinkle yeast over and let stand 10 minutes. Stir well.

Add 2 cups cold water, sugar and salt. Add all-purpose flour and buckwheat flour and beat until smooth. Cover with transparent wrap and refrigerate overnight.

Stir in soda and cream shortly before serving time. Let stand 30 minutes at room temperature.

Bake on a lightly greased griddle until browned underneath and bubbles form on top. Serve with warm maple syrup. (Makes about 25 large.)

Advance preparation: Refrigerate batter overnight as directed.

## Bread Pancakes

4 cups milk, scalded
4 cups fresh white bread
 crumbs
4 egg yolks
1³/4 cups sifted all-purpose
 flour
2 tsp. baking powder
¹/2 tsp. salt
³/4 cup butter or margarine,
 melted
4 egg whites
syrup, honey or jelly

Pour hot milk over bread crumbs and let stand until cool.

Beat egg yolks in a small bowl until thick and lemon colored. Stir into milk mixture.

Sift flour, baking powder and salt together into batter and mix thoroughly. Stir in melted butter or margarine. Beat egg whites stiff and fold into batter.

Bake on a lightly greased hot griddle, turning when pancakes are puffed and bubbly. Serve hot with syrup, honey or jelly. (Makes 40.)

*Note:* These are very light and tender pancakes. The recipe is large but can be cut in half if you wish.

## Apple-Honey Griddle Cakes

1 egg
³/4 cup milk
3 tbsp. cooking oil or melted
 shortening
2 tbsp. liquid honey
1¹/4 cups sifted all-purpose
 flour
2¹/2 tsp. baking powder
³/4 tsp. salt
¹/4 tsp. ground cinnamon
1 cup coarsely grated apple
Honey Butter (recipe follows)

Combine egg, milk, oil or shortening and honey in a mixing bowl and beat until well blended.

Sift flour, baking powder, salt and cinnamon together into mixture and stir to blend. Stir in apple.

Bake as for regular pancakes, spreading batter as thinly as possible. Serve very hot with Honey Butter. (Makes 8 large.)

## Honey Butter

¹/2 cup soft butter
¹/2 cup liquid honey

Cream butter. Beat in honey gradually. Beat until fluffy. Chill. (Makes 1 cup.)

24

### French Toast with Pineapple

3 eggs
3 tbsp. pineapple juice
1/4 tsp. salt
dash black pepper
butter or margarine
8 slices day-old bread
1 lb. sausages, cooked
Pineapple Garnish
 (recipe follows)
Pineapple Sauce
 (recipe follows)

Beat eggs, pineapple juice, salt and pepper together with a fork in a flat dish (a pie plate is good). Heat about 2 tbsp. butter or margarine in a large heavy skillet.

Dip bread slices quickly into egg mixture to coat both sides (dip only the number that will fit in the pan at one time). Fry in butter or margarine until golden on both sides. Add more butter or margarine as needed. Keep toast warm in low oven until all slices are fried.

Overlap slices of toast on a hot serving plate. Garnish plate with sausages and Pineapple Garnish. Put hot Pineapple Sauce in a pitcher and let guests help themselves. (Serves 8.)

*Note:* If you wish you can make the toast in the oven. Heat oven to 500°F. Put toast that has been dipped in egg mixture on a greased cookie sheet and bake until browned, about 10 minutes.

Advance preparation: Make Pineapple Sauce and have Pineapple Garnish ready for broiler.

### Pineapple Garnish

8 slices bacon
8 slices canned sweetened
 pineapple

Wrap bacon slices around and through the hole in the pineapple slices in a spiral. Put on broiler rack, place low in the oven and broil until bacon is cooked, about 10 minutes. Turn after first 5 minutes.

### Pineapple Sauce

1 1/2 cups packed brown sugar
2 tbsp. cornstarch
1 cup syrup drained from 19-oz.
 can sweetened pineapple
 slices (add water if necessary
 to make the 1 cup)
2 tbsp. butter or margarine

Combine brown sugar and cornstarch thoroughly in a medium saucepan. Stir in pineapple syrup gradually. Set over high heat and stir until boiling, thickened and smooth. Turn heat to low. Stir in butter or margarine. Keep hot. (Makes 1 3/4 cups.)

### Toasted Cheesies

8 slices bacon, cut in half
4 English muffins
250 g pkg. process cheese
 slices
2 tbsp. finely chopped onion
1 tsp. Worcestershire sauce
2 or 3 large tomatoes, sliced

Cook bacon until crisp, drain on paper toweling and keep warm. Heat broiler.

Pry muffins apart with the tines of a fork and lay them, cut side down, on a cookie sheet. Slip under broiler and toast undersides of muffins lightly. Remove from oven and turn muffins so cut sides are up.

Top each half with a slice of cheese. Combine onion and Worcestershire and put a small amount of mixture on top of each slice of cheese. Top each with a tomato slice.

Broil until hot and bubbly. Slip 2 pieces of muffin onto each of 4 serving plates and garnish each piece of muffin with 2 pieces of bacon. Serve immediately. (Serves 4.)

## Hashed Brown Potatoes

6 medium potatoes
2 tbsp. flour
1 tsp. salt
dash black pepper
$^1/_4$ cup chopped parsley
$^1/_2$ cup light cream
1 tbsp. butter or margarine
1 tbsp. cooking oil

Cook potatoes in their jackets until barely tender. (They are best if they are a little firm in the middle.) Cool until they can be handled, peel and grate on the coarse grater. (You should have about 4 cups.)

Add flour, salt, pepper and parsley to grated potatoes and toss lightly with a fork. Add cream and toss again lightly.

Heat butter or margarine and oil in a large heavy skillet. Add potatoes and spread evenly. Pack down lightly with an egg turner. Cook over low heat until golden underneath, 10 to 15 minutes.

Turn with egg turner. (If you wish, you may invert the skillet on a large flat plate, then slip potatoes back into skillet in one piece, unbrowned side down. However, I find it easier to cut potato mixture into large pieces and turn pieces with egg turner.) Pack down again lightly.

Add a little more butter or oil if necessary and continue cooking slowly until browned on second side. Cut into 6 wedges and serve immediately. (Serves 6.)

## Scalloped Mushrooms

1 lb. (2 pt.) fresh mushrooms, sliced
2 cups small soft French bread cubes
$^1/_3$ cup butter or margarine, melted
salt and pepper
$^1/_3$ cup chicken stock (recipe p. 48)
pinch dried leaf tarragon

Heat oven to 350°F. Butter a 1$^1/_2$-qt. casserole.

Put about $^1/_3$ of the mushrooms in prepared casserole. Sprinkle with $^1/_3$ of the bread cubes and drizzle with $^1/_3$ of the butter or margarine. Sprinkle lightly with salt and pepper.

Repeat these layers once, then top with a final layer of mushrooms and a sprinkling of salt and pepper. (You will have $^1/_3$ of the bread cubes and $^1/_3$ of the butter or margarine left to use later.) Combine chicken stock and tarragon and pour over all. Cover and bake 20 minutes.

Combine remaining bread cubes and melted butter or margarine and sprinkle over top of mushroom mixture. Bake, uncovered, 10 minutes more. (Serves 6.)

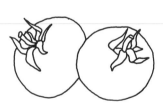

## Broiled Tomatoes

6 medium tomatoes
salt and pepper
dried leaf chervil
$^1/_2$ cup fine dry bread crumbs
2 tbsp. melted butter or margarine

Cut each tomato into halves crosswise. Sprinkle with salt and pepper and lightly with chervil. Combine bread crumbs and melted butter or margarine and sprinkle thickly onto top of each piece of tomato, patting down lightly. Put on broiler pan and broil about 4 inches from heat until topping is lightly browned and tomatoes are just warm, about 3 minutes. (Serves 6.)

# Breads

What is nicer than hot breads, no matter what the time of day? For breakfast they are a special treat so, since they all freeze well, why not make up a batch of muffins, or perhaps a yeast loaf or coffee cake, when there is time and freeze all or part of it to produce like magic just when you need it or crave it most.

## Popovers

1 cup sifted all-purpose flour
$^1/_2$ tsp. salt
2 eggs
1 cup milk
butter or margarine

Heat oven to 425°F. Grease six 6-oz. custard cups generously.

Mix flour and salt in a mixing bowl. Add eggs and milk and beat with an electric mixer or egg beater just until smooth.

Pour batter into prepared cups, filling about half full. Set on a baking sheet and bake until dark golden brown and dry to the touch, 40 to 45 minutes. Serve immediately with butter or margarine. (Makes 6.)

For a change: Substitute 1 cup whole wheat flour for all-purpose and sprinkle batter in cups with 1 tsp. wheat germ. Or use $^3/_4$ cup rye flour and $^1/_4$ cup all-purpose flour instead of the 1 cup all-purpose.

## Sesame Corn Muffins

1 egg
$1^1/_4$ cups milk
$^1/_2$ cup whole wheat flour
$1^1/_4$ cups cornmeal
2 tbsp. sugar
3 tsp. baking powder
1 tsp. salt
3 tbsp. cooking oil
sesame seeds

Heat oven to 450°F. Grease twenty-four 2-inch muffin cups. Put pans in oven to heat while preparing batter.

Beat egg. Add remaining ingredients except sesame seeds and beat with a rotary beater until blended.

Spoon into prepared pans, filling about $^2/_3$ full. Sprinkle each generously with sesame seeds. Bake until nicely browned, about 12 minutes. Serve hot. (Makes 24 small.)

## Strawberry Muffins

$^1/_2$ cup chopped strawberries
2 tbsp. sugar
milk
1 egg
$^1/_4$ cup cooking oil
2 cups sifted all-purpose flour
$^3/_4$ tsp. baking soda
$^1/_2$ tsp. salt
$^1/_4$ cup sugar

Combine strawberries and 2 tbsp. sugar and let stand 1 hour, stirring often.

Heat oven to 400°F. Grease 12 large muffin cups.

Put strawberries in a 2-cup measuring cup and add milk to make $1^1/_4$ cups liquid. Put this mixture, egg and oil in a mixing bowl and beat with a fork to blend well.

Sift flour, soda, salt and $^1/_4$ cup sugar together into first mixture and stir lightly with a fork just until dry ingredients are moistened, about 30 strokes.

Spoon into prepared muffin cups, filling about $^2/_3$ full. Bake until well browned, about 15 minutes. (Makes 12 large.)

## Pineapple Muffins

Heat oven to 400°F. Grease 12 large muffin cups.

Beat egg lightly with a fork. Beat in milk, molasses and oil. Stir in pineapple, bran and wheat germ. Mix flour, soda and salt together with a fork and add to first mixture. Stir just to blend (batter should be a little lumpy).

Spoon into prepared muffin cups, filling about 2/3 full. Bake until muffins are well browned and tops spring back when touched lightly, 15 to 20 minutes. Serve warm. (Makes 12.)

1 egg
1 1/4 cups milk
1/2 cup molasses
2 tbsp. cooking oil
3/4 cup well-drained crushed
   pineapple
1 1/2 cups natural bran
1/2 cup toasted wheat germ
1 cup whole wheat flour
1 tsp. baking soda
1 tsp. salt

## Herbed Muffins

Heat oven to 400°F. Grease 30 large muffin cups very well.

Beat eggs and buttermilk or soured milk together very well. Beat in oil.

Sift flour, sugar, salt and baking powder together into a medium bowl. Add whole wheat flour, herbs, spices and orange rind. Mix well with a fork. Add egg mixture and stir with a fork just until blended, about 30 strokes (batter should be lumpy).

Spoon into prepared muffin cups, filling about 2/3 full. Bake about 20 minutes. Serve warm. (Makes 30 large.)

4 eggs
1 3/4 cups buttermilk or soured
   milk
1/2 cup cooking oil
2 cups sifted all-purpose flour
1/4 cup sugar
1 1/2 tsp. salt
4 tsp. baking powder
1 1/4 cups whole wheat flour
2 tbsp. finely chopped parsley
1 tsp. dried leaf marjoram
1/2 tsp. ground coriander
1/2 tsp. ground allspice
1/8 tsp. black pepper
1 tsp. grated orange rind

## Apple Muffins

Heat oven to 375°F. Grease 12 large muffin cups.

Beat eggs, milk, butter or margarine and 1/3 cup sugar together well. Combine flour, salt, baking powder, 1/4 tsp. cinnamon and nutmeg in a bowl, mixing lightly with a fork. Add to egg mixture and stir just until dry ingredients are dampened (batter should be lumpy). Fold in apples.

Spoon into prepared muffin cups, filling about 2/3 full. Mix 1/4 cup sugar and 1/4 tsp. cinnamon and sprinkle over muffin batter. Bake about 30 minutes. Serve warm. (Makes 12 large.)

2 eggs
1 cup milk
2 tbsp. melted butter or
   margarine
1/3 cup sugar
2 cups whole wheat flour
1/2 tsp. salt
4 tsp. baking powder
1/4 tsp. ground cinnamon
1/4 tsp. ground nutmeg
2 medium apples, peeled,
   cored and finely chopped
   (about 2 cups)
1/4 cup sugar
1/4 tsp. ground cinnamon

## Cheese Muffins

Heat oven to 400°F. Grease 12 large muffin cups.

Sift flour, baking powder and salt together into a medium bowl. Add ²/₃ cup cheese and toss with a fork until cheese is coated with flour mixture. Beat egg, milk and oil together lightly with a fork. Add to flour mixture and stir with fork just to blend (batter should be a little lumpy).

Spoon into prepared muffin cups, filling ²/₃ full. Combine ¹/₄ cup cheese and wheat germ and sprinkle some of mixture on top of each muffin. Bake until nicely browned, 20 to 25 minutes. Serve warm. (Makes 12 large.)

1³/₄ cups sifted all-purpose flour
3 tsp. baking powder
¹/₂ tsp. salt
²/₃ cup grated old Cheddar cheese
1 egg
1 cup milk
2 tbsp. cooking oil
¹/₄ cup grated old Cheddar cheese
2 tbsp. wheat germ

## Oatmeal-Date Muffins

Heat oven to 400°F. Grease 12 large muffin cups.

Beat egg, milk, oil and honey together to blend well. Sift flour, baking powder and salt together into mixture. Add rolled oats and dates. Stir just to blend (batter should be a little lumpy).

Spoon into prepared muffin cups, filling ²/₃ full. Bake until golden, 20 to 25 minutes. Serve warm. (Makes 12 large.)

1 egg
1 cup milk
¹/₃ cup cooking oil
¹/₄ cup liquid honey
1¹/₂ cups sifted all-purpose flour
3 tsp. baking powder
1 tsp. salt
1 cup quick-cooking rolled oats
¹/₂ cup chopped dates

## Granola Muffins

Heat milk to scalding. Remove from heat. Stir in butter or margarine, ¹/₄ cup sugar and salt and stir until butter is melted. Cool to lukewarm.

Measure water into a mixing bowl. Add 1 tsp. sugar and stir to dissolve. Sprinkle yeast over water and let stand 10 minutes. Stir well.

Stir in milk mixture and eggs. Add flour and 1 cup granola. Beat with a wooden spoon until batter is smooth and fairly thick. Cover with a damp cloth and let rise in a warm place until very light, about 1¹/₄ hours.

Grease 24 large muffin cups very well. Beat batter again very well. Spoon into prepared muffin cups, filling them about half full. Sprinkle tops of muffins with ¹/₂ cup granola. Let rise again until double, about 30 minutes

Heat oven to 425°F. Bake 10 minutes. Reduce heat to 350°F and continue baking until nicely browned, about 5 minutes more. Serve warm. (Makes 24 large.)

2 cups milk
¹/₂ cup soft butter or margarine
¹/₄ cup sugar
1 tsp. salt
¹/₄ cup warm water
1 tsp. sugar
1 pkg. dry yeast
2 eggs, beaten
4¹/₂ cups sifted all-purpose flour
1 cup granola cereal
¹/₂ cup granola cereal

## Banana Muffins

1 egg
1/2 cup milk
1 cup mashed ripe bananas
  (2 to 3)
1 1/2 cups bran flakes
  (ready-to-eat cereal)
1/4 cup soft shortening
1 cup sifted all-purpose flour
2 1/2 tsp. baking powder
1/2 tsp. salt
1/4 cup sugar

Heat oven to 400°F. Grease 12 large muffin cups.

Beat egg lightly in a mixing bowl. Stir in milk, mashed bananas and bran flakes. Add shortening and beat well. Sift flour, baking powder, salt and sugar together into mixture and stir just to blend (batter should be a little lumpy).

Spoon into prepared muffin cups, filling 2/3 full. Bake until tops spring back when touched lightly, about 20 minutes. Serve warm. (Makes 12 large.)

## Wheat Germ Muffins

1 cup sifted all-purpose flour
2 tsp. baking powder
1/2 tsp. salt
2 tbsp. sugar
1/2 cup wheat germ
1/2 cup whole wheat flour
1 cup cut-up soft prunes
1 tsp. grated lemon rind
1 cup milk
1 egg
2 tbsp. cooking oil

Heat oven to 400°F. Grease 12 large muffin cups.

Sift flour, baking powder, salt and sugar together into a bowl. Add wheat germ and whole wheat flour and mix with a fork. Add prunes and lemon rind.

Combine milk, egg and salad oil and beat together lightly with a fork. Add to mixture in bowl and stir just to blend (batter should be a little lumpy).

Spoon into prepared muffin cups, filling 2/3 full. Bake about 20 minutes. (Makes 12 large.)

## Oat-Raisin Scones

1 1/2 cups sifted all-purpose
  flour
4 tsp. baking powder
1/2 tsp. salt
1/4 tsp. ground nutmeg
1/3 cup shortening
1/2 cup quick-cooking rolled
  oats
1/2 cup seedless raisins
1/4 cup molasses
1 cup milk (approx.)
1 tbsp. milk
2 tsp. sugar

Heat oven to 450°F. Grease a cookie sheet.

Sift flour, baking powder, salt and nutmeg together into a mixing bowl. Add shortening and cut in finely. Add rolled oats and raisins and stir lightly with a fork. Add molasses and enough of the 1 cup milk to make a soft, puffy dough. Stir lightly with a fork.

Turn dough out onto a floured board and knead gently 10 times. Divide dough into 2 equal parts and shape each part into a ball. Pat each ball into a round about 3/4 inch thick. Put on prepared sheet. Mark each round into 6 wedges with the tines of a fork.

Combine 1 tbsp. milk and sugar, stirring until sugar is dissolved. Brush mixture over rounds.

Bake until golden brown, 12 to 15 minutes. Break rounds apart along fork marks and serve warm. (Makes 12.)

### Potato-Bacon Scones

6 slices bacon
1/4 cup bacon fat or melted
   butter or margarine
1 cup plain mashed potatoes
1/4 cup milk
2 cups sifted all-purpose flour
3 tsp. baking powder
1/2 tsp. salt
1 tbsp. sugar
1 egg
3/4 cup milk (approx.)

Fry bacon until crisp. Drain well, crumble and set aside.

Measure out 1/4 cup of the fat (add melted butter or margarine to make up the amount if necessary). Combine fat with potatoes and 1/4 cup milk in a small saucepan. Heat gently until well blended. Cool.

Heat oven to 425°F. Grease a cookie sheet.

Sift flour, baking powder, salt and sugar into a bowl. Beat egg and 3/4 cup milk together. Add potatoes, egg mixture and bacon bits to dry ingredients. Stir with a fork just to blend. Add a little more milk if necessary to make a fairly soft dough.

Turn out onto a floured board and knead gently 12 times. Pat into a round about 3/4 inch thick on waxed paper. Invert on cookie sheet. Mark into 8 wedges with a knife.

Bake 25 to 30 minutes. Break into wedges and serve warm. (Makes 8.)

### Sally Lunn

1 tsp. sugar
1/4 cup warm water
1 pkg. dry yeast
1 cup milk
1/4 cup soft butter or margarine
1/4 cup sugar
1 tsp. salt
2 eggs, beaten
3 1/3 cups sifted all-purpose
   flour
butter

Add 1 tsp. sugar to 1/4 cup warm water and stir to dissolve. Sprinkle yeast over and let stand 10 minutes. Stir well.

While yeast is soaking, heat milk to scalding. Remove from heat and stir in butter or margarine, 1/4 cup sugar and salt. Stir until butter or margarine is melted. Pour into a large bowl and cool to lukewarm.

Stir in eggs and yeast mixture. Add flour gradually, beating until smooth after each addition.

Scrape down sides of bowl, cover with a damp cloth and let rise in a warm place until double, about 1 hour.

Beat dough down with a wooden spoon and turn it into a well-greased 2-qt. tube pan, Turk's-head mold or bundt pan (see note). Level it off by patting with a floured hand. Cover and let rise in a warm place until very light (about 1 inch from top of pan or mold).

Heat oven to 350°F. Bake until very well browned and loaf sounds hollow when tapped on top, about 45 minutes. (Cover loaf loosely with aluminum foil if top begins to brown too much.) Turn out onto a rack to cool. Serve Sally Lunn slightly warm or cold with butter.

*Note:* You can check the size of your pan or mold by pouring 2 quarts of water into it. Water should fill it to the brim.

## Whole Wheat Raisin Bread

1/2 cup warm water
2 tsp. sugar
2 pkg. dry yeast
1 1/2 cups milk
1/4 cup sugar
1 tbsp. salt
1/4 cup soft butter or
  margarine
3 eggs, lightly beaten
7 1/2 cups whole wheat flour
  (approx.)
2 cups seedless raisins
melted butter or margarine
sugar

Put 1/2 cup warm water in a large mixing bowl. Add 2 tsp. sugar and stir until sugar is dissolved. Sprinkle yeast over and let stand 10 minutes.

Heat milk to scalding. Remove from heat and stir in 1/4 cup sugar, salt and 1/4 cup butter or margarine, stirring until butter or margarine is melted. Cool to lukewarm.

Stir yeast mixture well. Stir in milk mixture and eggs. Add half of the flour and beat very well with a wooden spoon. Beat in raisins. Add enough of remaining flour to make a dough that is firm but not stiff. Mix first with spoon, then with hand.

Turn out onto a floured board and knead until smooth and elastic, about 10 minutes.

Put in a large greased bowl, turn over once so top is greased, cover with a damp cloth and let rise in a warm place until double, about 1 1/2 hours.

Punch dough down and let rise again until nearly double, about 45 minutes.

Grease three 9 × 5 × 3-inch loaf pans.

Punch dough down again and divide into 3 equal parts. Shape each part into a loaf and put into prepared pans. Let rise again until double, about 1 hour.

Heat oven to 425°F. Brush loaves lightly with melted butter or margarine and sprinkle with sugar. Bake until loaves sound hollow when tapped on top, 25 to 30 minutes. (Cover loaves loosely with aluminum foil if they start to brown too much.) Turn out onto racks to cool. (Makes 3 loaves.)

## Fried Pies

shortening or oil for deep
  frying
2 eggs
1/2 cup milk (approx.)
3 tbsp. cooking oil
1 tsp. vanilla extract
2 1/2 cups sifted all-purpose
  flour
4 tsp. baking powder
1 1/4 tsp. salt
1/2 cup sugar
1/2 tsp. ground mace
jam or jelly
milk
sugar

Heat shortening or oil for deep frying to 370°F.

Beat eggs well. Stir in 1/2 cup milk, 3 tbsp. oil and vanilla. Sift flour, baking powder, salt, 1/2 cup sugar and mace together and stir into liquid ingredients, adding a little more milk if necessary to make a soft dough that is easy to handle.

Turn dough out onto a floured board and knead lightly about 8 times to smooth up. Roll to 1/4 inch thick. Cut into 2 1/2-inch rounds with a cookie cutter.

Put a small spoonful of jam or jelly in the centre of each round. Dampen edges of rounds with milk and fold rounds in half, pinching edges together well to completely enclose jam or jelly.

Put turnovers a few at a time into hot fat and fry until golden, turning once. Drain on paper toweling. Roll in sugar while warm. (Makes about 2 dozen.)

### Petites Brioches

$2/3$ cup warm water
1 tbsp. sugar
2 pkg. dry yeast
$2/3$ cup milk
$2\frac{1}{2}$ tsp. salt
6 cups sifted all-purpose flour
$1\frac{1}{3}$ cups soft butter or
  margarine
6 eggs
1 egg yolk
1 tbsp. water

Measure warm water into a large bowl. Add sugar and stir until dissolved. Sprinkle yeast over and let stand 10 minutes.

Heat milk to scalding. Remove from heat and cool to lukewarm. Add salt.

Stir yeast mixture well. Add milk and 2 cups of the flour and beat well with a wooden spoon. Add butter or margarine and beat to blend. Beat in eggs one at a time. Blend in remaining flour. Dough should be soft.

Continue beating with a wooden spoon as long as possible or until dough begins to firm up. Then pick it up and slap it down on a lightly floured board again and again until dough is fairly firm. Put in a greased bowl, turn over once so top is greased, cover with a damp cloth and let rise until double, about 3 hours. Stir down and chill overnight.

Grease well 24 fluted individual brioche molds or custard cups, or 30 large muffin cups.

Pinch off about $1/5$ of the dough and set aside. Divide remaining dough into 24 to 30 pieces and shape each piece into a round (whatever size mold you use should be filled about half full with the round of dough). Put rounds into baking pans. Snip a small X about $1/4$ inch deep in top of each round with kitchen shears. Push points of X down with tips of shears to make a hole.

Divide dough you set aside into 24 or 30 equal parts. Shape these pieces into teardrop shapes and drop pointed ends into holes on top of dough rounds, pressing them in firmly. Cover with waxed paper and let rise in a warm place until double, about 2 hours.

Heat oven to 425°F. Beat egg yolk and 1 tbsp. water together with a fork and brush over tops of buns (try to keep egg yolk mixture from running down between dough and pan).

Bake until browned, about 20 minutes. Cover loosely with foil if tops begin to brown too much. (Makes 2 to $2\frac{1}{2}$ dozen.)

## Raised Doughnuts

2 cups milk
1 cup sugar
1/2 cup shortening
1 1/2 tsp. salt
1 cup freshly mashed
   unseasoned potatoes
   (2 medium)
1/2 cup warm water
2 tsp. sugar
2 pkg. dry yeast
3 eggs, beaten
1 tsp. ground nutmeg
8 cups sifted all-purpose flour
oil for deep frying
icing sugar or sugar-cinnamon
   mixture

Scald milk. Add 1 cup sugar, shortening and salt and stir until shortening is melted. Add potatoes and stir to blend. Cool to lukewarm.

Measure water into a large bowl. Add 2 tsp. sugar and stir until sugar is dissolved. Sprinkle yeast over and let stand 10 minutes. Stir well.

Stir in cooled milk mixture, eggs and nutmeg. Add half of the flour and beat well with a wooden spoon. Blend in remaining flour. Turn out onto a lightly floured board and knead until smooth and elastic, about 5 minutes.

Put in a large greased bowl, turn dough over once so top is greased, cover with a damp cloth and let rise in a warm place until double, about 1 1/2 hours.

Punch dough down and let rise again until nearly double, about 30 minutes.

Roll dough slightly less than 1/2 inch thick and cut with a doughnut cutter. (If you don't have a doughnut cutter, cut the dough into strips 1/2 inch wide by 8 inches long and twist ends of each strip in opposite directions until it forms into a figure 8, sealing ends together. Or twist the strips as for figure 8s and tie each one in a loose knot.)

Set doughnuts on a lightly floured pastry board or counter top and let stand, uncovered, until very light, 30 to 45 minutes.

Heat oil to 375°F. Fry doughnuts a few at a time until golden on both sides. Drain on paper toweling. Roll in icing sugar or a mixture of sugar and cinnamon while warm. (Makes about 4 dozen large.)

## Prune-Bran Coffee Cake

1 cup sifted all-purpose flour
1/4 cup sugar
2 1/2 tsp. baking powder
1 tsp. ground cinnamon
1/2 tsp. salt
1 cup natural bran (not
   prepared cereal)
1 cup chopped cooked prunes
1 egg
1 cup milk
2 tbsp. cooking oil
1/4 cup sugar
1/2 tsp. ground cinnamon

Heat oven to 375°F. Grease an 8-inch square cake pan.

Sift flour, 1/4 cup sugar, baking powder, 1 tsp. cinnamon and salt into a mixing bowl. Add bran and prunes and mix lightly with a fork.

Beat egg, milk and oil together and add to first mixture. Stir just to blend. Spoon into prepared pan. Combine 1/4 cup sugar and 1/2 tsp. cinnamon and sprinkle over batter.

Bake until a toothpick stuck in the centre comes out clean, about 30 minutes. Serve warm.

## Rich Coffee Cake

Combine brown sugar, walnuts and cardamom in a small bowl. Set aside. Dry pieces of orange well by letting them stand on paper toweling.

Heat oven to 375°F. Grease a 10-inch tube pan (one with a solid bottom if possible).

Cream butter or margarine. Add sugar gradually, creaming well after each addition. Add eggs one at a time, beating well after each addition.

Sift flour, baking powder, soda and salt together and stir into creamed mixture alternately with sour cream.

Spoon half of batter into prepared tube pan. Sprinkle with brown sugar-nut mixture, then with orange bits. Spoon remaining batter on top and spread evenly.

Bake until a toothpick stuck in the centre comes out clean, about 1 hour. Cool 10 minutes in pan. Turn out onto a rack and drizzle with Orange Glaze, letting glaze run down sides. Serve warm or cold, cut in wedges.

1/2 cup packed brown sugar
1/2 cup chopped walnuts
1/2 tsp. ground cardamom
1 cup chopped orange
    sections
1/2 cup soft butter or
    margarine
1 cup sugar
3 eggs
3 cups sifted all-purpose flour
3 tsp. baking powder
1 tsp. baking soda
1/2 tsp. salt
1 1/2 cups sour cream
Orange Glaze (recipe follows)

## Orange Glaze

Blend until a smooth, rather thin icing is formed.

3/4 cup sifted icing sugar
1 tsp. grated orange rind
1 tbsp. orange juice

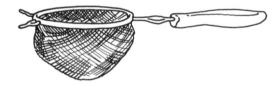

## Quick Orange Breakfast Ring

Heat oven to 375°F. Grease a small cookie sheet.

Unroll crescent roll dough and separate into triangles as directed on package. Brush each lightly with melted butter or margarine. Combine sugar and cinnamon and sprinkle a little of this mixture on each triangle.

Peel and section oranges, holding them over a bowl to catch any juice. Dry sections on paper toweling and lay 2 on the wide end of each triangle of dough. Roll dough up around orange sections and shape into crescents. Form 5 of the crescents into a small circle (about 8 inches in diameter) on prepared cookie sheet.

Fill centre of circle with remaining 3 crescents. (The crescents should be touching so they bake into a single unit.) Brush tops lightly with melted butter or margarine.

Bake until well browned, 15 to 18 minutes. Remove from cookie sheet immediately and put onto a cake rack. Drizzle with Orange Glaze while hot. Serve warm.

1 pkg. refrigerated crescent
    rolls
melted butter or margarine
4 tsp. sugar
1/4 tsp. ground cinnamon
2 medium oranges
melted butter or margarine
Orange Glaze (see Rich Coffee
    Cake)

# Sweets

Who wants toast without something on top? Maybe your favorite is peanut butter or honey. But if you are a jam lover, here are some special breakfast spreads that will make your whole day sweeter.

## Apricot-Orange Jam

1 lb. dried apricots, cut up
3 cups cold water
3 medium oranges
sugar
1/2 cup slivered blanched almonds

Put apricots in a bowl and add the 3 cups cold water. Let stand overnight.

Cut oranges into paper thin slices (skin and all) and cut slices into very fine strips. Combine with apricots and their liquid. Measure fruit and liquid. Return to bowl. Add 1/2 cup sugar for each 1 cup of fruit. Stir, cover bowl and let stand overnight.

Put fruit mixture in a large shallow saucepan (see note). Bring to a boil over moderate heat, stirring often. Turn heat to moderately low and cook slowly, stirring occasionally, until a few drops of the liquid thicken when dropped on a cold plate, about 45 minutes. Remove from heat. Stir in almonds.

Ladle into hot sterilized jars and seal with paraffin. (Makes about six 8-oz. jars.)

*Note:* If you use a large shallow saucepan the jam will cook faster than if it is cooked in a deep narrow saucepan with a smaller bottom surface. Over-cooking will make the jam dark.

## Rhubarb-Pineapple Jam

8 cups cut-up rhubarb (about 2 lb.)
2 cups 1/4-inch cubes fresh pineapple
4 cups sugar

Combine rhubarb and pineapple in a large heavy saucepan. Put over low heat and stir until juice begins to form in pan. Turn up heat and bring to a boil. Boil, uncovered, 15 minutes, stirring often. Add sugar and continue boiling gently until thick, about 30 minutes.

Ladle into hot sterilized jars and seal with paraffin. (Makes about six 8-oz. jars.)

## Rhubarb-Raspberry Jam

two 15-oz. pkg. frozen raspberries, thawed
6 cups cut-up rhubarb
8 cups sugar
1 bottle liquid pectin

Press thawed raspberries through a sieve to remove seeds. Discard seeds and combine raspberry purée with cut-up rhubarb in a large saucepan. Bring to a boil, cover and simmer gently until rhubarb is just tender.

Measure mixed fruit and return 6 cups to saucepan (add a little water if you don't have the full 6 cups). Add sugar and stir until sugar is dissolved. Bring to a full rolling boil and boil 1 minute. Remove from heat and immediately stir in pectin. Stir and skim 5 minutes (this cools jam slightly so rhubarb doesn't float).

Ladle into hot sterilized jars and seal with paraffin. (Makes ten 8-oz. jars.)

## Spring Jam

1 medium pineapple
2 cups cut-up rhubarb
1 tbsp. grated orange rind
4 cups hulled strawberries
pinch salt
4¹/₂ cups sugar

Trim, peel and core pineapple and grate coarsely. (You should have about 3 cups.)

Put in a large heavy kettle and cook gently, covered, 10 minutes, stirring often.

Add rhubarb and orange rind and continue cooking, covered, 10 minutes.

Add berries, salt and sugar and cook rapidly, uncovered, stirring often, until a small amount thickens quickly when dropped on an ice-cold plate. Skim.

Ladle into hot sterilized jars and seal with paraffin. (Makes about six 9-oz. jars.)

## Ginger Marmalade

3 large lemons
4 lb. sweet apples (about 16 medium)
6 cups sugar
2 cups water
1 tbsp. finely chopped fresh ginger

Wash lemons and slice paper thin, discarding seeds. Peel and core apples and chop with the food processor or food chopper.

Boil sugar and water rapidly in a large saucepan 5 minutes. Add apple, lemon and ginger, bring back to a boil, lower heat and cook gently, uncovered, until thick and clear, about 1¹/₄ hours.

Ladle into hot sterilized jars and seal with paraffin. Let stand for at least a week before tasting. (Makes about nine 8-oz. jars.)

## Peach Conserve

3 medium oranges
1 cup water
8 cups peeled, cubed ripe peaches
9 cups sugar
3 tbsp. maraschino cherry juice
¹/₂ cup coarsely chopped maraschino cherries

Put oranges, skin and all, through the coarse blade of the food chopper. Put in a large flat-bottomed preserving kettle. Add 1 cup water, cover and simmer until orange is tender, about 20 minutes.

Remove cover and add peaches, sugar and cherry juice. Cook fairly rapidly, stirring often, until thickened, about 20 minutes. Add cherries and boil gently 5 minutes more.

Ladle into hot sterilized jars and seal with paraffin. (Makes about ten 9-oz. jars.)

## Honey Jelly

2¹/₂ cups liquid honey
³/₄ cup water
1 tbsp. grated orange rind
¹/₂ bottle liquid pectin

Put honey, ³/₄ cup water and orange rind in a large saucepan over high heat. Mix well. Bring to a boil, remove from heat and strain.

Return to heat and bring back to a full rolling boil. Add pectin, stirring constantly, and let return to a full rolling boil. Remove from heat and skim.

Ladle into hot sterilized jars and seal with paraffin. (Makes five 6-oz. jars.)

## Cranberry Jam

2 lb. raw cranberries
2 oranges
1 lemon
1 cup seedless raisins
6 cups sugar
4 cups water

Look over and wash berries. Squeeze oranges and lemon, then cut rinds into pieces and cut away and discard membrane and most of white from inside.

Put cranberries, raisins and pieces of orange and lemon rind through the fine blade of the food chopper and put into a large kettle along with orange and lemon juice, sugar and 4 cups water. Cook slowly, stirring often, until thick, about 30 minutes.

Pour into hot sterilized jars and seal with paraffin. (Makes about eight 8-oz. jars.)

## Apricot-Pineapple Jam

$1/2$ lb. dried apricots
2 cups diced fresh pineapple
$1 1/2$ cups dates
3 cups water
3 cups sugar
$1/4$ cup lemon juice
$1/2$ cup blanched almonds

Soak apricots in hot water until tender and puffed. Drain well.

Put apricots, pineapple and dates through the fine blade of the food chopper. Put in a large saucepan and add 3 cups water. Cover and cook slowly 25 minutes, stirring occasionally.

Uncover and add sugar and lemon juice and continue cooking until mixture thickens, about 30 minutes. Add almonds.

Ladle into hot sterilized jars and seal with paraffin. (Makes about four 8-oz. jars.)

### Soups

Eighteen appealing, hearty soups. Have a lunch of sandwiches and tasty Cock-a-Leekie, or build a supper 'round a robust ham and lentil combination.

### Salads

Twenty-five different and health-ful ways to combine vegetables or fruit with other ingredients. Special dressings add the final touch.

### Sandwiches and Breads

Twenty-five delightful recipes for homemade breads, buns, turnovers and sandwiches — sure to please everyone.

### Main Dishes

Thirty-three appetizing casseroles and other lunch or supper dishes. Pick something to please all from this great variety that includes Bulgarian Moussaka, Turkey Cakes, Crab Crêpes and Stir-Fried Vegetables.

### Desserts

Eighteen ways to light and easy-to-make desserts that end a meal perfectly.

# 2
# Lunch
# & Supper

While lunches are always in style, suppers may not be as popular as they once were because so many of us have our big meal at night. However, there are times when a light meal in the evening is perfect — especially on weekends. These recipes have been chosen to make whichever is the smaller meal of the day something to look forward to. There are soups, salads and sandwiches, many of which are a meal in themselves. And there are delicious casseroles and other light main dishes, as well as simple yet tantalizing desserts. While many of the recipes are intended for quick family meals, others make very nice company fare.

# Soups

Homemade soups are relatively economical and wonderfully satisfying to make and to eat. These are especially hearty and are intended, in most cases, to be a meal in a bowl. Many of them do not require stock (although for convenience I have included recipes for chicken and beef stock), and since most can be made ahead they are perfect for the cook in a hurry. One or two have been marked with special advance preparation instructions since they don't reheat well, and in general fish soups are better if made at serving time, since reheating will toughen fish. Otherwise the soups can be nearly or completely made, refrigerated and reheated as needed. The only things to watch for are recipes that call for milk, cream, yogurt, eggs or cheese to be added just before serving. Don't add them if you are precooking — add them at reheating time.

## Macaroni and Cheese Soup

3 tbsp. butter or margarine
1 1/2 cups thinly sliced onion
  (1 extralarge)
2 tbsp. flour
1 tsp. salt
dash black pepper
1/2 tsp. dry mustard
dash cayenne
5 cups milk
1 cup grated process cheese
  (use medium grater)
1/2 cup elbow macaroni,
  cooked and drained
chopped parsley

Melt butter or margarine in a medium saucepan. Add onion and cook gently, stirring, until golden, about 5 minutes. Sprinkle in flour, salt, pepper, mustard and cayenne and stir to blend. Remove from heat.

Add milk all at once and stir to blend. Return to moderate heat and cook, stirring constantly, until boiling, slightly thickened and smooth. Turn heat to low and continue cooking, stirring often, 5 minutes.

Add cheese and cooked macaroni and heat gently, stirring, until cheese is melted.

Ladle into soup bowls and sprinkle each serving with chopped parsley. (Serves 5 or 6.)

## Cheddar Soup

1/4 cup butter or margarine
1 clove garlic, peeled and cut
  in half
1/4 cup finely chopped onion
2 medium carrots, coarsely
  grated
1/2 cup finely chopped celery
1/4 cup flour
1 tsp. salt
1/4 tsp. black pepper
3 cups milk
2 cups grated old Cheddar
  cheese

Melt butter or margarine in a saucepan. Add garlic and cook gently 3 minutes. Remove and discard garlic.

Turn heat to low. Add onion, carrots and celery. Cover tightly and cook gently just until vegetables are tender, about 7 minutes.

Sprinkle in flour, salt and pepper and stir to blend. Remove from heat and add milk all at once. Return to heat and cook, stirring constantly, until boiling, thickened and smooth.

Add cheese and continue heating gently, stirring constantly, until cheese is melted and blended. Serve immediately. (Serves 4.)

### Mehlsuppe (Browned Flour Soup)

Melt butter or margarine in a large saucepan. Add flour and onion and cook over moderately high heat, stirring constantly, until mixture is dark golden brown, about 15 minutes. (Be sure to stir constantly and turn down heat if necessary so mixture doesn't scorch.)

Remove from heat and stir in 5 cups hot water gradually. Return to heat. Add bouillon cubes, 1/2 tsp. salt and 1/8 tsp. pepper, then stir until boiling, slightly thickened and smooth. Turn heat to low, cover and simmer 30 minutes, stirring occasionally. Add salt and pepper to taste.

Ladle into soup bowls and top each serving with 1 tbsp. cheese. (Serves 6.)

1/4 cup butter or margarine
1/3 cup flour
1 large onion, chopped
 (about 1 cup)
5 cups hot water
4 beef bouillon cubes
1/2 tsp. salt
1/8 tsp. black pepper
6 tbsp. grated Swiss cheese
salt and pepper

### Potato-Mushroom Soup

Cook mushrooms and onion in butter or margarine in a heavy saucepan 3 minutes. Add potato cubes and 1 cup water. Bring to a boil. Cover and simmer until potatoes are tender, about 10 minutes. Remove from heat.

Beat milk and egg yolks together with a fork. Combine with sour cream or yogurt, salt, pepper, thyme, mace and nutmeg. Stir into hot mixture gradually. Heat just until mixture is ready to boil but do not boil. Serve immediately, sprinkled with parsley. (Serves 6.)

3 cups coarsely chopped
 mushrooms
1 medium onion, chopped
1/4 cup butter or margarine
1 cup 1/2-inch raw potato
 cubes
1 cup boiling water
2 cups milk
2 egg yolks
2 cups sour cream or plain
 yogurt
2 tsp. salt
1/4 tsp. black pepper
1/4 tsp. dried leaf thyme
pinch ground mace
pinch ground nutmeg
chopped parsley

### Corn and Tomato Soup

Heat butter or margarine in a large saucepan. Add onion and curry powder and cook gently 5 minutes, stirring. Sprinkle in flour and stir to blend. Remove from heat.

Stir in sugar, seasoned salt, salt and pepper. Add 2 cups water all at once and stir to blend. Return to moderate heat and bring to a boil, stirring constantly. Add bay leaf, corn and tomatoes. Bring back to a boil, turn down heat, cover and simmer 30 minutes. Discard bay leaf.

Beat evaporated milk and egg yolks together with a fork and stir into hot mixture gradually. Simmer 3 minutes, stirring constantly. Stir in lemon juice.

Ladle into soup bowls and sprinkle each serving with parsley. (Serves 4 to 6.)

1/4 cup butter or margarine
1/2 cup finely chopped Spanish
 onion
1/8 tsp. curry powder
2 tbsp. flour
1 tbsp. sugar
1 tsp. seasoned salt
1/2 tsp. salt
1/4 tsp. black pepper
2 cups water
1 bay leaf
2 cups fresh corn (cut from
 cobs) or 12-oz. can whole
 kernel corn
2 cups peeled, chopped
 tomatoes
2/3 cup evaporated milk
 (1 small can)
2 egg yolks
2 tbsp. lemon juice
chopped parsley

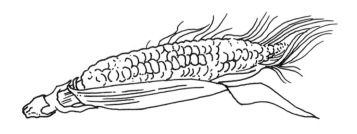

## Minestra

Put carrots, potatoes, celery, cabbage, onion, leek, garlic and parsley in a large kettle. Add salt and 8 cups water. Bring to a boil, turn down heat, cover and simmer 1 hour.

Ladle mixture into glass of blender, part at a time, and buzz until almost smooth. Return soup to kettle.

Add tomatoes, basil, oil and pepper. Return to a boil, turn down heat, cover and simmer 1 hour, stirring occasionally and breaking up any large pieces of tomato. Add beans for last 15 minutes of cooking.

Ladle into soup bowls and pass the grated Parmesan cheese. (Serves 10 to 12.)

4 medium carrots, peeled and coarsely cut up
4 medium potatoes, peeled and coarsely cut up
4 large stalks celery with leaves, coarsely chopped
3 cups coarsely cut cabbage
1 medium onion, coarsely chopped
1 leek (white and pale green parts only), coarsely chopped
1 clove garlic, chopped
$1/2$ cup coarsely chopped parsley
2 tsp. salt
8 cups cold water
19-oz. can tomatoes
1 tsp. dried leaf basil
1 tbsp. olive oil
$1/4$ tsp. black pepper
19-oz. can kidney beans
grated Parmesan cheese

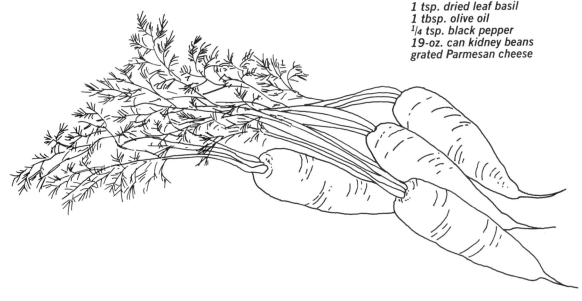

## Red Bean Soup

Soak beans overnight in 4 cups water or bring them to a boil in the water, boil 2 minutes, remove from heat and let stand, covered, 1 to 2 hours.

Pour beans and soaking water into a medium saucepan, bring to a boil, turn down heat, cover and simmer until beans are tender, about 1 hour. Drain, saving cooking liquid. Add water to cooking liquid, if necessary, to make 3 cups liquid.

Combine beans, tomatoes, carrots, onions, celery leaves and 3 cups liquid in a saucepan. Simmer 1 hour.

Buzz in glass of blender a little at a time (or press through a coarse sieve). Return to saucepan. Heat well. Add salt and pepper to taste.

Ladle into soup bowls and sprinkle each serving with some of the parsley and bacon bits. (Serves 6.)

1 cup dry kidney beans
4 cups water
28-oz. can tomatoes
$1/2$ cup diced carrots
$1/3$ cup chopped green onions
$1/3$ cup chopped celery leaves
$1 1/2$ tsp. salt (approx.)
$1/4$ tsp. black pepper (approx.)
$1/4$ cup chopped parsley
4 slices bacon, cooked and crumbled

## Ham-Lentil Soup

1½ cups dried lentils
2 lb. ready-to-eat ham shank
8 cups water
3 tbsp. butter or cooking oil
½ cup finely chopped celery
½ cup finely chopped leeks
    (white and pale green parts)
½ cup finely chopped onion
1 small clove garlic, minced
¼ tsp. dried leaf thyme
¼ tsp. black pepper
3 wieners, thinly sliced
salt

Rinse lentils under cold running water. Soak in cold water overnight. Drain.

Trim excess fat from ham shank. Put ham in a large saucepan or Dutch oven and add 8 cups water. Add lentils. Bring to a boil, turn down heat, cover and simmer until ham is very tender, about 1½ hours. Lift out ham, cool and dice.

Cool ham stock until fat settles on top. Skim off fat and discard. Heat ham stock to boiling.

Heat butter or oil in a skillet. Add celery, leeks, onion and garlic and cook gently, stirring, 5 minutes. Add to ham stock along with thyme and pepper. Cover and simmer 30 minutes.

Mash vegetables with a potato masher. Add ham and wiener slices. Bring back to a boil and add salt to taste.

Turn down heat. Simmer, uncovered, until slightly thickened, about 30 minutes. Serve immediately. (Serves 8.)

## Vegetable-Lentil Soup

1 cup dried lentils
1 to 1½ lb. neck of lamb
2 tsp. salt
bunch celery leaves
4 sprigs parsley
6 cups boiling water
1 tbsp. olive oil
1 clove garlic, peeled and
    cut in half
1 bay leaf
½ tsp. dried leaf basil
1 tbsp. olive oil
1 large onion, chopped
2 cups cut-up carrots
1 cup cut-up celery
2 cups cut-up cabbage
2 cups boiling water
10-oz. bag spinach, torn up
¼ cup chopped parsley
1½ tsp. salt (approx.)
¼ tsp. black pepper (approx.)
1 tbsp. butter or margarine
1½ tsp. flour

Wash and look over lentils the day before you want to make the soup. Cover with cold water and let stand overnight.

Trim fat from lamb and discard. Cut meat off bones and set aside. Put bones, 2 tsp. salt, celery leaves, parsley sprigs and 6 cups boiling water in a large saucepan. Bring to a boil, turn down heat, cover and simmer 1½ hours. Strain, discarding bones and vegetables. Return stock to saucepan.

Cut lamb meat into thin, short strips. Heat 1 tbsp. olive oil in a small skillet and add lamb strips and pieces of garlic. Cook, stirring constantly, until lamb is lightly browned. Discard garlic.

Add lamb to stock. Drain lentils and add them to stock along with bay leaf and basil. Cover and simmer until lentils and lamb are nearly tender, about 1 hour.

Heat 1 tbsp. olive oil in skillet. Add onion. Cook 3 minutes. Add to soup along with carrots, celery, cabbage and 2 cups boiling water. Cover and simmer until vegetables are nearly tender, about 15 minutes.

Add spinach, chopped parsley and salt and pepper to taste and simmer 5 minutes more.

Cream butter or margarine and flour together and stir into hot mixture bit by bit. Serve immediately. (Serves 8.)

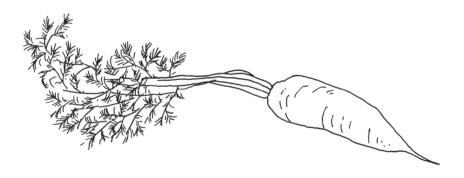

## Pea Soup with Pork

1 lb. split peas
1 bay leaf
8 cups water
2½ lb. pork shoulder,
  including bone
1 cup finely chopped onion
4 cups water
1 tbsp. salt
¼ tsp. black pepper
1 tsp. dried leaf marjoram
¼ tsp. dried leaf thyme
½ tsp. ground ginger
lemon slices
mustard (optional)
rye bread (optional)

Combine peas, bay leaf and 8 cups water in a large kettle. Bring to boiling. Turn down heat, cover and simmer 1 hour, stirring occasionally.

Add pork, onion, 4 cups water, salt, pepper, marjoram, thyme and ginger. Bring back to boiling. Turn down heat, cover and simmer, stirring occasionally, until pork is tender, about 2½ hours.

Lift pork out onto a platter. Serve soup very hot, topped with lemon slices. Cut meat into thin slices and serve with mustard and rye bread or save for another day. (Serves 6 to 8.)

## Barley Broth

1½ lb. stewing lamb
12 cups cold water
⅓ cup dried split peas
  (see note)
⅓ cup pearl barley
3 tsp. salt
¼ tsp. black pepper
1 medium onion, chopped
1 leek (white and pale green
  parts only), chopped
1 cup small cubes turnip
1 cup small cubes carrot
2 cups finely shredded cabbage
1 medium carrot, grated
salt and pepper
2 tbsp. chopped parsley

Trim all excess fat from meat and put meat into a large kettle. Add 12 cups cold water, peas, barley, 3 tsp. salt and ¼ tsp. pepper. Bring to a boil and skim.

Add onion, leek and cubes of turnip and carrot. Bring to a boil again, turn down heat, cover and simmer 3 hours.

Lift out meat and discard any fat or bones. Break or cut meat into small pieces. Add back into soup along with shredded cabbage and grated carrot. Simmer about 30 minutes. Add salt and pepper to taste. Stir in parsley and ladle into soup bowls. (Serves 6 to 8.)

*Note:* Most split peas do not need soaking. Check package directions.

## Yogurt-Meatball Soup

¼ lb. ground beef
1½ tsp. grated onion
¼ tsp. salt
⅛ tsp. black pepper
1 tbsp. butter or margarine
2 cups plain yogurt
  (three 175 g cartons)
1½ tsp. cornstarch
1 egg
¾ tsp. salt
⅛ tsp. black pepper
2 tbsp. regular long-grain rice
2½ cups chicken stock
  (recipe p. 48)
¼ cup chopped parsley
¼ cup chopped green onions
½ cup finely grated carrots
½ tsp. dried dill weed

Combine beef, grated onion, ¼ tsp. salt and ⅛ tsp. pepper and shape mixture into tiny meatballs, about ½ inch in diameter. Heat butter or margarine in a small skillet, add meatballs and brown lightly.

Put yogurt into a heavy saucepan. Add cornstarch, egg, ¾ tsp. salt and ⅛ tsp. pepper and beat well to blend. Add rice and chicken stock. Set over moderate heat and cook, stirring constantly, until just beginning to boil. Turn down heat. Add meatballs, cover and simmer 15 minutes, lifting lid and stirring once.

Add vegetables and dill weed, cover again and simmer until vegetables and rice are tender, about 5 minutes. Serve immediately. (Serves 4.)

Advance preparation: Make and brown meatballs.

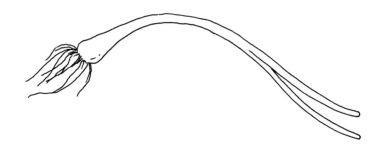

### Garbure

1 cup dried baby lima beans
3 cups water
3 cups beef stock or 3 cups water and 2 beef bouillon cubes
2 medium carrots, sliced
2 cups diced rutabaga (yellow turnip)
3 medium potatoes, sliced
2 cups shredded cabbage
19-oz. can tomatoes
2 tsp. salt (approx.)
1/4 tsp. black pepper (approx.)
2 tbsp. butter or margarine
6 thick slices French bread
butter or margarine
1 cup grated old Cheddar cheese

Soak beans overnight in 3 cups water or bring them to a boil in the water, boil 2 minutes, remove from heat and let stand, covered, 1 to 2 hours.

Pour into a large saucepan along with soaking water and add beef stock or water and bouillon cubes, carrots, rutabaga and potatoes. Cover and cook until beans are tender, about 1 hour. Add cabbage and tomatoes and simmer 10 minutes.

Buzz mixture in glass of blender a little at a time (or press through a coarse sieve). Return to saucepan. Thin with water or more beef stock if desired. (Soup should be quite thick.) Heat and add salt and pepper to taste. Add 2 tbsp. butter or margarine.

Toast one side of the bread under the broiler. Turn pieces of bread and butter untoasted side. Sprinkle thickly with cheese. Broil until cheese is bubbling.

Put a piece of bread in each bowl and add soup. (Serves 6 to 8.)

Advance preparation: Complete soup except for cheese-topped toast and refrigerate.

### Cock-a-Leekie

3-lb. chicken (whole)
10 cups water (approx.)
6 leeks (white and pale green parts only), cut in 1/2-inch slices
2 large stalks celery, chopped
4 large sprigs parsley, chopped
1/2 cup pearl barley
1 bay leaf, crumbled
6 peppercorns
1/4 tsp. dried leaf thyme
1 tbsp. salt
chopped parsley

Wash chicken and tie legs and wings close to the body. Put in a large kettle. Add the 10 cups water or enough to cover chicken. Bring to a boil. Add leeks, celery, parsley, barley, bay leaf, peppercorns, thyme and salt. Cover and simmer until chicken is very tender, 1 to 1 1/2 hours.

Lift chicken out of stock and put on a platter. Cool until it can be handled, then remove meat from bones, discarding skin and bones. Cut meat into short slivers, return to soup and heat well. Sprinkle with chopped parsley and serve very hot. (Serves 6 to 8.)

## Turkey-Vegetable Soup

Put broken-up turkey carcass in a large kettle. Add 12 cups water, celery leaves, bay leaf and carrot. Bring to a boil, turn down heat, cover and simmer 2 hours.

Strain and return stock to kettle. Strip turkey meat off bones, cut into small pieces and set aside to add to soup later. Discard all bones and vegetables.

Add tomatoes, celery, onion, 1 1/2 tbsp. salt, 1/4 tsp. pepper and poultry seasoning to stock in kettle. Bring to a boil and simmer 30 minutes. Add rice and simmer 20 minutes. Add turkey meat and mixed vegetables and simmer 20 minutes. Add salt and pepper to taste. Serve immediately. (Serves 8.)

turkey carcass (from 15- to
  20-lb. turkey)
12 cups water
large bunch celery leaves
1 bay leaf
1 carrot, coarsely cut up
19-oz. can tomatoes
2 cups sliced celery
1 cup chopped onion (1 large)
1 1/2 tbsp. salt
1/4 tsp. black pepper
1/2 tsp. poultry seasoning
1/2 cup regular long-grain rice
11-oz. pkg. frozen mixed
  vegetables
salt and pepper

## Deep-Sea Bisque

Put block of frozen fish in a saucepan large enough to hold it flat on the bottom. Add 3 cups boiling water and salt. Cover and simmer until fish flakes easily with a fork, about 10 minutes. Turn block of fish after first 5 minutes cooking. (Be careful not to overcook — the fish will cook a little longer when the soup is heating just before serving.) Lift fish out of water with a slotted spoon. Break up into bite-size chunks.

Add vegetables and chervil to fish cooking water and bring to a boil. Cook until just tender, about 10 minutes. Do not drain.

Blend flour and about 1/2 cup of the milk until smooth. Add to boiling vegetables gradually, stirring constantly. Add pepper and simmer 2 minutes.

Stir in remaining milk and cream gradually. Add fish pieces and parsley and heat but do not boil. Stir in lemon juice, being careful not to break up fish. Add butter or margarine. Serve immediately. (Serves 4.)

1 lb. frozen cod fillets
3 cups boiling water
2 tsp. salt
4 small carrots, thinly sliced
1 large potato, cubed
1 leek (white and pale green
  parts only), thinly sliced
1 medium onion, chopped
1/2 tsp. dried leaf chervil
2 tbsp. flour
2 cups milk
1/8 tsp. black pepper
1 cup light cream
2 tbsp. chopped parsley
1 1/2 tsp. lemon juice
1 tbsp. butter or margarine

## Down East Bouillabaisse

Thaw fish enough so it cuts easily. Cut fish fillets into 2-inch squares. Cut very large scallops into halves.

Heat butter or margarine in a large kettle and add onion, celery and garlic. Cook gently until onion is transparent but not brown. Add clam and tomato juice cocktail, tomatoes, 1 cup water, thyme, bay leaf and saffron. Bring to a boil.

Add fish pieces (not scallops) and simmer 10 minutes. Add scallops and simmer 10 minutes more. Add salt and pepper to taste.

While soup is cooking, remove meat from lobsters and dice. Add to soup just before serving. Put a slice of toasted French bread into each bowl and ladle soup over, or serve bread separately. (Serves 8.)

1 lb. fresh or frozen haddock
   fillets
1 lb. fresh or frozen cod fillets
1 lb. fresh or frozen ocean
   perch fillets
1 lb. fresh or frozen scallops
$1/3$ cup butter or margarine
$3/4$ cup chopped onion
$3/4$ cup thinly sliced celery
1 clove garlic, finely chopped
1 L bottle clam broth and
   tomato juice cocktail
19-oz. can tomatoes
1 cup water
$1/2$ tsp. dried leaf thyme
1 large bay leaf, crushed
$1/8$ tsp. powdered saffron
   (optional)
$1/2$ tsp. salt (approx.)
$1/4$ tsp. black pepper (approx.)
2 small cooked lobsters
   (optional)
toasted French bread

## Haddock Chowder

Heat oil in a large saucepan. Add leeks, carrots and garlic and cook gently, stirring, 3 minutes.

Cut haddock into bite-size pieces. Add to pan along with tomatoes, 2 cups water, bay leaf, thyme, salt and pepper. Heat to boiling, turn down heat, cover and simmer until fish is tender, about 10 minutes.

Add lemon juice and simmer 5 minutes. Sprinkle in parsley and serve immediately. (Serves 4 to 6.)

*Note:* If using frozen fish, thaw only until it can be cut easily.

$1/4$ cup cooking oil
2 leeks (white and pale green
   parts only), very thinly sliced
2 medium carrots, chopped
1 clove garlic, crushed
$1^1/2$ to 2 lb. haddock (see note)
2 cups peeled, chopped
   tomatoes
2 cups water
1 small bay leaf
$1/8$ tsp. dried leaf thyme
$1^1/2$ tsp. salt
$1/4$ tsp. black pepper
1 tbsp. lemon juice
$1/4$ cup chopped parsley

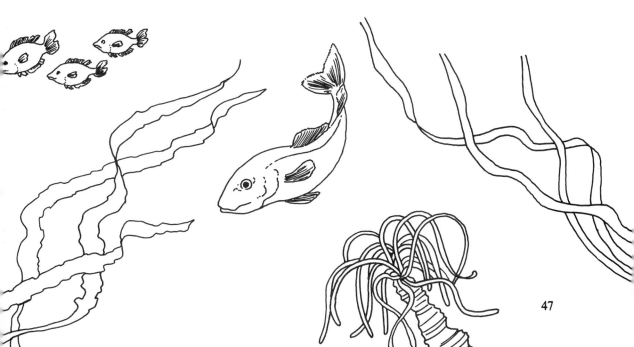

## Beef Stock

2 whole cloves
1 large onion
3 lb. lean brisket of beef, cut up
3 lb. beef shank, cut up
2 lb. veal shank, cut up
4 leeks (white and pale green parts only), coarsely cut up
2 large stalks celery with leaves, coarsely cut up
6 large sprigs parsley
2 carrots, scrubbed and coarsely cut up
1 bay leaf
5 qt. water
2 tsp. salt

Stick cloves into onion and put all ingredients except salt into a large kettle. Bring to a boil, skimming as needed. Cover, lower heat and simmer 2 hours. Add salt and simmer 2 hours more.

Strain through several thicknesses of cheesecloth and chill. Remove fat and clarify as directed below. Refrigerate for 2 or 3 days or put in jars (leaving plenty of headroom) and freeze. (Makes about 12 cups.)

## Chicken Stock

5-lb. stewing hen, cut up
1 lb. veal shank, cut up
5 qt. water
2 tbsp. salt
6 peppercorns
3 whole cloves
1 medium onion
4 leeks (white and pale green parts only), coarsely cut up
4 large carrots, scrubbed and coarsely cut up
2 large stalks celery with leaves, coarsely cut up
1 bay leaf
1/4 tsp. dried leaf thyme

Put stewing hen, veal, 5 qt. water, salt and peppercorns in a large kettle. Bring to a boil over high heat, lower heat and simmer 1 hour, skimming as needed.

Stick cloves into onion and add to kettle along with remaining ingredients. Cover and cook until meat falls off bones, 2½ to 3 hours.

Strain through several thicknesses of cheesecloth and chill. Remove fat and clarify as directed below. Refrigerate for 2 or 3 days or put in jars (leaving plenty of headroom) and freeze. (Makes about 12 cups.)

## To Clarify Stock

Most stocks jell when cold, and this jelly can be lifted out. Still, there will be sediment in the jelly. Here's how to get rid of it.

For every 5 cups of stock, beat 1 cup of it and 2 egg whites together with a wire whip. Bring remaining stock to a boil in a large saucepan, then gradually pour some of it into egg white mixture, beating constantly. Pour back into saucepan, set over moderate heat and bring to simmering, stirring slowly with the whip. Lower heat, stop stirring and simmer gently 15 minutes.

Strain through several thicknesses of cheesecloth, ladling it into the sieve gently rather than dumping it. (It is important to keep the egg whites together, since they hold the sediment.) Discard cheesecloth and egg. Refrigerate clarified stock until needed.

# Salads

A salad for lunch is what many people prefer, and here are salads for every taste. In almost every case the salads are chilled at some point, making advance preparation planning easy. Dressings can nearly always be made ahead, too. For everyday salads, as well as for greens to include with any of these recipes, a plastic bag of washed mixed greens with paper toweling between the layers gives a real helping hand to the cook. I find the leafy lettuces, rather than head lettuce, will keep a week if stored this way in the refrigerator.

## Carrot-Sprout Salad

Combine mayonnaise, parsley, soya sauce, sugar, salt and pepper and refrigerate. Add a small amount of boiling water to green beans in a saucepan. Bring to a boil, cover and boil 1 minute. Drain immediately. Chill.

At serving time, rinse bean sprouts under cold running water and drain well. Combine with carrots and beans. Add mayonnaise mixture, toss lightly and serve on lettuce. (Serves 4.)

*1/3 cup mayonnaise*
*1 tbsp. chopped parsley*
*1 tsp. soya sauce*
*1/2 tsp. sugar*
*1/2 tsp. salt*
*1/8 tsp. black pepper*
*10-oz. pkg. frozen frenched green beans*
*2 cups fresh bean sprouts*
*1 1/2 cups grated carrots (use medium grater)*
*lettuce*

## Far East Salad

Rinse bean sprouts well with cold running water. Put them, cabbage and green beans in a large saucepan. Add 1 tsp. salt and cover with boiling water. Cover saucepan and bring to a boil. Boil 5 minutes. Drain, saving 1/2 cup of the cooking water. Chill vegetables.

Heat oil in a small skillet and add onion. Cook gently 2 minutes, stirring. Remove from heat. Stir in peanut butter, peanuts, soya sauce, lemon juice, brown sugar, 1/4 tsp. salt and enough of the 1/2 cup vegetable cooking water to make a dressing about the consistency of heavy cream.

Combine chilled vegetables, radish slices and zucchini in a large bowl at serving time. Pour peanut butter mixture over vegetables and toss lightly. Serve immediately. (Serves 4 to 6.)

*3 cups fresh bean sprouts*
*3 cups finely sliced cabbage*
*2 cups fresh green beans, cut in 1-inch pieces on the diagonal*
*1 tsp. salt*
*1 tsp. cooking oil*
*1 green onion, sliced paper thin*
*3 tbsp. smooth peanut butter*
*2 tbsp. chopped salted peanuts*
*1/2 tsp. soya sauce*
*1/2 tsp. lemon juice*
*1 tsp. brown sugar*
*1/4 tsp. salt*
*1 cup paper thin slices radishes*
*1 small zucchini, sliced paper thin*

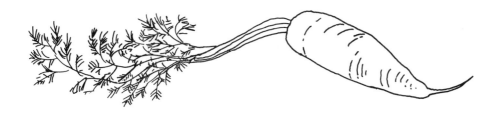

### Bean and Chick Pea Salad

Cook green beans until tender-crisp. Drain immediately and cool. Combine with kidney beans and chick peas in a large bowl and chill.

To make dressing, shake salad oil, vinegar, salt, paprika, mustard, relish and pimento together in a small jar with a tight lid.

At serving time, add celery, onion and green pepper to bean mixture and toss gently. Drizzle on enough dressing to coat vegetables lightly. Toss again and pile into a lettuce-lined bowl. (Serves 6 to 8.)

12-oz. pkg. frozen cut green
  beans or 1 lb. fresh beans,
  trimmed and cut
14-oz. can kidney beans,
  drained
19-oz. can chick peas, drained
1/2 cup salad oil
1/4 cup red wine vinegar
1/2 tsp. salt
1/2 tsp. paprika
1/4 tsp. dry mustard
2 tbsp. drained sweet pickle
  relish
1 tbsp. chopped pimento
1 cup celery, thinly sliced on
  the diagonal
1/2 small Spanish onion, sliced
  paper thin
1/2 cup slivered green pepper
lettuce

### Swiss Radish Salad

Put cheese and radishes in a bowl. Shake remaining ingredients except lettuce together in a small jar with a tight lid. Pour over salad and toss lightly. Chill. Serve on lettuce. Especially good with cold leftover roast. (Serves 4.)

2 cups coarsely grated Swiss
  cheese (about 1/2 lb.)
2 cups coarsely grated radishes
3 tbsp. salad oil
2 tbsp. white vinegar
1/4 tsp. salt
dash black pepper
pinch dry mustard
pinch paprika
lettuce

### Potato-Cheese Salad in Tomato Cups

Put potatoes, onions and dill in a bowl. Shake oil, lemon juice, 1 1/2 tsp. salt, pepper and garlic powder together in a small jar with a tight lid. Pour over potato mixture, mix lightly with a fork, cover and let stand in refrigerator at least 1 hour.

Add cheese. Mix mayonnaise and sour cream and add to potato mixture and toss again lightly with a fork. Chill until serving time.

Cut tops from tomatoes and hollow out. Sprinkle insides of tomatoes lightly with salt and invert on paper toweling to drain.

Set tomatoes on a bed of watercress or lettuce at serving time and fill with potato mixture. Garnish each with a sprig of watercress and serve immediately. (Serves 6.)

2 cups hot diced cooked
  potatoes
1/4 cup thinly sliced green
  onions
2 tsp. finely chopped fresh dill
1/4 cup salad oil
2 tbsp. lemon juice
1 1/2 tsp. salt
1/4 tsp. black pepper
1/8 tsp. garlic powder
2 cups tiny cubes Gruyère
  cheese
2 tbsp. mayonnaise
2 tbsp. sour cream
6 large ripe tomatoes
salt
watercress or lettuce
watercress sprigs

### Ham and Egg Salad

Combine peas, celery, green pepper, onion and pickle in a large bowl and toss together lightly. Chill.

Add ham and eggs at serving time. Combine mayonnaise, cream and mustard and pour over salad. Toss lightly. Serve immediately. (Serves 4.)

2 cups cooked peas
1 cup thinly sliced celery
1/4 cup chopped green pepper
2 tbsp. finely chopped onion
1/4 cup chopped sweet pickle
2 cups diced cooked ham
4 hard-cooked eggs, chopped
1/3 cup mayonnaise
2 tsp. light cream
1 tsp. prepared mustard

### Mushroom-Cheese Salad

Wash, trim and slice mushrooms very thinly. Separate onion into rings. Toss together in a medium bowl.

Shake 1/3 cup olive oil, vinegar, salt, sugar, chervil, tarragon and cayenne together in a small jar with a tight lid. Pour over mushroom mixture and toss to blend. Cover and chill several hours.

Heat 2 tbsp. oil in a small skillet over moderate heat. Add bread cubes and fry, stirring, until browned and crisp. Cool.

Add cheese cubes, fried bread cubes and watercress to salad at serving time and toss to blend. Spoon into lettuce cups on salad plates. (Serves 6.)

1 lb. (2 pt.) fresh mushrooms
1 small red onion, sliced
    paper thin
1/3 cup olive oil
1/4 cup red wine vinegar
1/2 tsp. salt
1/2 tsp. sugar
1/2 tsp. dried leaf chervil
pinch dried leaf tarragon
dash cayenne
2 tbsp. olive oil
2 slices whole wheat bread,
    cut in small cubes
1/4 lb. old Cheddar cheese,
    cut in tiny cubes (about
    1 cup)
1/2 cup watercress leaves
lettuce

### Leftover Lamb Salad

Combine lamb, potatoes and green onions and season with salt and pepper.

Pour Mint Dressing over and chill well. Serve on lettuce. (Serves 4.)

2 cups slivered leftover lamb
    roast
2 cups diced cooked potatoes
2 tbsp. finely chopped green
    onions
1/2 tsp. salt
1/8 tsp. black pepper
Mint Dressing (recipe follows)
lettuce

### Mint Dressing

Combine all ingredients in a small jar with a tight lid and shake to combine thoroughly. (Makes 3/4 cup.)

Note: If fresh mint is not available, combine the lemon juice and 1/4 cup mint jelly and heat until jelly is melted. Cool and shake with remaining ingredients as directed above.

1/2 cup olive or salad oil
1/4 cup lemon juice
1/2 tsp. salt
1 tbsp. finely chopped fresh
    mint (see note)
1 tbsp. finely chopped parsley
1/2 tsp. dry mustard
1/2 tsp. paprika

## Wiener and Potato Salad

Wash potatoes and cook them in their jackets in boiling salted water until just tender. Cool to lukewarm and peel. Cube into a large bowl. (You should have about 4 cups.)

While potatoes are cooking, heat 1 tbsp. oil in a large heavy skillet. Add wiener rounds and cook, stirring constantly, until lightly browned. Add to potatoes. Add celery, dill pickle and onion and toss lightly.

Combine 1/3 cup oil, vinegar, pickle liquid, mustard, salt, pepper, basil and celery seeds in a small jar with a tight lid. Shake to blend thoroughly. Pour over salad and toss lightly. Good served immediately while still warm and also good if well chilled before serving. (Serves 6.)

6 medium potatoes
1 tbsp. cooking oil
1 lb. wieners, sliced in thin rounds
2 cups chopped celery
1/2 cup chopped dill pickle
1 medium Spanish onion, chopped (about 1 cup)
1/3 cup salad oil
1/4 cup cider vinegar
3 tbsp. dill pickle liquid
2 tsp. dry mustard
1 1/2 tsp. salt
1/4 tsp. black pepper
1 tsp. dried leaf basil
1 tsp. celery seeds

## Macaroni and Cheese Salad

Cook macaroni in plenty of boiling salted water until just tender, about 7 minutes. Drain and rinse thoroughly with cold water.

Combine macaroni, eggs and vegetables in a large bowl. Sprinkle with salt and pepper.

Combine mayonnaise, lemon juice and cream and add to salad. Toss lightly to mix. Chill.

Add cheese and meat and toss again lightly at serving time. (Serves 4.)

1 cup uncooked macaroni
3 hard-cooked eggs, chopped
1 cup chopped celery
1/2 cup chopped green pepper
1/4 cup chopped pimento
2 tbsp. thinly sliced green onions
1/2 tsp. salt
1/8 tsp. black pepper
1/2 cup mayonnaise
1 tsp. lemon juice
1 tsp. light cream
1 cup grated old Cheddar cheese
1 cup slivered cooked ham or luncheon meat

## Bean and Ham Salad

Cook beans in boiling salted water just until they are tender-crisp. Cool.

Combine beans, carrots, onions and ham in a bowl and toss lightly. Cover and chill until just before serving time.

Combine remaining ingredients except lettuce at serving time and add to bean mixture, tossing lightly. Spoon into lettuce cups on serving plates. (Serves 4.)

2 cups 1-inch pieces fresh green beans
1 cup grated raw carrots (use medium grater)
2 tbsp. chopped green onions
1 1/2 cups diced cooked ham
1/2 cup sour cream
1 tbsp. white vinegar
1/4 tsp. Worcestershire sauce
1/4 tsp. dry mustard
1/2 tsp. sugar
1/4 tsp. salt
dash black pepper
lettuce

## Spanish Chicken Salad

3 cups diced cooked chicken
1 Spanish onion, sliced paper thin and separated into rings
5 cups thinly sliced iceberg lettuce (1 small head)
1 cup paper thin slices radishes
3 medium tomatoes
2 oranges
2 avocados
1/3 cup olive oil
1/4 cup red wine vinegar
1 tsp. salt
1/4 tsp. black pepper
pinch dried leaf tarragon
lettuce

Combine chicken, onion, sliced lettuce and radishes in a large bowl. Quarter tomatoes, seed and chop coarsely. Peel oranges and avocados and chop coarsely. Add tomatoes, oranges and avocados to chicken mixture in bowl.

Combine oil, vinegar, salt, pepper and tarragon in a small jar with a tight lid. Shake to blend well. Pour over salad and toss lightly to blend.

Line a large salad bowl with lettuce. Pile in the chicken mixture. Serve immediately. (Serves 8.)

Advance preparation: Mix and chill chicken, onion, lettuce and radishes. Combine dressing ingredients and chill.

## Chicken and Melon Salad

2 cups bite-size pieces cooked chicken
5-oz. can water chestnuts, sliced
1 cup halved seedless green grapes
1/2 cup sliced celery
1/2 cup slivered toasted almonds
2/3 cup mayonnaise
1/2 tsp. curry powder
1/4 tsp. salt
1 tsp. soya sauce
1 1/2 to 2 melons (see note)
lettuce
1/4 cup slivered toasted almonds

Combine chicken, water chestnuts, grapes, celery and 1/2 cup almonds. Mix mayonnaise, curry powder, salt and soya sauce. Add to chicken mixture and toss lightly. Chill.

Cut melons into 6 thick slices crosswise. Remove seeds and peel slices. Put each slice on a bed of lettuce on a serving plate. Put a spoonful of the chicken mixture in the centre of each slice of melon and sprinkle with some of the 1/4 cup almonds. Serve immediately. (Serves 6.)

Note: Cantaloupe can be used for this salad but why not try one of the more unusual melons such as Persian, casaba or cranshaw.

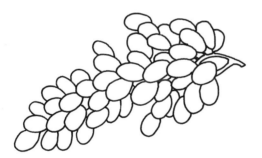

## Grapefruit and Turkey Salad

3 medium grapefruit
2 1/2 cups bite-size pieces cooked turkey
1/2 cup chopped green pepper
1/2 cup chopped celery
1/4 cup finely chopped pimento
2/3 cup mayonnaise
2 tbsp. finely chopped green onions
2 tsp. prepared mustard
lettuce

Peel and section grapefruit and put sections in a sieve to drain well.

Combine turkey, green pepper, celery and pimento in a large bowl. Combine mayonnaise, onions and mustard.

Choose 12 perfect grapefruit sections and set aside. Dry remaining sections on paper toweling and cut them into halves. Add to turkey mixture and toss together lightly with a fork. Add mayonnaise mixture and toss again to blend. Chill.

At serving time, spoon onto lettuce and top each serving with 3 of the grapefruit sections you set aside. (Serves 4.)

## Fish Salad

Cut haddock into pieces and put in a saucepan. Add 1 cup boiling water and 1 tsp. salt. Cover and simmer gently until fish flakes easily with a fork, about 7 minutes. Drain well and chill.

Flake fish and combine with celery. Sprinkle lightly with salt and pepper and toss gently.

Combine mayonnaise, sour cream, French dressing, capers, curry powder and lemon juice.

Line a shallow bowl with lettuce. Pile in fish mixture. Pour mayonnaise mixture over and sprinkle with parsley. Garnish bowl with tomatoes and lemon wedges. Serve immediately, tossing gently at the table. (Serves 4 to 6.)

*1½ lb. fresh or frozen
  haddock fillets
1 cup boiling water
1 tsp. salt
1 cup chopped celery
salt and pepper
⅔ cup mayonnaise
3 tbsp. sour cream
1 tbsp. French dressing
1 tbsp. chopped capers
2 tsp. curry powder
1 tbsp. lemon juice
lettuce
chopped parsley
cherry tomatoes
lemon wedges*

## Rice and Tuna Salad

Cook rice according to package directions. Put in a large bowl and cool. Add tuna, carrots, celery, cabbage, parsley and onion. Toss lightly and chill.

Combine mayonnaise, lemon juice, Worcestershire, salt, savory and marjoram and add to salad at serving time. Toss lightly. (Serves 6.)

*1 cup regular long-grain rice
7-oz. can solid tuna, drained
  and broken up
1½ cups grated carrots
1 cup diced celery
1 cup very finely shredded
  cabbage (red cabbage
  if possible)
¼ cup chopped parsley
2 tbsp. chopped onion
¾ cup mayonnaise
1 tbsp. lemon juice
¼ tsp. Worcestershire sauce
¼ tsp. salt
⅛ tsp. dried leaf savory
⅛ tsp. dried leaf marjoram*

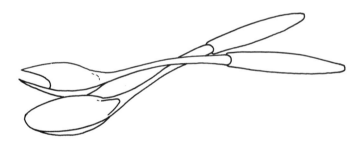

## Piquant Cauliflower-Salmon Salad

Separate cauliflower into flowerets, cutting large ones into thick slices. Cook in small amount of boiling salted water until just tender-crisp, 3 to 5 minutes. Drain immediately and put in a bowl.

Combine oil, vinegar, stuffed olives, relish, sugar, 1 tsp. salt, paprika and dash pepper in a jar with a tight lid. Shake to blend well. Pour over cauliflower, stir so cauliflower is coated with mixture, cover and chill several hours, stirring occasionally.

Drain off excess oil-vinegar mixture at serving time. Add chopped tomato and salmon and toss lightly. Add salt and pepper to taste.

Line a shallow bowl with lettuce and pile in the salad. Sprinkle with ripe olives and garnish with egg slices. (Serves 6.)

*1 medium cauliflower
¾ cup salad oil
⅓ cup white vinegar
2 tbsp. chopped stuffed olives
1 tbsp. drained sweet pickle
  relish
1 tsp. sugar
1 tsp. salt
1 tsp. paprika
dash black pepper
1 large tomato, peeled,
  seeded and chopped
7¾-oz. can pink salmon,
  drained and broken up
salt and pepper
lettuce
¼ cup slivered ripe olives
2 hard-cooked eggs, sliced*

## Smoky Caesar Salad

3³/₄-oz. can smoked salmon
salt
1 clove garlic, peeled and cut
  in half
8 cups torn-up salad greens
2 tbsp. olive oil
2 tsp. lemon juice
1 raw egg
dash salt
dash black pepper
¹/₄ cup butter or margarine,
  melted
2 tbsp. grated Parmesan
  cheese
Salad Croutons (recipe follows)

Drain salmon and break up coarsely. Set aside.

Sprinkle a large salad bowl generously with salt and rub all over with cut sides of garlic clove. Discard garlic. Put torn-up greens in bowl.

Beat olive oil, lemon juice, egg, salt and pepper together with a fork. Pour over greens along with melted butter or margarine. Toss lightly and quickly to coat greens well.

Add salmon pieces, Parmesan and Salad Croutons and toss again lightly. Serve immediately. (Serves 4.)

Advance preparation: Make Salad Croutons. Wash greens and store in the refrigerator.

## Salad Croutons

2 cloves garlic
2 tbsp. olive oil
1 cup day-old bread cubes
  (¹/₄-inch cubes)

Peel garlic and cut each clove into 4 pieces. Add to oil, cover and let stand several hours. Discard garlic.

Toss bread cubes with oil until well coated. Spread cubes on a cookie sheet.

Heat oven to 325°F. Heat cubes in oven, stirring often, until golden, about 15 minutes. Cool. (Makes 1 cup.)

## Cheese, Crab and Potato Salad

4 cups ¹/₄-inch cubes Swiss
  cheese (about 1 lb.)
5-oz. can crab, drained and
  broken up
4 cups cooked, peeled, diced
  potatoes
3 hard-cooked eggs, diced
¹/₂ cup chopped celery
¹/₂ cup chopped green onions
¹/₂ cup chopped radishes
¹/₄ cup chopped green pepper
¹/₂ cup mayonnaise
¹/₂ cup plain yogurt
1 tbsp. prepared horseradish
1 tsp. lemon juice
¹/₂ tsp. salt

Toss cheese, crab, potatoes, eggs, celery, onions, radishes and green pepper together in a large bowl.

Blend mayonnaise, yogurt, horseradish, lemon juice and salt. Pour over salad and toss again lightly. Chill well. (Serves 6 to 8.)

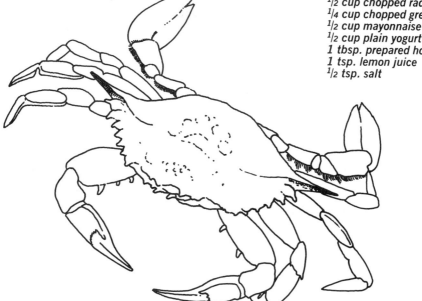

## Seafood Salad

Combine lobster, shrimp, chopped eggs, celery, pickle, onion and 2 tbsp. pimento strips. Shake olive oil, vinegar, mustard, salt and pepper together in a small jar with a tight lid. Pour over seafood mixture and toss lightly. Chill for a few minutes.

Serve on lettuce, garnished with sliced egg and more pimento strips if desired. (Serves 4 to 6.)

two 5-oz. lobster tails, cooked,
  shelled and coarsely chopped
1/2 lb. shrimp, cooked, shelled
  and coarsely chopped
3 hard-cooked eggs, chopped
1/2 cup paper thin slices celery
2 tbsp. chopped sweet pickle
1 medium onion, sliced paper
  thin
2 tbsp. short thin strips
  pimento
1/4 cup olive oil
2 tbsp. red wine vinegar
1/4 tsp. dry mustard
1/2 tsp. salt
1/4 tsp. black pepper
lettuce
egg slices (optional)
pimento strips (optional)

## Thousand Island Mold with Shrimp

Add gelatin to 1/3 cup water and let stand 5 minutes. Set in simmering water and heat until gelatin is dissolved.

Combine mayonnaise, chili sauce, Worcestershire and salt. Stir into gelatin. Chill by setting in ice water until beginning to set. Fold in olives, celery, chives and eggs. Spoon into a 1-qt. ring mold and chill until set.

Combine cream cheese, blue cheese, horseradish and Tabasco, blending until smooth. Spread this mixture down the backs of the shrimp and dip each one into chopped parsley to coat the cheese mixture. Chill until serving time.

Unmold jellied mixture onto salad greens at serving time. Fill centre with shrimp and sprinkle with ripe olives. (Serves 6.)

*Note:* For a party the recipe can be tripled and molded in a bundt pan or an 11-cup ring mold.

1 envelope (1 tbsp.)
  unflavored gelatin
1/3 cup water
3/4 cup mayonnaise
3/4 cup bottled chili sauce
1 1/2 tsp. Worcestershire sauce
1/2 tsp. salt
1/2 cup chopped stuffed olives
1/2 cup chopped celery
1 tbsp. chopped chives
2 hard-cooked eggs, chopped
125 g pkg. cream cheese
  (room temperature)
1/4 cup crumbled blue cheese
1 tsp. prepared horseradish
dash Tabasco
Cooked Shrimp (recipe follows)
1/4 cup finely chopped parsley
salad greens
1/4 cup slivered ripe olives

## Cooked Shrimp

Shell and clean shrimp.

Put about 2 inches boiling water in a saucepan. Add all ingredients except shrimp and simmer 5 minutes.

Drop in shrimp, add water to cover if necessary and simmer until shrimp are bright red, about 4 minutes. Remove from heat, drain and chill.

1 lb. large raw shrimp
small slice onion
bunch celery leaves
small piece bay leaf
1 tsp. salt
1/4 tsp. dried leaf thyme
1/4 tsp. dried leaf chervil
4 peppercorns
2 tbsp. lemon juice

## Tomato Aspic with Vegetables

10-oz. pkg. frozen mixed
  vegetables
3 envelopes (3 tbsp.) unflavored
  gelatin
$3/4$ cup cold water
$2^{1}/2$ cups tomato juice
$1^{1}/2$ tsp. dried leaf basil or
  1 tbsp. fresh basil
1 tsp. salt
1 tsp. sugar
$1/8$ tsp. black pepper
$1/4$ tsp. grated onion
$5^{1}/2$-oz. can tomato paste
$1/4$ cup white vinegar
3 tbsp. lemon juice
$1/2$ tsp. Worcestershire sauce
1 cup chopped celery
$1/2$ cup chopped green pepper
1 avocado, cut in small cubes
lettuce
Boiled Dressing (recipe follows)

Cook frozen mixed vegetables until barely tender, about 5 minutes. Drain, saving cooking water.

Soak gelatin in $3/4$ cup cold water 5 minutes. Heat tomato juice, vegetable cooking water, basil, salt, sugar, pepper and onion to boiling. Remove from heat and add gelatin, stirring until gelatin is dissolved.

Stir in tomato paste, vinegar, lemon juice and Worcestershire. Chill by setting in ice water, stirring constantly, until beginning to thicken. Remove from ice water.

Fold in cooked mixed vegetables, celery, green pepper and avocado. Spoon into an 8-cup mold and chill until firm. Unmold on lettuce and serve with Boiled Dressing. (Serves 8.)

## Boiled Dressing

1 egg
2 tbsp. sugar
2 tbsp. flour
$1/2$ tsp. salt
$1/2$ tsp. dry mustard
$1/4$ tsp. paprika
$1/4$ cup white vinegar
$1^{1}/4$ cups milk
2 tsp. prepared horseradish
light cream or milk (optional)

Beat egg, sugar, flour, salt, mustard and paprika together in a medium saucepan. Stir in vinegar, milk and horseradish, blending until smooth. Set over moderate heat and cook, stirring constantly, until boiling, thickened and smooth.

Store in a covered jar in the refrigerator. Thin, when used, with a little light cream or milk if desired. (Makes $1^{1}/2$ cups.)

## Jellied Potato Salad

5 cups diced cooked potatoes
$1/2$ cup chopped green onions
1 cup diced cucumber
2 hard-cooked eggs, chopped
$1/2$ cup sliced stuffed olives
1 tbsp. white vinegar
2 tsp. salt
1 tbsp. celery seeds
$1^{1}/2$ cups mayonnaise
2 envelopes (2 tbsp.)
  unflavored gelatin
$1/2$ cup cold water
2 cups boiling water
$1/4$ cup white vinegar
9 green pepper rings
1 hard-cooked egg, sliced
radish slices

Toss potatoes, onions, cucumber, chopped hard-cooked eggs, olives, 1 tbsp. vinegar, salt, celery seeds and mayonnaise together lightly in a large bowl. Chill.

Soak gelatin in $1/2$ cup cold water 5 minutes. Add 2 cups boiling water and stir until gelatin is dissolved. Stir in $1/4$ cup vinegar and cool (do not chill).

Spoon into a 9-inch square pan just enough of gelatin mixture to cover the bottom. Arrange green pepper rings, sliced eggs and radish slices in a design in gelatin. Chill until set.

Chill remaining gelatin mixture until beginning to thicken. Beat with a rotary beater or electric mixer until fluffy. Add to chilled potato mixture and fold to blend well. Pour over design in pan and chill until set.

Turn out onto a plate and cut into squares to serve. (Serves 9.)

57

### Jellied Avocado Salad with Strawberries

Have ready a 6-cup ring mold.

Put jelly powder and salt in a bowl and add 2 cups hot water. Stir until jelly powder is dissolved. Add 1½ cups cold water and chill by setting in ice water until syrupy.

While jelly is chilling, peel, pit and cut up avocados into a bowl. Add lemon juice and mash with a fork until very smooth. Blend in mayonnaise and cayenne. Stir into thickened jelly. Pour into jelly mold and chill until firm.

Unmold on salad greens and fill centre with strawberries. Pass the Honey Dressing. (Serves 6.)

*two 3-oz. pkg. lime-flavored*
  *jelly powder*
*½ tsp. salt*
*2 cups hot water*
*1½ cups cold water*
*2 very ripe avocados*
*3 tbsp. lemon juice*
*⅓ cup mayonnaise*
*dash cayenne*
*salad greens*
*3 cups whole strawberries*
*Honey Dressing (recipe follows)*

### Honey Dressing

Blend all ingredients and chill well. (Makes ½ cup.)

*¼ cup sour cream*
*¼ cup mayonnaise*
*2 tsp. liquid honey*

### Confetti Salad

Combine fruit and chill well. Cover 6 salad plates with leaf lettuce at serving time. Spoon melon mixture onto lettuce. Spoon a little of the Poppy Seed Dressing over each salad and garnish with a sprig of mint. Serve immediately. Pass remaining dressing. (Serves 6.)

*3 cups cantaloupe cubes*
  *(1 medium)*
*3 cups watermelon cubes*
*2 cups honeydew melon cubes*
  *(½ small)*
*1 cup halved strawberries*
*leaf lettuce*
*Poppy Seed Dressing*
  *(recipe follows)*
*mint sprigs*

### Poppy Seed Dressing

Combine all ingredients in a small jar with a tight lid and shake to blend well. (Makes about 1½ cups.)

*1 cup salad oil*
*⅓ cup orange juice*
*¼ cup liquid honey*
*1 tsp. salt*
*½ tsp. dry mustard*
*½ tsp. paprika*
*1 tbsp. poppy seeds*

# Sandwiches and Breads

How would we manage without sandwiches to make good hurry-up meals? Since sandwiches are basically all fast food, there isn't a lot of advance preparation to be done. However, the meat can be mixed with other ingredients ahead of time and refrigerated for special hamburgers; meats and cheeses can be sliced and wrapped in transparent wrap for quick fillings; eggs can be hard cooked; some fillings can be completed. For turnovers or pasties, make, bake and refrigerate, then reheat either wrapped in foil in a 450°F oven for about 10 minutes or wrapped loosely in paper toweling in the microwave for 1 to 4 minutes, depending on the number being heated.

For really extraspecial hamburgers and other sandwiches, I have included homemade buns and bread that make up in goodness for the time that's needed to create them.

## Favorite Whole Wheat Bread

1 cup milk
1 tbsp. liquid honey
$^1$/2 cup margarine or shortening
1$^1$/4 cups warm water
  (preferably water drained
  from cooked potatoes)
2 tsp. sugar
2 pkg. dry yeast
4 cups whole wheat flour
3 tsp. salt
$^1$/2 cup soy flour
$^1$/2 cup wheat germ
$^1$/2 cup sesame seeds
$^1$/2 cup wheat flakes (optional)
1$^1$/2 cups all-purpose flour
  (approx.)

Combine milk, honey and margarine or shortening in a small saucepan. Heat, stirring occasionally, until mixture is almost boiling. Cool to lukewarm.

Measure water into a large mixing bowl. Stir in sugar until dissolved. Sprinkle yeast over and let stand 10 minutes. Stir well.

Stir in cooled milk mixture, a little more than 2 cups of the whole wheat flour and the salt. Beat hard with a wooden spoon until smooth.

Add remaining whole wheat flour, soy flour, wheat germ, sesame seeds, wheat flakes and enough of the all-purpose flour to make a firm but not stiff dough. Mix thoroughly with hand, squeezing dough through your fingers until it is well blended.

Turn out onto a floured board and knead until smooth and very elastic and small bubbles appear under the surface, about 10 minutes.

Round up in a greased bowl, turn over so top of dough is greased, then cover with a damp cloth. Set in a warm place and let rise until double, about 1$^1$/2 hours. Punch down and let rise again until nearly double, about 45 minutes.

Grease two 9 × 5 × 3-inch loaf pans or three 8 × 4 × 2$^1$/2-inch loaf pans (I prefer the latter size). Divide dough into equal pieces and shape into loaves. Put in prepared pans, set in a warm place and let rise until double, about 1 hour.

Heat oven to 375°F. Bake loaves until they're well browned and sound hollow when tapped on top, about 50 minutes for large ones, 40 minutes for smaller. Turn out onto racks to cool. (Makes 2 large or 3 small loaves.)

## Oat-Bran Bread

Heat oven to 350°F. Grease two 7½ × 3½ × 2-inch loaf pans.

Beat eggs lightly in a mixing bowl. Stir in milk, molasses and oil. Sift flour, soda and salt together into mixture. Add remaining ingredients, stir to blend well and spoon into prepared pans.

Bake until a toothpick stuck in the centres comes out clean, about 50 minutes. Turn out onto a rack to cool. (Makes 2 small loaves.)

2 eggs
1⅓ cups buttermilk or
  soured milk
½ cup molasses
¼ cup cooking oil
2 cups sifted all-purpose flour
1 tsp. baking soda
1½ tsp. salt
1½ cups quick-cooking
  rolled oats
1 cup All-Bran cereal
½ cup raisins

## Wheat Germ Hamburger Buns

Put 1 cup water in a large bowl. Add 2 tsp. sugar and stir to dissolve. Sprinkle yeast over and let stand 10 minutes. Stir well.

While yeast is soaking, heat milk to scalding. Remove from heat. Add butter or margarine, 2 tbsp. sugar and salt and stir until butter or margarine is melted. Cool to lukewarm.

Add milk mixture, egg, wheat germ, Parmesan, dill weed and half of the flour to the yeast mixture. Beat to blend well. Add enough of remaining flour to make a soft dough.

Turn dough out onto a floured board and knead until smooth and elastic, about 10 minutes, kneading in enough of remaining flour to make dough easy to handle.

Divide dough into 12 equal pieces, cover with a towel and let stand about 20 minutes.

Grease a large cookie sheet. Shape each piece of dough into a round ball and put on sheet. Flatten slightly with hand. Brush with oil. Cover loosely with transparent wrap and refrigerate at least 2 hours (or as long as 24 hours).

Heat oven to 400°F when ready to bake buns. Let buns stand at room temperature 10 minutes. Beat egg and 1 tsp. water together and brush over buns.

Bake until buns are nicely browned, 20 to 25 minutes. (Makes 12.)

1 cup warm water
2 tsp. sugar
2 pkg. dry yeast
1 cup milk
¼ cup butter or margarine
2 tbsp. sugar
2 tsp. salt
1 egg
½ cup toasted wheat germ
½ cup grated Parmesan cheese
1 tbsp. snipped fresh dill or
  1 tsp. dried dill weed
5 cups whole wheat flour
  (approx.)
cooking oil
1 egg
1 tsp. water

## Pita Bread

*1/2 cup warm water*
*2 tsp. sugar*
*2 pkg. dry yeast*
*7 cups all-purpose flour*
*2 tsp. salt*
*1/4 cup olive oil*
*1 3/4 cups warm water*
*cornmeal*

Put the 1/2 cup warm water in a medium bowl. Add sugar and stir to dissolve. Sprinkle yeast over and let stand 10 minutes. Stir well.

Mix flour and salt in a large bowl. Make a well in centre and add yeast mixture, oil and 1 3/4 cups warm water. Gradually beat flour into liquids, adding a little more warm water if necessary to make a firm ball. Mix with a spoon, then with hand. Turn out onto a floured board and knead until very smooth and elastic, 15 to 20 minutes. Shape into a ball.

Put in a large oiled bowl. Turn over so top is oiled. Cover with a damp cloth and let rise in a warm place until double, about 1 hour.

Punch dough down and divide into 8 equal pieces. Shape each piece into a ball and put on a lightly floured board. Cover again with a damp cloth and let rise 30 minutes.

Lightly grease 2 large cookie sheets and sprinkle generously with cornmeal. Roll 4 of the dough balls into circles 8 inches in diameter and about 1/8 inch thick. (The other 4 dough balls will be used when these are baked.) Put 2 of these rounds on opposite corners of each cookie sheet, leaving a little space between them. Cover with a towel and let stand 30 minutes.

While the dough is rising, arrange oven racks so one is at bottom of oven and the other just above the centre. Heat oven to 500°F.

Bake one sheet of breads on lower rack 5 minutes. Move to upper rack and bake until puffed and browned, about 5 minutes more. Remove breads from cookie sheet and slip into plastic bags or wrap loosely in foil to keep moist and pliable — do not seal closed. Bake second sheet of breads and wrap the same way.

Use bread while warm. Repeat rolling, rising and baking with remaining 4 dough rounds. (Makes 8.)

Advance preparation: Wrap cooled bread airtight to store or freeze. To reheat, wrap in foil and place in a 400°F oven 10 to 15 minutes.

## Chicken Pockets

Combine mayonnaise, ketchup, onion, green pepper and olives. Spread inside of warm pita breads lightly with butter or margarine. Fill each with 2 overlapping chicken slices, a cheese slice, 3 overlapping tomato slices and some shredded lettuce. Spread with some mayonnaise mixture and serve immediately. (Makes 6.)

$^1/_2$ cup mayonnaise
2 tbsp. ketchup
$^1/_2$ tsp. grated onion
2 tbsp. very finely chopped
green pepper
1 tbsp. very finely chopped
stuffed olives
6 pita breads, heated and split
(recipe p. 61)
soft butter or margarine
12 thin slices chicken breast
6 slices Swiss cheese
18 thin slices tomato
shredded lettuce

## Italian-Style Pockets

Cream butter or margarine with mustard and spread lightly inside warm pita breads. Fill each with 2 overlapping salami slices, a Gruyère cheese slice, 2 overlapping tomato slices, 2 overlapping salami slices, a provolone cheese slice, a prosciutto or cooked ham slice and some shredded lettuce. (Makes 6.)

3 tbsp. butter or margarine
$^1/_4$ tsp. Dijon mustard
6 pita breads, heated and split
(recipe p. 61)
12 thin slices Italian salami
6 thin slices Gruyère cheese
12 paper thin slices tomato
12 thin slices Italian salami
6 thin slices provolone cheese
6 thin slices prosciutto or
cooked ham
shredded lettuce

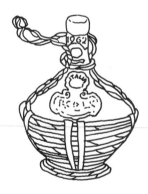

## Curried Beef Pockets

Heat oil in a heavy skillet over moderate heat. Add beef, onion and curry powder and stir until meat is lightly browned. Add apple, raisins, salt and 2 tbsp. of the yogurt. Lower heat and cook gently 5 minutes, stirring often. Spoon into warm pita breads. Add a tablespoonful of yogurt to each and serve immediately. (Makes 6.)

1 tbsp. cooking oil
1 lb. ground beef
$^1/_2$ cup chopped onion
2 tsp. curry powder
1 apple, peeled and chopped
$^1/_2$ cup seedless raisins
1 tsp. salt
$^2/_3$ cup plain yogurt
(one 175 g carton)
6 pita breads, heated and split
(recipe p. 61)

## Spinach Pasties

12-oz. pkg. frozen cut spinach
2 tbsp. water
2 tbsp. finely chopped onion
1/4 tsp. dried leaf rosemary
2 tbsp. butter or margarine
1 cup sliced mushrooms
1 tbsp. flour
1/2 cup chicken stock
  (recipe p. 48)
1 cup grated Swiss cheese
1/2 tsp. salt
dash black pepper
dash cayenne
dash ground nutmeg
Whole Wheat Biscuit Dough
  (recipe follows)
1 egg yolk
1 tbsp. water

Put spinach, 2 tbsp. water, onion and rosemary in a saucepan. Cover tightly and warm over moderate heat until spinach is thawed, breaking it apart with a fork as it begins to thaw. Turn spinach into a sieve and drain very well, pressing with the back of a spoon to remove all excess water. Put in a bowl.

Melt butter or margarine in same saucepan over high heat. Add mushrooms and stir 3 minutes. Sprinkle in flour and stir to blend. Remove from heat.

Stir in chicken stock. Return to heat and stir until boiling, thickened and smooth. Stir into spinach and let cool. Add cheese, salt and seasonings and toss together.

Heat oven to 400°F. Roll Whole Wheat Biscuit Dough into an 18-inch square. Cut into 6-inch squares and divide filling evenly among them. Fold into triangles, pressing edges firmly to seal. Put on large ungreased cookie sheets.

Beat egg yolk and 1 tbsp. water together with a fork and brush over tops of turnovers. Prick several times with a fork. Bake until well browned, 15 to 20 minutes. (Makes 9.)

## Whole Wheat Biscuit Dough

3 cups whole wheat flour
6 tsp. baking powder
1 1/2 tsp. salt
1/2 cup shortening
1 1/2 cups milk (approx.)

Measure flour into a bowl. Add baking powder and salt and blend well with a fork. Add shortening and cut in finely. Add enough of the milk to make a soft puffy dough that is easy to handle, mixing lightly with a fork. Turn out onto a floured board and knead gently 20 times.

## Meat and Potato Pasties

1 lb. lean ground beef
4 medium potatoes, peeled
  and cut in small cubes
1 cup small cubes turnip
1 large onion, finely chopped
1 tsp. salt
1/4 tsp. black pepper
double recipe of pastry for
  2-crust 9-inch pie
  (recipe p. 172)
1 egg yolk
1 tbsp. cold water

Combine beef, vegetables, salt and pepper in a bowl, mixing well. Heat oven to 400°F.

Roll pastry very thin, part at a time, and cut 5 1/2-inch rounds (you should have 24).

Put about 1/4 cup of filling on each round, moisten pastry edges with water and fold over to completely enclose filling. Press edges with fork tines to seal. Put on a large ungreased cookie sheet.

Beat egg yolk and 1 tbsp. water together with a fork. Brush tops of pasties with mixture. Prick several times with fork and bake 15 minutes. Reduce temperature to 350°F and continue baking until well browned, about 40 minutes. (Makes 2 dozen.)

## Soybean Turnovers

1 cup cold cooked soybeans
$^1/_4$ cup toasted sesame seeds
$^1/_4$ cup chopped water
  chestnuts
2 tbsp. tomato paste
2 tbsp. chopped ripe olives
$1^1/_2$ tbsp. finely chopped onion
$^1/_2$ tsp. salt
1 tbsp. wheat germ
pastry for 2-crust 9-inch pie
  (recipe p. 172)
1 egg yolk
1 tbsp. cold water

Mash soybeans until quite smooth. Mix in sesame seeds, water chestnuts, tomato paste, olives, onion and salt. Heat oven to 425°F.

Add wheat germ to dry ingredients for pastry. Roll pastry very thin and cut into 6-inch rounds (you should have 8).

Divide filling among rounds. Moisten edges of pastry with water and fold pastry over filling, sealing by pressing firmly with fork tines. Put on ungreased cookie sheets.

Beat egg yolk and 1 tbsp. water together with a fork and brush over tops of turnovers. Prick several times with fork. Bake until well browned, about 20 minutes. (Makes 8.)

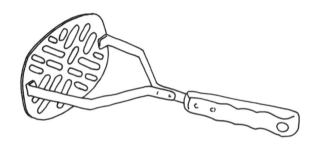

## Carrot and Egg Turnovers

2 tbsp. butter or margarine
3 cups grated raw carrots
  (use medium grater)
1 tsp. salt
$^1/_8$ tsp. black pepper
$^1/_8$ tsp. ground allspice
4 hard-cooked eggs, chopped
$^1/_4$ cup chopped parsley
2 tbsp. light cream
pastry for 2-crust 9-inch pie
  (recipe p. 172)
1 egg yolk
1 tbsp. cold water

Heat butter or margarine in a large heavy skillet. Add carrots and stir over low heat until carrots are getting tender, about 10 minutes. Remove from heat and stir in seasonings, eggs, parsley and cream. Cool.

Heat oven to 425°F. Roll pastry into an 18 × 12-inch rectangle and cut into 6-inch squares (you should have 6).

Divide filling among the squares. Moisten edges of pastry squares with water and fold pastry over filling, sealing by pressing firmly with fork tines. Put on an ungreased cookie sheet.

Beat egg yolk and 1 tbsp. water together with a fork and brush over tops of turnovers. Cut a small slit in the top of each to allow steam to escape. Bake until well browned, about 12 minutes. Serve hot or cold. (Makes 6.)

## Deviled Western Sandwiches

2 eggs
1 tbsp. milk
$2^1/_4$-oz. can deviled ham
2 tbsp. minced onion
2 tbsp. minced green pepper
$^1/_4$ tsp. salt
$^1/_8$ tsp. black pepper
2 tbsp. butter or margarine
4 slices hot buttered toast

Beat eggs, milk and ham together until well blended. Stir in onion, green pepper, salt and pepper.

Heat butter or margarine in a heavy skillet. Add egg mixture and cook over moderate heat until browned. Cut into 2 pieces and turn to brown second side.

Put each part of egg mixture between 2 slices of toast and serve immediately. (Makes 2.)

## French-Toasted Ham Sandwiches

Combine ham, cheese, olives, onion, chili powder and mayonnaise. Spread mixture between slices of bread to make 6 sandwiches.

Heat butter or margarine in a large heavy skillet.

Beat eggs and milk in a flat dish (a pie plate is good). Dip sandwiches quickly into mixture to coat both sides (don't let sandwiches soak in liquid).

Fry sandwiches slowly in hot butter or margarine, adding more if needed, until bread is golden brown and filling is very hot. Serve immediately. (Makes 6.)

Advance preparation: Make ham mixture and refrigerate.

1 1/2 cups ground cooked ham
1/2 cup grated process cheese
1/4 cup chopped ripe olives
1 tbsp. finely chopped green onion
1 tsp. chili powder
1/4 cup mayonnaise
12 slices whole wheat bread
1/4 cup butter or margarine (approx.)
2 eggs, lightly beaten
1/3 cup milk

## Broiled Bacon and Onion Sandwiches

Lay bread on a cookie sheet and toast one side under the broiler. Remove from oven and turn.

Fry bacon until crisp. Drain, cool and crumble. Drain almost all of drippings from pan bacon was cooked in and add onion. Cook gently until yellow.

Combine bacon bits, onion, Swiss cheese, Parmesan, mayonnaise and seasonings. Spread on untoasted side of bread, covering bread well.

Put low under broiler and broil until browned and bubbling. (Makes 4.)

4 slices bread
4 slices bacon
1 medium onion, chopped
1 cup grated Swiss cheese
1/4 cup grated Parmesan cheese
1/2 cup mayonnaise
1/4 tsp. ground nutmeg
1/4 tsp. salt
1/8 tsp. black pepper

## Swiss Broiled Sandwiches

Heat butter or margarine in a small heavy skillet. Add onions and mushrooms and cook gently, stirring, 3 minutes. Add ham and cook gently, stirring, until lightly browned. Sprinkle in flour, 1/4 tsp. salt and dash of pepper. Stir to blend. Remove from heat.

Dissolve bouillon cube in 1 cup boiling water and add to first mixture along with cream. Stir to blend. Return to moderate heat and cook, stirring constantly, until thick and smooth.

Put slices of toast in a single layer in a large shallow baking dish. Top each slice of toast with a slice of cheese. Pour sauce over all.

Lay a slice of tomato on top of each sandwich and sprinkle with salt and pepper and a little grated cheese.

Put low under broiler and broil until sauce is bubbling well. Serve immediately. (Makes 6.)

Advance preparation: If it is to be used within a couple of hours, the ham-mushroom mixture can be made down to the point of cooking until thick, then refrigerated.

1/4 cup butter or margarine
1/2 cup chopped green onions
1 cup sliced fresh mushrooms
1 1/2 cups cubed cooked ham
1/4 cup flour
1/4 tsp. salt
dash black pepper
1 chicken bouillon cube
1 cup boiling water
1 cup light cream
6 slices buttered white toast
6 thin slices Swiss cheese
6 slices tomato
salt and pepper
1/2 cup grated Swiss cheese

### Grilled Peanut Butter Sandwiches

4 slices bacon
1/2 cup smooth peanut butter
1 cup grated process cheese
8 slices whole wheat bread
soft butter or margarine

Fry bacon until crisp. Drain on paper toweling and crumble.

Blend peanut butter, cheese and bacon bits. Spread thickly on 4 of the slices of bread. Top with remaining slices. Spread top of sandwich thickly with soft butter or margarine.

Heat a large heavy skillet and put sandwiches in it, butter side down (do 2 at a time if necessary). Spread butter or margarine on upper side of sandwiches.

Cook slowly until sandwiches are golden brown on one side, then turn and brown second side. Serve hot. (Makes 4.)

### Grilled Tofu Sandwiches

3/4 lb. tofu (soybean curd)
2 tbsp. soybean or other
   vegetable oil
2 green onions, chopped
2 tbsp. salted peanuts
1 tbsp. chopped parsley
1 tbsp. finely chopped celery
1/2 tsp. salt
grating fresh black pepper
12 slices whole wheat bread
1/2 cup soft butter or margarine
1/4 cup sesame seeds

Put all ingredients except whole wheat bread, butter or margarine and sesame seeds in glass of blender and buzz until smooth. Spread between slices of bread to make 6 sandwiches.

Cream butter or margarine with sesame seeds and spread half the mixture on one side of sandwiches.

Put buttered side down in a hot heavy skillet over moderate heat and cook until browned, then butter second side, turn and brown. Serve hot. (Makes 6.)

### Club House Wieners

6 wieners
6 slices bacon
6 hot dog buns
commercial sandwich spread
   (see note)
butter or margarine
shredded lettuce
12 thin slices tomato

Split wieners almost through lengthwise and spread open. Lay on a broiler pan. Put slices of bacon on broiler pan.

Slip under hot broiler and broil until bacon is crisp and wieners are heated through. Put a slice of bacon in the slit of each wiener.

Split hot dog buns and toast lightly under broiler. Spread one half of buns generously with sandwich spread and the other half with butter or margarine. Add some shredded lettuce, 2 slices tomato and one of the bacon-stuffed wieners to each bun and serve immediately. (Makes 6.)

Note: The sandwich spread we used is the kind that looks like mayonnaise with pickle relish in it.

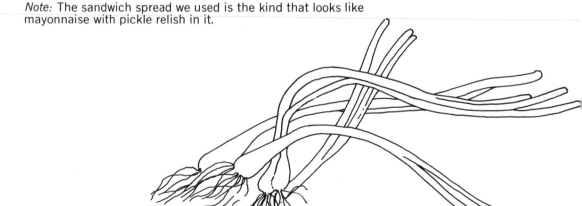

## Corn Burgers

Combine meat, milk, corn, egg, bread crumbs, ketchup, onion and seasonings and blend well with a fork (mixture will be quite soft). Shape into 12 thin patties.

Heat butter or margarine and oil in a heavy skillet. Fry patties quickly until browned on both sides. Lower heat and cook until done the way you like them, 3 to 5 minutes more. Serve patties in toasted buns. (Makes 12.)

$1^1/_2$ lb. ground chuck
$^2/_3$ cup evaporated milk
  (1 small can)
12-oz. can whole kernel corn
1 egg, lightly beaten
$^2/_3$ cup fine dry bread crumbs
$^1/_4$ cup ketchup
2 tbsp. grated onion
1 tsp. salt
$^1/_8$ tsp. black pepper
$1^1/_2$ tsp. chili powder
1 tsp. paprika
1 tbsp. butter or margarine
2 tbsp. cooking oil
12 toasted hamburger buns

## Butterfly Burgers

Heat broiler. Have ready a cookie sheet and lightly oil a broiler pan.

Split hamburger buns into halves crosswise. Cut a $^1/_4$-inch slice from top of top half of each bun. Butter all cut sides of buns lightly. Lay bottom halves on cookie sheet.

Combine meat, onions, milk or water, salt and pepper and mix lightly with a fork. Shape into 6 patties about the size of the buns. Put on broiler pan.

Broil 3 minutes a side. (If you prefer, pan fry them in a little oil for the same time.) Put meat patties on bun bottoms. Top with bun tops.

Set oven temperature at 400°F.

Combine pickle relish, cheese, mustard and enough mayonnaise to make a mixture that is easy to spread. Spread mixture over cut surface on top of each bun.

Cut the thin slice you trimmed from the top of each bun into halves and set it in the cheese mixture, cut side up, so it looks like a butterfly. Cut onion slices into halves and slip a half slice under each butterfly wing. Put a tomato wedge or a strip of pimento between the wings.

Bake until very hot and wings have browned lightly along the edges, about 10 minutes. (Makes 6.)

6 hamburger buns
butter or margarine
$1^1/_2$ lb. ground chuck
$^1/_2$ cup chopped green onions
  (optional)
$^1/_2$ cup milk or water
1 tsp. salt
$^1/_4$ tsp. black pepper
$^1/_4$ cup drained sweet pickle
  relish
1 cup grated old Cheddar
  cheese
1 tsp. prepared mustard
2 tbsp. mayonnaise (approx.)
6 thin slices onion
1 small tomato, cut in 6 wedges
  or 6 strips pimento about
  $1^1/_2$ inches long

### Hashed Brown Burgers

Combine meat, potatoes, onion, parsley, milk, salt, pepper and mustard, mixing lightly with a fork. Shape into 6 patties about 3/4 inch thick.

Heat oil and 1 tbsp. butter or margarine in a large heavy skillet and add patties. Cook slowly until very well browned on both sides and potatoes are tender, about 15 minutes a side.

Toast buns lightly just before meat is ready and spread with butter or margarine. Serve meat patties in buns. (Makes 6.)

1 lb. ground chuck
2 cups grated raw potatoes
  (use medium grater)
1/4 cup finely chopped onion
1/4 cup chopped parsley
3 tbsp. milk
1 1/2 tsp. salt
1/8 tsp. black pepper
1/2 tsp. dry mustard
2 tbsp. cooking oil
1 tbsp. butter or margarine
6 hamburger buns
butter or margarine

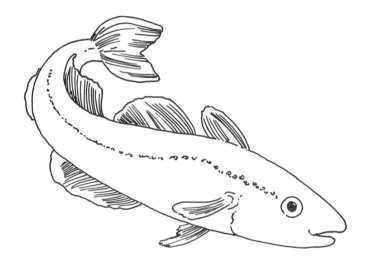

### Fish Burgers

Thaw fish until fillets can be separated if it is frozen. Heat oven to 350°F.

Split hamburger buns, butter and wrap them in aluminum foil. Put in oven to heat while preparing filling for sandwiches.

Cut fish into pieces the size of the buns. Put fish pieces in a shallow dish and drizzle lemon juice over. Let stand a few minutes.

Combine flour and 1 tsp. salt. Dip fish in this mixture to coat both sides. Mix mayonnaise, onions, pickle and mustard.

Heat about 1/4 inch cooking oil in a large heavy skillet. Drop in fish pieces and fry quickly just until they are lightly browned and flake easily with a fork. Lift fish out of pan as it cooks and drain on paper toweling.

Spread bottom of each bun with some of the mayonnaise mixture. Top with a portion of fish. Lay a tomato slice on each and sprinkle lightly with salt and pepper. Add tops of buns and serve immediately. (Makes 6.)

1 lb. fresh or frozen white fish
  fillets (sole, haddock, etc.)
6 hamburger buns
butter or margarine
1 tbsp. lemon juice
1/4 cup flour
1 tsp. salt
3 tbsp. mayonnaise
1/4 cup finely chopped green
  onions
2 tbsp. finely chopped sweet
  pickle
1 tbsp. prepared mustard
cooking oil
6 slices tomato
salt and pepper

### Salmon French Toast Sandwiches

Drain salmon, collecting liquid in a flat dish (a pie plate is good). Set liquid aside to use later.

Put salmon, including bones and skin, into a bowl. Mash bones with a fork and break up salmon well. Add mayonnaise, onions, parsley, salt, pepper and curry powder and blend together well.

Spread salmon mixture on buttered side of 4 slices of bread. Top with remaining slices.

Break eggs into salmon liquid in flat dish and beat lightly with a fork.

Heat butter or margarine in a large heavy skillet. Dip sandwiches into egg mixture quickly to coat both sides. Put sandwiches in skillet and brown slowly on both sides, adding more butter or margarine if necessary to keep from burning. Serve hot. (Makes 4.)

7³/₄-oz. can salmon
3 tbsp. mayonnaise
2 tbsp. finely chopped green onions
1 tbsp. chopped parsley
¹/₄ tsp. salt
¹/₈ tsp. black pepper
¹/₂ tsp. curry powder
8 slices whole wheat bread, buttered
2 eggs
2 tbsp. butter or margarine (approx.)

### Puffy Tuna Sandwiches

Blend tuna, 2 tbsp. mayonnaise and lemon juice. Toast bread on one side under broiler. Turn and toast other side very lightly. Spread toast with tuna mixture.

Beat egg white until stiff. Fold in 2 tbsp. mayonnaise, cayenne, parsley and pickle. Spread over tuna.

Put low under broiler and broil until tops of sandwiches are lightly browned and puffed. Sprinkle lightly with paprika and serve immediately. (Makes 4.)

6¹/₂-oz. can flaked tuna
2 tbsp. mayonnaise
2 tsp. lemon juice
4 slices bread
1 egg white
2 tbsp. mayonnaise
dash cayenne
1 tbsp. chopped parsley
2 tbsp. finely chopped sweet pickle, well drained
paprika

### Lobster Sandwiches

Combine all ingredients except butter or margarine and bread, using enough mayonnaise to make a mixture that will spread easily.

Butter bread and spread lobster filling between slices, using a generous ¹/₄ cup filling for each sandwich and spreading the filling to ¹/₄ inch of the edge. Trim off crusts and cut sandwiches into quarters to serve. (Makes 8.)

10-oz. can lobster, finely chopped or 2 cups chopped fresh-cooked lobster
2 hard-cooked eggs, finely chopped
1 large tomato, peeled, seeded and finely chopped
2 tsp. finely chopped green onion
1 tsp. snipped fresh dill
¹/₂ tsp. salt
¹/₈ tsp. black pepper
¹/₄ cup mayonnaise (approx.)
butter or margarine
16 slices whole wheat bread

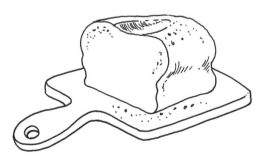

# Main Dishes

For substantial lunches or suppers, it's hard to beat a good casserole or a nice mixture of vegetables cooked with a small amount of meat. Casseroles, besides being both good and satisfying, are useful, since nearly all can be prepared completely and refrigerated to be heated when needed, allowing about 15 minutes extra baking time to make up for the refrigerator chill. Quickly made dishes suggested include some that are cooked Chinese style, some fast pasta sauces and some creamed foods served on toast. For the host or hostess with a little more time, there are some inviting entertaining ideas.

## Ground Beef and Noodles

Heat oil in a large heavy skillet. Add ground beef and onion and cook gently until beef is lightly browned, stirring constantly and breaking the meat apart. Spread meat and onion evenly in pan and put uncooked noodles in a layer on top.

Combine tomato juice, salt, celery salt, pepper and Worcestershire and pour over noodles. Bring to a boil, turn heat to simmer, cover and cook 20 minutes. Add celery and green pepper, cover again and simmer until noodles are tender and vegetables are tender-crisp, about 10 minutes.

Stir in sour cream or yogurt and mushrooms and heat just to boiling, stirring. Serve immediately. (Serves 4.)

2 tbsp. cooking oil
1 lb. ground beef
1 cup chopped onion (1 large)
3 cups medium noodles
3 cups tomato juice
1 tsp. salt
1$^1$/$_2$ tsp. celery salt
dash black pepper
2 tsp. Worcestershire sauce
1 cup thinly sliced celery
$^1$/$_2$ cup chopped green pepper
1 cup sour cream or plain
  yogurt
4$^1$/$_2$-oz. can sliced mushrooms,
  drained

## Leftover Beef and Macaroni

Heat oven to 350°F. Butter a 2$^1$/$_2$-qt. casserole.

Cook macaroni in plenty of boiling salted water until just tender, about 7 minutes. Drain.

Melt $^1$/$_4$ cup butter or margarine in a saucepan. Sprinkle in flour, salt, pepper, nutmeg and mustard and stir to blend. Remove from heat.

Add milk all at once, stirring to blend. Return to moderate heat and cook, stirring constantly, until boiling, thickened and smooth. Add cheese and heat gently, stirring, until cheese is melted. Remove from heat.

Heat 2 tbsp. butter or margarine in a medium skillet and add meat cubes. Cook gently, stirring, until lightly browned. Add mushrooms and stir 3 minutes. Remove from heat.

Combine macaroni, meat and mushrooms and tomatoes in prepared casserole, tossing together lightly with a fork. Pour sauce over and mix lightly with a fork. Combine bread crumbs and melted butter or margarine and sprinkle over all.

Bake until browned on top and bubbling well, about 35 minutes. (Serves 6.)

2 cups elbow macaroni
$^1$/$_4$ cup butter or margarine
$^1$/$_4$ cup flour
1$^1$/$_2$ tsp. salt
$^1$/$_4$ tsp. black pepper
$^1$/$_8$ tsp. ground nutmeg
$^1$/$_4$ tsp. dry mustard
2 cups milk
1$^1$/$_2$ cups grated Swiss cheese
2 tbsp. butter or margarine
2 cups diced leftover roast beef
2 cups sliced mushrooms
2 large tomatoes, peeled
  and chopped
$^1$/$_2$ cup fine dry bread crumbs
$^1$/$_4$ cup butter or margarine,
  melted

## Swiss Spaghetti

1/4 cup butter or margarine
1 medium onion, chopped
1 green pepper, chopped
1 small clove garlic, crushed
1 lb. ground beef
19-oz. can tomatoes
1 1/2 tsp. salt
1/2 tsp. black pepper
1 tsp. sugar
1/2 tsp. dried leaf basil
500 g pkg. spaghetti
3/4 lb. Swiss cheese, cut in
    1/4-inch cubes

Melt butter or margarine in a large saucepan. Add onion, green pepper and garlic. Cook gently, stirring, 3 minutes. Add beef and cook, stirring and breaking apart, until lightly browned. Add tomatoes, salt, pepper, sugar and basil. Cover and simmer 1 hour, stirring occasionally.

Cook spaghetti in plenty of boiling salted water shortly before sauce is ready. Drain. Add cheese cubes and hot spaghetti to sauce. Stir lightly to blend and serve immediately. (Serves 6.)

## New Zealand Macaroni and Cheese Loaf

1 cup elbow macaroni
2 tbsp. cooking oil
1 small onion, finely chopped
1 lb. ground beef
1/2 tsp. salt
1/4 tsp. black pepper
2 tbsp. chopped parsley
2 tbsp. cooking oil
2 tbsp. flour
1 cup milk
2 eggs
1 cup grated old Cheddar
    cheese
1/4 cup milk
fine dry bread crumbs

Cook macaroni in plenty of boiling salted water until just tender, about 7 minutes. Drain.

Heat 2 tbsp. oil in a medium saucepan over high heat. Add onion and beef and stir until meat is lightly browned. Stir in salt, pepper, parsley and macaroni and set aside.

Heat 2 tbsp. oil in a second saucepan over moderate heat. Sprinkle in flour and stir to blend. Remove from heat. Add 1 cup milk all at once and stir to blend. Return to heat and stir until thick and smooth. Remove from heat.

Separate one of the eggs and add yolk and 1/2 cup of the cheese to sauce, stirring until blended. Add egg white, whole egg, 1/4 cup milk and 1/4 cup of the cheese to meat mixture. Mix well.

Heat oven to 350°F. Grease a 9 × 5 × 3-inch glass loaf pan and sprinkle with bread crumbs, shaking them around to coat the bottom and sides.

Put half of meat mixture in pan. Add half of sauce. Repeat layers and sprinkle top with remaining cheese. Bake 45 minutes, then cut into thick slices and serve hot right from the pan. Or chill, unmold and slice thinly. (Serves 6.)

## Mince and Barley

1 tbsp. beef drippings or butter
1 lb. ground beef
1 tsp. salt
dash black pepper
1/2 cup water
1 small whole onion
1 cup pearl barley
3 cups cold water
2 tsp. salt
1 tbsp. butter

Heat beef drippings or butter in a heavy skillet. Add ground beef and brown lightly, stirring constantly. Add 1 tsp. salt, pepper, the 1/2 cup water and onion and cover tightly. Simmer 30 minutes, stirring occasionally.

Cover barley with 3 cups cold water. Add 2 tsp. salt. Bring to a boil, turn down heat and simmer, stirring occasionally, until water has disappeared and barley is tender, about 30 minutes. Add butter and toss lightly with a fork.

Serve beef on hot barley. (Serves 4.)

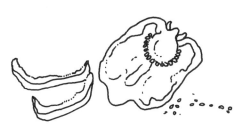

## Stuffed Zucchini with Tomato Sauce

2 tbsp. cooking oil
2 medium onions, chopped
4 medium tomatoes, peeled
  and chopped
$1/4$ cup tomato paste
$1/2$ cup water
$1/2$ tsp. salt
$1/4$ tsp. black pepper
$1/2$ tsp. sugar
$1/2$ tsp. dried leaf basil
2 tbsp. cooking oil
$1/2$ lb. ground beef
1 tsp. salt
$1/4$ tsp. black pepper
4 medium zucchini

Heat 2 tbsp. oil in a medium saucepan. Add onion and cook gently, stirring, until limp, about 5 minutes. Add tomatoes, tomato paste, $1/2$ cup water, $1/2$ tsp. salt, $1/4$ tsp. pepper, sugar and basil. Bring to a boil, turn down heat and simmer, uncovered, 30 minutes, stirring often.

Heat oven to 350°F. Grease a 13 × 9 × 2-inch baking dish.

Heat 2 tbsp. oil in a small skillet. Add ground beef, 1 tsp. salt and $1/4$ tsp. pepper and cook until meat loses its pink color, about 5 minutes.

Trim ends off zucchini and cut each one into halves lengthwise. Scoop out centres with a spoon to make a dish to hold filling. Be sure to leave a wall at least $1/4$ inch thick. Chop pieces you scooped out finely and add to tomato sauce.

Set zucchini halves in prepared baking dish. Spoon meat mixture into cavities. Spoon tomato sauce over all. Bake until zucchini is tender, 30 to 45 minutes. (Serves 4 to 8.)

Advance preparation: Make sauce and brown meat. Chill until ready to complete dish.

## Chili-Stuffed Tomatoes

6 large tomatoes
1 tbsp. cooking oil
$1/2$ lb. ground beef
$1/2$ cup chopped onion
$3/4$ tsp. salt
$1/8$ tsp. black pepper
1 tsp. chili powder
1 cup cooked rice (see note)
$3/4$ cup grated old
  Cheddar cheese
paprika

Heat oven to 375°F. Have ready a baking dish that will just hold the 6 tomatoes.

Cut tops from tomatoes and hollow out with a spoon, leaving a fairly thick wall so tomatoes will not break apart during baking. Invert on paper toweling to drain.

Heat oil in a skillet. Add beef and onion and cook gently, stirring, until beef is lightly browned. Remove from heat. Stir in salt, pepper, chili powder, rice and $1/2$ cup of the cheese.

Set tomatoes in baking dish and spoon meat mixture into them. Sprinkle remaining $1/4$ cup cheese evenly over tops of tomatoes and shake a little paprika on each.

Bake until stuffing is very hot and tomatoes are tender, about 30 minutes. (Serves 6.)

Note: You can use leftover rice for this recipe. If you are using quick-cooking rice, use $1/2$ cup and prepare it according to package directions.

## Beef and Vegetables

Cut beef into thin strips across grain. Combine $1/2$ cup water, cornstarch, soya sauce and honey. Rinse sprouts under cold running water and drain immediately.

Heat oil in a large heavy skillet over high heat. Add beef and cook until it loses its pink color. Lift out with a slotted spoon.

Add mushrooms, green pepper and onion to pan and stir 3 minutes. Add Chinese cabbage and stir 1 minute. Add peas, cover and cook 1 minute.

Stir soya sauce mixture, then stir into vegetables. Add meat, cover and simmer just until peas are tender, about 3 minutes. Add bean sprouts and stir until warm, about 1 minute. Serve immediately over brown rice. (Serves 4.)

$1/2$ lb. round steak, cut
   $1/2$ inch thick
$1/2$ cup water
1 tbsp. cornstarch
2 tbsp. soya sauce
1 tbsp. liquid honey
2 cups fresh bean sprouts
2 tbsp. cooking oil
$3/4$ lb. fresh mushrooms, sliced
2 green peppers, cut in 1-inch
   squares
1 medium onion, thinly sliced
3 large stalks Chinese cabbage,
   sliced on the diagonal
$1/4$ lb. Chinese pea pods
   (snow peas)
hot cooked brown rice

## Bulgarian Moussaka

Wash eggplants and slice $1/4$ inch thick (do not peel unless skin is marked and tough). Lay slices out on waxed paper and sprinkle lightly with salt on both sides. Let stand 1 hour.

Heat 2 tbsp. oil in a large heavy skillet. Add onions, green pepper and garlic and fry gently, stirring, 3 minutes. Add meat and stir, breaking meat apart, until meat browns lightly. Drain off excess fat. Add 1 tsp. salt, pepper and paprika. Blend well and set aside.

Heat a small amount of oil in a heavy skillet. Dry eggplant pieces with paper toweling and dip in $1/4$ cup flour to coat both sides. Fry pieces a few at a time, adding oil to pan in small amounts as needed.

Heat oven to 350°F. Butter a 13 × 9 × 2-inch baking dish.

Put a layer of about $1/3$ of the eggplant in prepared baking dish. Add $1/3$ of the meat mixture. Repeat layers twice more. Cover pan with foil.

Bake 1 hour. Uncover pan. Mix yogurt, egg yolks and $1/2$ cup flour, blending well. Spread over eggplant-meat layers. Bake 15 minutes. Turn on broiler and broil until topping browns lightly. Serve immediately. (Serves 4.)

Advance preparation: Cook meat mixture.

1 extralarge or 2 medium
   eggplants (about $1^{1}/_{2}$ lb.
   in all)
salt
2 tbsp. cooking oil
2 medium onions, finely
   chopped
1 medium green pepper, finely
   chopped
3 cloves garlic, minced
$1^{1}/_{2}$ lb. ground lean lamb
1 tsp. salt
dash black pepper
2 tsp. paprika
cooking oil
$1/4$ cup flour (approx.)
2 cups plain yogurt
   (three 175 g cartons)
4 egg yolks, lightly beaten
$1/2$ cup sifted all-purpose flour

## Broccoli and Ham Casserole

Heat oven to 350°F. Butter a 1¹/₂-qt. casserole.

Cook macaroni in plenty of boiling salted water until just tender, about 7 minutes. Drain.

Cook broccoli according to package directions, using the minimum time suggested. Drain, saving cooking water. Add milk to cooking water to make 2 cups liquid.

Melt 3 tbsp. butter or margarine in a medium saucepan. Sprinkle in flour and let bubble up. Stir in salt and pepper. Remove from heat.

Add the 2 cups liquid all at once to saucepan, stirring to blend. Return to moderate heat. Stir until boiling, thickened and smooth. Stir in liquid from mustard pickles, chopped pickle, ham or luncheon meat, macaroni and broccoli. Pour into prepared casserole.

Add bread cubes to 2 tbsp. melted butter or margarine and toss together with a fork. Add cheese and toss with fork. Sprinkle on top of broccoli mixture.

Bake until bubbling and browned on top, about 25 minutes. (Serves 6.)

1 cup elbow macaroni
10-oz. pkg. frozen chopped broccoli
milk
3 tbsp. butter or margarine
3 tbsp. flour
1 tsp. salt
¹/₄ tsp. black pepper
1 tbsp. liquid from mustard pickles
2 tbsp. chopped mustard pickle
1 cup diced cooked ham or luncheon meat
³/₄ cup ¹/₄-inch bread cubes
2 tbsp. butter or margarine, melted
¹/₂ cup grated old Cheddar cheese

## Corned Beef Hash Cakes

Heat oven to 450°F. Grease a cookie sheet.

Beat egg whites until stiff and set aside. Beat egg yolks with same beaters until thick. Combine with corned beef, potatoes, onion, parsley, salt and pepper, mixing very well. Fold in egg whites.

Make 6 equal mounds of mixture on prepared cookie sheet. Flatten cakes to about 1 inch thick. Bake until bottoms are well browned, about 15 minutes.

While cakes are baking, heat ketchup, ¹/₄ cup water and relish in a small pan. Invert hash cakes onto hot serving plates and spoon a little of the ketchup mixture over each. (Serves 6.)

2 egg whites
2 egg yolks
12-oz. can corned beef, broken up
1¹/₂ cups small cubes cooked potatoes
¹/₂ cup finely chopped onion
¹/₄ cup chopped parsley
1 tsp. salt
¹/₄ tsp. black pepper
¹/₃ cup ketchup
¹/₄ cup water
2 tbsp. sweet pickle relish

## Scalloped Potatoes and Wieners

Heat oven to 350°F. Butter a 2-qt. casserole.

Melt butter or margarine in a small skillet. Add onion and cook gently, stirring, until onion is tender but not browned, about 5 minutes.

Put yogurt in a large bowl. Stir in flour, salt, pepper and paprika, blending well. Add cottage cheese, 1 cup Swiss cheese, parsley, potatoes and about ³/₄ of the wieners. Turn mixture into prepared casserole. Cover and bake 1¹/₂ hours.

Remove cover. Sprinkle top of potatoes with remaining wiener pieces and ¹/₂ cup Swiss cheese. Continue baking, uncovered, until potatoes are tender, about 15 minutes more. (Serves 6.)

2 tbsp. butter or margarine
1 cup chopped onion
2 cups plain yogurt (three 175 g cartons)
2 tbsp. all-purpose flour
1¹/₂ tsp. salt
¹/₈ tsp. black pepper
¹/₈ tsp. paprika
1 cup cream-style cottage cheese (one 250 g carton)
1 cup grated Swiss cheese
¹/₄ cup chopped parsley
4 cups thinly sliced raw potatoes
1 lb. wieners, cut in ¹/₂-inch pieces on the diagonal
¹/₂ cup grated Swiss cheese

## Chicken with Almonds

1 large whole chicken breast
(about 1 lb.)
1/2 cup water
2 tbsp. soya sauce
1/2 tsp. ground ginger
1 tbsp. cornstarch
2 tbsp. cooking oil
1/2 tsp. salt
1 tbsp. cooking oil
1 large onion, sliced paper thin
1 1/2 cups celery, cut in 1/2-inch
pieces on the diagonal
1 cup sliced mushrooms
1/2 large green pepper, cut in
strips lengthwise
1/4 cup water
12-oz. pkg. frozen peas
salt
1 cup water
1/2 cup toasted slivered
almonds

Bone chicken breast, remove skin and cut meat into thin strips.

Blend 1/2 cup water, soya sauce, ginger and cornstarch in a small bowl.

Heat 2 tbsp. oil to very hot in a large heavy skillet or wok. Add chicken pieces and 1/2 tsp. salt. Cook over high heat 2 minutes, stirring constantly. Lift chicken out of pan with a slotted spoon and keep hot.

Add 1 tbsp. oil to pan. Add onion, celery, mushrooms and green pepper and cook over high heat 1 minute, stirring constantly. Add 1/4 cup water and peas. Cover tightly and cook 2 minutes. Sprinkle with salt. Turn out onto a deep platter.

Add chicken pieces to pan and heat 30 seconds, stirring. Spoon on top of vegetables.

Add 1 cup water to pan and heat to boiling. Stir in cornstarch mixture gradually. Cook until thick and clear, stirring constantly. Pour over vegetables and chicken. Sprinkle with almonds. Serve immediately. (Serves 4.)

Advance preparation: Bone and cut up chicken breast. Refrigerate.

## Turkey Cakes

2 cups ground cooked turkey
2 1/2 cups mashed potatoes
(about 4 large)
1 tbsp. finely grated onion
1/4 cup chopped parsley
1/2 cup milk
1 egg, lightly beaten
1 tsp. salt
1/4 tsp. black pepper
flour
2 tbsp. butter or margarine
(approx.)
Mushroom Sauce (optional)

Combine turkey, potatoes, onion, parsley, milk, egg, salt and pepper, mixing lightly with a fork. Shape into 8 cakes about 1 inch thick. Dip cakes in flour to coat both sides.

Heat 2 tbsp. butter or margarine in a large heavy skillet. Add turkey cakes and fry until golden brown on both sides, about 5 minutes a side. Add more butter or margarine if needed. Serve immediately, 2 per person. Top with Mushroom Sauce if desired. (Serves 4.)

Advance preparation: Grind turkey. Cook and mash potatoes. Make sauce. Refrigerate everything. Reheat sauce in a double boiler over simmering water.

## Mushroom Sauce

3 tbsp. butter or margarine
1 cup chopped mushrooms
2 tbsp. flour
1 1/2 cups water
1 chicken bouillon cube
1/8 tsp. black pepper
1/4 tsp. dried leaf thyme
3/4 tsp. salt (optional)
2 tbsp. dry sherry

Heat butter or margarine in a medium saucepan. Add mushrooms and stir 3 minutes. Sprinkle in flour and stir to blend. Remove from heat.

Add 1 1/2 cups water all at once and stir to blend. Add bouillon cube, pepper and thyme. Set over moderate heat and stir until sauce is boiling, thickened and smooth. Add salt to taste (some bouillon cubes are very salty, so be sure to taste before adding more salt). Turn down heat and simmer 3 minutes. Stir in sherry. (Makes about 2 cups.)

## Turkey-Stuffed Avocados

Heat oven to 350°F. Have ready a large shallow baking dish.

Heat soup and milk in a small saucepan. Stir in turkey, peas, parsley, lemon juice, pimento and pepper. Combine bread cubes and melted butter or margarine.

Cut avocados into halves and set them in baking dish. Add 1/4 inch water to dish. Spoon turkey mixture into hollows in avocados. Sprinkle with bread cubes.

Heat in oven until everything is hot and bread cubes are lightly browned, about 20 minutes. Turn on broiler for a minute to brown cubes if necessary. (Serves 6.)

10-oz. can cream of chicken soup
1/4 cup milk
1 cup cubed cooked turkey
1 cup frozen peas, cooked
2 tbsp. chopped parsley
1 tbsp. lemon juice
2 tbsp. chopped pimento
1/8 tsp. black pepper
1 cup small bread cubes (use day-old bread)
2 tbsp. butter or margarine, melted
3 medium avocados

## Chicken Liver Spaghetti Sauce

Heat oil in a heavy saucepan. Add onion and cook gently 10 minutes, stirring often. Stir in tomato sauce, 1/2 tsp. salt, thyme and red pepper. Cover and cook gently 15 minutes, stirring occasionally. Stir in 1/2 cup grated Parmesan and simmer 5 minutes more.

Melt butter or margarine in a heavy skillet. Add chicken livers and mushrooms and cook gently, stirring constantly, until livers are cooked, about 5 minutes. Add 1/2 tsp. salt and blend lightly. Add to tomato mixture and serve immediately spooned over hot spaghetti and sprinkled with more Parmesan. (Serves 4.)

1/4 cup olive oil
2 medium onions, chopped
two 7 1/2-oz. cans tomato sauce
1/2 tsp. salt
1/4 tsp. dried leaf thyme
1/4 tsp. crushed dried red pepper
1/2 cup grated Parmesan cheese
1/4 cup butter or margarine
1 lb. chicken livers, cut in half
2 cups sliced fresh mushrooms
1/2 tsp. salt
hot cooked spaghetti
grated Parmesan cheese

## Quick Pasta Sauce

Heat oil in a large heavy skillet and add bacon. Fry, stirring constantly, until bacon bits are very crisp. Lift out with a slotted spoon and set aside.

Drain off and discard all but 2 tbsp. of fat left in pan. Add mushrooms and garlic and cook gently, stirring, 3 minutes. Add tomatoes, basil, 1/2 tsp. salt and 1/4 tsp. pepper and continue stirring until tomatoes are soft and sauce is fairly thick.

Stir in bacon bits, add salt and pepper to taste and serve immediately over hot pasta. (Serves 4.)

1 tbsp. olive oil
1/2 lb. lean bacon, cut in small pieces
1/2 lb. (1 pt.) fresh mushrooms, sliced
1 clove garlic, crushed
6 medium tomatoes, peeled and coarsely chopped
1/4 tsp. dried leaf basil
1/2 tsp. salt
1/4 tsp. black pepper
salt and pepper
hot cooked noodles, spaghetti or macaroni

### Ham and Eggs à la King

2 tbsp. butter or margarine
2 cups cubed cooked ham
1 cup sliced fresh mushrooms
1/4 cup butter or margarine
1/4 cup flour
1/2 tsp. salt
1/4 tsp. black pepper
1 1/2 cups milk
1 chicken bouillon cube
1/4 cup slivered pimento
1/2 cup slivered green pepper
6 hard-cooked eggs, quartered
   lengthwise
Corn Bread (recipe follows)

Heat 2 tbsp. butter or margarine in a heavy skillet. Add ham cubes and mushrooms and cook gently, stirring, until ham is lightly browned. Lift out ham and mushrooms with a slotted spoon.

Add 1/4 cup butter or margarine to pan. Sprinkle in flour, salt and pepper and let bubble up. Remove from heat and add milk all at once, stirring to blend. Add bouillon cube. Return to moderate heat and cook, stirring constantly, until thickened and smooth.

Add pimento and green pepper and simmer gently, stirring constantly, 10 minutes.

Add eggs, ham and mushrooms and heat gently. Spoon over large pieces of Corn Bread. (Serves 6.)

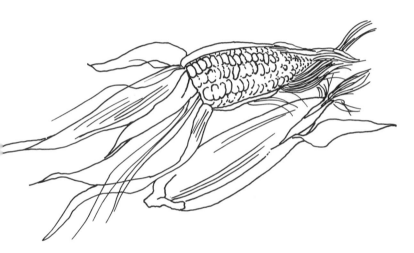

### Corn Bread

1 egg
1 cup plus 2 tbsp. milk
1/4 cup sifted all-purpose flour
1 1/4 cups cornmeal
3 tsp. baking powder
1 tsp. salt
3 tbsp. bacon drippings

Heat oven to 450°F. Grease a 9-inch square cake pan.

Beat egg. Add remaining ingredients and beat with a rotary beater until smooth. Pour into pan and bake until set and lightly browned, about 20 minutes. Serve hot.

### Deviled Eggs on Toast

2 tbsp. butter or margarine
2 tbsp. chopped green pepper
2 tbsp. flour
1/4 tsp. salt
1 1/2 cups milk
2 tbsp. bottled chili sauce
1 tbsp. Worcestershire sauce
1 tsp. prepared mustard
dash Tabasco
6 hard-cooked eggs, quartered
   lengthwise
4 slices hot buttered toast

Heat butter or margarine in a medium saucepan. Add green pepper and cook gently, stirring, 3 minutes. Sprinkle in flour and salt. Stir to blend. Remove from heat and add milk all at once. Stir to blend.

Return to heat and cook, stirring constantly, until boiling, thickened and smooth. Stir in chili sauce, Worcestershire, mustard and Tabasco. Add eggs and heat gently.

Put toast on serving plates and spoon egg mixture over. (Serves 4.)

## Scalloped Eggs and Cheese

Heat oven to 375°F. Butter a 1-qt. casserole.

Heat 2 tbsp. butter or margarine in a medium saucepan. Stir in flour, salt, pepper and paprika and let bubble up a little.

Remove from heat and add milk all at once. Stir to blend. Stir in Worcestershire and add bouillon cube. Return to heat and cook, stirring constantly, until boiling, thickened and smooth.

Put a thin layer of sauce in bottom of prepared casserole. Add 1/2 cup of the bread cubes, half the eggs and 1/4 cup of the cheese. Pour half of the remaining sauce over the cheese layer, add another 1/2 cup bread cubes, remaining eggs and another 1/4 cup of the cheese. Pour remaining sauce over all.

Combine remaining 1/2 cup bread cubes, 1/4 cup cheese and melted butter or margarine and sprinkle over.

Bake until bubbling well, about 20 minutes. (Serves 4.)

2 tbsp. butter or margarine
2 tbsp. flour
1/2 tsp. salt
1/8 tsp. black pepper
1/8 tsp. paprika
1 1/2 cups milk
1/2 tsp. *Worcestershire sauce*
1 chicken bouillon cube
1 1/2 cups 1/4-inch soft bread cubes
6 hard-cooked eggs, sliced
3/4 cup grated *Swiss cheese*
2 tbsp. butter or margarine, melted

## Zucchini Omelet Italian Style

Heat oil and butter or margarine in a large heavy skillet. Add zucchini and cook gently, stirring often, until zucchini is just tender, about 3 minutes.

Beat eggs, salt, pepper and marjoram together with a fork. Spread zucchini evenly in pan and pour egg mixture over. Cook over moderate heat until beginning to set around edges. Stir around once with a fork as if you were scrambling the eggs. Spread evenly again and let cook gently just until eggs are set but still soft on top. Remove from heat.

Heat broiler while eggs are cooking. Sprinkle top of egg mixture with Parmesan and slip under hot broiler for a minute to just lightly brown the cheese. Cut into wedges and serve immediately. (Serves 4 to 6.)

2 tbsp. olive oil
2 tbsp. butter or margarine
6 small zucchini, sliced 1/4 inch thick
6 eggs
1 tsp. salt
1/4 tsp. black pepper
1/4 tsp. dried leaf marjoram
1/2 cup grated *Parmesan cheese*

## Crab Crêpes

crêpes (recipe p. 22)
1/4 cup butter or margarine
1/4 cup flour
1 1/2 cups milk
3/4 tsp. salt
dash black pepper
pinch dried leaf tarragon
1 tbsp. butter or margarine
1 green onion, finely chopped
1 tsp. curry powder
6-oz. can crab, broken up
1/4 cup dry white wine
3 hard-cooked eggs, chopped
1/4 cup chopped parsley
1/2 tsp. paprika
1/8 tsp. ground ginger
1/4 tsp. dry mustard
1/2 cup heavy cream
1/2 cup grated Parmesan cheese
dash black pepper

Make crêpes and keep soft by putting waxed paper between them and wrapping in transparent wrap.

Melt 1/4 cup butter or margarine in a medium saucepan. Sprinkle in flour and stir to blend. Remove from heat and add milk, salt, dash pepper and tarragon. Return to moderate heat and cook until thick and smooth, stirring constantly. Remove from heat.

Heat oven to 350°F. Butter a 13 × 9 × 2-inch baking dish.

Melt 1 tbsp. butter or margarine in a small skillet. Add onion and curry powder and cook gently 3 minutes, stirring. Stir in crab and wine and heat. Add 1 cup of the white sauce, hard-cooked eggs, parsley, paprika and ginger.

With well-browned sides of crêpes facing down, spoon a rounded tablespoonful of mixture on each of 12 crêpes and fold around filling. Put in prepared baking dish and cover with foil. Bake until crêpes and filling are very hot, about 20 minutes. Remove from oven and turn on broiler.

Combine remaining white sauce with dry mustard, cream, Parmesan and dash of pepper. Bring to a boil and pour over hot crêpes. Put low under hot broiler and brown lightly. Serve immediately. (Serves 6.)

Advance preparation: Make crêpes, put waxed paper between them, wrap in foil and freeze until needed.

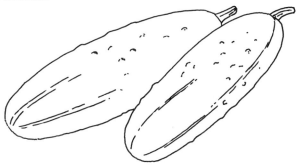

## Shrimp and Cucumbers

1 lb. raw jumbo shrimp
1 tbsp. sherry
2 tsp. salt
1 tsp. sugar
2 tsp. cornstarch
2 large cucumbers
2 tbsp. cooking oil
1 tbsp. cooking oil
1 cup sliced fresh mushrooms
2 green onions, sliced
  paper thin

Shell and remove veins from shrimp. Wash and put in a medium bowl. Combine sherry, salt, sugar and cornstarch and pour over shrimp. Stir to coat shrimp with mixture as much as possible.

Peel cucumbers, cut into quarters lengthwise and scrape out seeds. Cut into pieces about 1 1/2 inches long.

Heat 2 tbsp. oil to very hot in a large heavy skillet or wok. Add shrimp and cook quickly, stirring, until bright pink, about 2 minutes. Lift out with a slotted spoon and keep hot.

Add 1 tbsp. oil to skillet or wok and add mushrooms and cook quickly 30 seconds. Add cucumbers and stir over high heat 2 minutes. Return shrimp to pan and heat 30 seconds, stirring. Serve immediately, sprinkled with green onion slices. (Serves 4.)

Advance preparation: Shell and clean shrimp and refrigerate, covered, until needed.

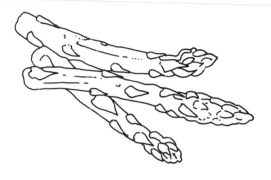

## Scallops and Asparagus

Thaw scallops if using frozen and rinse in cold water. Dry on paper toweling. Cut large scallops into 4 pieces and small scallops into 2 pieces. Wash asparagus and break off and discard tough ends. Cut stalks at a very sharp angle, making long thin bias slices.

Heat oil in a large skillet. Add pieces of garlic and cook, shaking pan constantly, about 2 minutes. Lift out and discard garlic.

Add asparagus pieces and 1/2 tsp. salt, cover and shake pan over high heat, holding pan just above heat source, until asparagus is tender, about 4 minutes. Set aside.

Heat butter or margarine in a medium saucepan. Add onion and cook gently 3 minutes. Sprinkle in flour, 1 tsp. salt and cayenne. Stir to blend. Remove from heat. Add milk all at once and stir to blend.

Return to moderate heat and cook, stirring constantly, until boiling, thickened and smooth. Stir in tomato paste and cream. Add scallops, cover and cook gently, stirring often, until scallops have lost their watery look and are milky white, about 5 minutes.

Stir in asparagus and heat for a minute. Add sherry and serve immediately in patty shells or over rice. (Serves 4.)

1 lb. scallops
1 lb. fresh asparagus
1 tbsp. cooking oil
1 small clove garlic, cut in half
1/2 tsp. salt
3 tbsp. butter or margarine
1 tbsp. finely chopped onion
3 tbsp. flour
1 tsp. salt
dash cayenne
1 1/3 cups milk
1 tbsp. tomato paste
1/4 cup light cream
1 tbsp. dry sherry
4 patty shells or hot cooked rice

## Salmon Supper

Heat oven to 350°F. Butter a 2 1/2-qt. casserole.

Peel potatoes and slice thinly. Cover with boiling water and let stand 5 minutes. Drain.

Drain salmon, saving liquid. Break into bite-size pieces, discarding skin and bones. Break peas apart and combine with carrots and onion.

Put half of potatoes in prepared casserole. Top with half of salmon and half of vegetables. Repeat layers.

Combine salmon liquid, egg, milk, salt, pepper and basil and beat together lightly with a fork. Pour over salmon and vegetables.

Combine butter or margarine and corn flakes and sprinkle over all.

Bake, covered, 45 minutes. Remove cover and continue baking until potatoes are tender and crumbs are crisp, about 15 minutes. (Serves 6.)

3 medium potatoes
15 1/2-oz. can salmon
12-oz. pkg. frozen peas
1 cup coarsely grated carrots
1/4 cup finely chopped onion
1 egg
1 cup milk
1 1/2 tsp. salt
1/2 tsp. black pepper
1/2 tsp. dried leaf basil
1/4 cup butter or margarine, melted
1 cup crushed corn flakes

## Egg-Tuna Bake

Heat oven to 375°F. Butter a 9-inch pie pan.

Heat 1/4 cup butter or margarine in a small saucepan. Add onion and cook gently, stirring, 1 minute. Sprinkle in flour, salt and pepper and stir to blend. Remove from heat and stir in milk all at once. Return to moderate heat and cook, stirring constantly, until boiling, thickened and smooth.

Remove from heat and stir in lemon juice, tuna, almonds, pimento and eggs. Spoon into prepared pan.

Combine bread cubes and 2 tbsp. butter or margarine, mixing until bread cubes are coated with butter or margarine, and sprinkle over top of dish.

Bake until bread cubes are nicely browned and tuna mixture is bubbling, about 15 minutes. Serve immediately. (Serves 4.)

1/4 cup butter or margarine
1 tsp. grated onion
1/4 cup flour
1/2 tsp. salt
1/4 tsp. black pepper
2 cups milk
1 tbsp. lemon juice
6 1/2-oz. can flaked tuna
1/4 cup chopped blanched
   almonds
1/4 cup slivered pimento
4 hard-cooked eggs, diced
1 cup small soft bread cubes
2 tbsp. butter or margarine,
   melted

## Creamed Tuna on Toast

Heat butter or margarine in a saucepan. Add onion and cook gently, stirring, 3 minutes. Sprinkle in flour, salt and pepper and stir to blend. Remove from heat.

Add wine, chicken stock and cream all at once and stir to blend. Return to moderate heat and cook, stirring constantly, until boiling, thickened and smooth. Stir in eggs, olives, dill and tuna. Heat thoroughly, stirring gently.

Spoon onto hot toast on serving plates and serve immediately. (Serves 6.)

1/4 cup butter or margarine
1/3 cup finely chopped onion
3 tbsp. flour
3/4 tsp. salt
1/8 tsp. black pepper
3/4 cup dry white wine
1/2 cup chicken stock or
   1 chicken bouillon cube
   dissolved in 1/2 cup
   boiling water
1 cup light cream
3 hard-cooked eggs, chopped
3 tbsp. chopped ripe olives
1/2 tsp. dried dill weed
two 6 1/4-oz. cans flaked tuna
6 slices hot buttered toast

## Cheese and Noodles

Cook noodles in plenty of boiling salted water until just tender, about 7 minutes. Drain.

Heat oven to 350°F. Butter a 2-qt. casserole.

Heat butter or margarine in a medium saucepan and add onion and green pepper. Cook gently, stirring, 3 minutes.

Sprinkle in flour, salt, pepper and celery seeds. Remove from heat and add milk all at once. Stir to blend, then return to moderate heat and cook, stirring constantly, until boiling. Boil 1 minute. Remove from heat. Stir in cottage cheese and lemon juice.

Put noodles in prepared casserole. Pour cheese sauce over and toss with a fork to blend. Sprinkle generously with paprika.

Bake until bubbling well and lightly browned on top, about 40 minutes. Serve with ham or bacon. (Serves 4 to 6.)

3 1/2 cups wide noodles,
   broken in 1 1/2-inch pieces
1/4 cup butter or margarine
1/4 cup finely chopped onion
1/4 cup finely chopped green
   pepper
3 tbsp. flour
2 tsp. salt
1/8 tsp. black pepper
1 tsp. celery seeds
1 1/3 cups milk
2 cups cottage cheese
   (one 500 g carton)
2 tbsp. lemon juice
paprika
fried ham or bacon

## Cheese Pie

*pastry for 1-crust 9-inch pie*
*(recipe p. 172)*
*4 strips bacon*
*1 cup cottage cheese*
*(one 250 g carton)*
*3 eggs*
*1/4 cup light cream*
*1 1/4 tsp. salt*
*1/8 tsp. black pepper*
*1/4 cup finely chopped parsley*
*1 tbsp. finely chopped chives*
*1/2 cup grated Swiss cheese*
*2 medium onions, thinly*
*sliced*

Heat oven to 475°F.

Line a 9-inch pie pan with pastry, building up a high fluted edge. Bake pie shell 5 minutes. Reduce oven temperature to 350°F.

Fry bacon until crisp. Lift out and drain on paper toweling and crumble. (Leave bacon fat in pan.)

Beat cottage cheese, eggs, cream, salt and pepper together well. Fold in parsley and chives.

Sprinkle Swiss cheese and bacon bits into prepared pie shell. Pour cottage cheese mixture over. Cover edge of pie with a narrow strip of aluminum foil to keep from browning too much. Bake 15 minutes.

Separate onion slices into rings. Fry gently until golden in bacon fat left in pan. Add a little butter or margarine if necessary. Lift out with a slotted spoon and drain on paper toweling. Sprinkle onions over baked pie filling.

Continue baking until a knife inserted 1 inch from edge comes out clean, about 30 minutes more. Serve hot. (Serves 4 to 6.)

## Vegetarian Pizza

*1 1/3 cups warm water*
*1/2 tsp. sugar*
*1 pkg. dry yeast*
*2 tbsp. cooking oil*
*2 tsp. salt*
*4 cups whole wheat flour*
*(approx.)*
*28-oz. can tomatoes*
*1/3 cup cooking oil*
*1/2 cup finely chopped onion*
*2 tsp. sugar*
*2 tsp. dried leaf oregano*
*1 tbsp. dried parsley*
*1/2 tsp. garlic salt*
*1/4 tsp. black pepper*
*2 cups cream-style cottage*
*cheese (one 500 g carton)*
*1 cup grated Parmesan cheese*

Measure water into a bowl. Add 1/2 tsp. sugar and stir until dissolved. Sprinkle yeast over and let stand 10 minutes. Stir well. Add 2 tbsp. oil, salt and 3 1/2 cups of the whole wheat flour. Mix well with a wooden spoon.

Turn out onto a floured board and knead in enough additional flour to make a stiff dough. Knead until smooth, about 5 minutes.

Shape dough into a round, place in a greased bowl, turn over so top of dough is greased and cover with a damp cloth. Let rise in a warm place until more than double in size, about 2 hours. Punch down.

Divide dough into 2 equal pieces and roll and stretch each piece to fit a 14-inch pizza pan. If dough is very bouncy, let it rest a few minutes until it will roll more easily. If dough isn't quite the right size when you get it in the pan, press and stretch it until you can seal it firmly to the sides of the pan. If you don't have pizza pans, roll dough into 14-inch rounds, put on large cookie sheets and roll edges under a little to make a raised edge to hold the filling.

Heat oven to 450°F.

Drain tomatoes well (refrigerate juice for another use) and chop tomato pulp coarsely. Drain again.

Combine tomatoes, 1/3 cup oil, onion, 2 tsp. sugar, oregano, parsley, garlic salt and pepper. Spread about 1/4 of this mixture on each round of dough. Spoon half of the cottage cheese on each pizza, spreading it evenly. Top each with half of the remaining tomato mixture. Sprinkle each pizza with half of the Parmesan.

Bake until crust is browned and filling is bubbling well, 20 to 25 minutes. (Makes 2.)

## Beans Italiano

Soak beans overnight in cold water to cover. Put beans and soaking liquid into a large saucepan. Add more water just to cover if needed. Add bay leaf, onions, garlic, parsley and dill weed. Bring to a boil, turn down heat, cover and boil gently until tender, about 1½ hours. Drain, saving cooking liquid.

Heat oven to 275°F. Grease a 2½-qt. casserole.

Heat oil in another saucepan. Add tomatoes, pickle, olives and celery and cook gently until tomatoes break up and mixture forms a sauce. Add pimento, salt and pepper.

Add tomato mixture to beans and pour into prepared casserole. Add enough of the bean cooking liquid to barely cover. Cover casserole and bake about 1 hour. Uncover and continue baking until liquid has nearly cooked away, about 1 hour more. Sprinkle with Parmesan and bake until it browns lightly. (Serves 6 to 8.)

1 lb. dried white pea beans
1 bay leaf
2 medium onions, grated
1 clove garlic, mashed
2 tbsp. chopped parsley
1 tsp. dried dill weed
½ cup cooking oil
2 cups peeled, seeded and chopped tomatoes
¼ cup chopped sweet pickle
½ cup slivered ripe olives
1 cup chopped celery
¼ cup chopped pimento
1½ tsp. salt
¼ tsp. black pepper
¼ cup grated Parmesan cheese

## Stir-Fried Vegetables

Heat oil in a large heavy skillet over high heat. Add cabbage, onions, celery, ginger and garlic and stir 3 minutes. Add 2 tbsp. water, cover and steam 1 minute. Add green pepper, carrots and water chestnuts, cover again and steam 1 minute more.

Rinse bean sprouts under cold water and drain well. Add to vegetables and stir until hot.

Combine ¼ cup water, soya sauce and cornstarch and stir into pan liquid, blending thickened liquid through vegetables. Serve immediately with brown rice. (Serves 4.)

2 tbsp. cooking oil
4 cups coarsely shredded cabbage
2 onions, thinly sliced
1 cup thin diagonal slices celery
1½ tsp. finely chopped fresh ginger
1 clove garlic, minced
2 tbsp. water
1 medium green pepper, cut in 1-inch squares
½ cup grated carrots (use medium grater)
½ cup sliced water chestnuts (optional)
½ lb. fresh bean sprouts
¼ cup water
1 tbsp. soya sauce
1 tbsp. cornstarch
cooked brown rice

### Vegetable Sukiyaki

Remove stems from mushrooms and put stems in a small saucepan with $1/2$ cup water. Bring to a boil, lower heat, cover and simmer 5 minutes. Drain, saving water and discarding stems. Slice mushroom caps thinly.

Cut tofu into $1/2$-inch cubes (you should have about $1^1/2$ cups). Let cubes stand on a plate a few minutes, then drain off any water that accumulates.

Heat oil in a large heavy saucepan over moderate heat. Add tofu and cook slowly, turning cubes carefully, 3 minutes. Lift out with a slotted spoon and set aside.

Turn heat to high and add sliced mushroom caps, green onions and leek to oil left in pan. Stir 2 minutes, adding more oil if necessary.

Add beans and celery and stir 3 minutes. Add mushroom liquid, honey and soya sauce and bring to a boil. Lower heat, add bamboo shoots and tofu, cover and simmer 5 minutes.

Mix $1/4$ cup water and cornstarch until smooth. Push vegetables to one side of pan and gradually stir mixture into boiling liquid. Cook until liquid is thick and clear, stir through vegetables and serve immediately. (Serves 6.)

$1/2$ lb. (1 pt.) fresh
  mushrooms
$1/2$ cup water
$1/2$ lb. tofu (soybean curd)
$1/4$ cup cooking oil
12 green onions, sliced very
  thinly
1 large leek (white and pale
  green parts only), sliced
  very thinly
two 10-oz. pkg. frozen cut
  green beans
2 stalks celery, sliced thinly
  on the diagonal
2 tbsp. liquid honey
$1/4$ cup soya sauce
two 7-oz. cans sliced bamboo
  shoots, drained
$1/4$ cup cold water
1 tbsp. cornstarch

# Desserts

Most people feel that a meal isn't a meal without at least a little sweet at the end. Very often some fresh fruit ends a lunch or supper well. But if you are looking for something different, there are recipes here for easy-to-make and light desserts. Most of them can be made at the last minute, many are fruit based, some are hot and others are chilly or icy.

## Strawberries Cardinal

Press raspberries through a sieve. Discard seeds. Add lemon juice and chill.

Wash and hull strawberries. Chill well.

Put strawberries in sherbet glasses at serving time and spoon raspberry purée over. Sprinkle with almonds. (Serves 4.)

15-oz. pkg. frozen raspberries, thawed
1 tbsp. lemon juice
1 pt. fresh strawberries
1/4 cup slivered toasted almonds

## Yogurt Topping

Blend yogurt, honey and cardamom and chill until serving time. Spoon over fresh fruit or berries. (Makes 1 cup.)

1 cup plain yogurt
2 tbsp. liquid honey
large pinch ground cardamom
fresh fruit or berries

## Strawberries with Raspberry Sherbet

Wash and hull strawberries. Set 8 perfect berries aside for garnish and slice the rest into a bowl. Add sugar and brandy and stir to blend. Let stand at room temperature 30 minutes.

Put scoops of sherbet into 8 sherbet glasses at serving time. Spoon sliced strawberries over. Press a little of the jelly through a coarse sieve onto each serving. Top with a dab of whipped cream and a whole berry. (Serves 8.)

1 qt. strawberries
1/4 cup sugar
2 tbsp. brandy
raspberry sherbet
1/4 cup red currant jelly
sweetened whipped cream

## Spiced Pineapple and Blueberries

Boil sugar, 1/2 cup water, lemon juice, cinnamon stick and cloves 2 minutes. Remove from heat. Stir in vanilla. Add pineapple cubes to hot mixture and cool, stirring often. Cover and chill well. Thaw blueberries and drain.

Remove and discard cinnamon stick and cloves and spoon spiced pineapple and some of the syrup into large sherbet glasses at serving time. Sprinkle generously with blueberries. (Serves 4.)

1/3 cup sugar
1/2 cup water
1 tbsp. lemon juice
1 small stick cinnamon
6 whole cloves
1 tsp. vanilla extract
3 cups 1/2-inch cubes fresh
    pineapple
11-oz. pkg. frozen blueberries

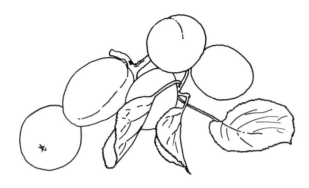

## Fresh Apricots and Peaches

Slice equal amounts of apricots and peaches into a bowl. Sprinkle lightly with fruit sugar and stir gently. Chill about 30 minutes. Serve topped with Honey Cream or Custard Sauce.

apricots
peaches
fruit sugar
Honey Cream (recipe follows)
    or Custard Sauce
    (recipe p. 168)

## Honey Cream

Fold ingredients together and chill. (Makes 1 cup.)

1 cup sour cream
2 tbsp. liquid honey
2 tbsp. chopped candied or
    preserved ginger

## Peach Crumble

Heat oven to 350°F. Line the inside of a 15 × 10 × 1-inch jelly roll pan with aluminum foil.

Beat egg and beat in sugar gradually. Stir in pecans. Spread mixture as thinly as possible in foil-lined pan.

Bake until lightly browned and crisp, 15 to 18 minutes. Cool.

Combine pudding mix, yogurt, milk and almond extract in a small mixer bowl. Beat for 2 minutes at low speed. Fold in peaches.

Crumble nut mixture coarsely. Put about half of crumbs in 6 large sherbet or parfait glasses. Add peach mixture, then remaining crumbs. Chill well before serving. (Serves 6.)

1 egg
1/2 cup sugar
1/2 cup chopped pecans
3 1/4-oz. pkg. instant vanilla
    pudding mix
2/3 cup plain yogurt
    (one 175 g carton)
1 1/4 cups milk
1/2 tsp. almond extract
1 cup diced peeled fresh
    peaches or well-drained
    canned peaches

## Banana Whip

2 egg whites
1/4 tsp. salt
1/4 cup sugar
1 tsp. vanilla extract
2 medium bananas
1/2 cup heavy cream
12 thin chocolate wafers

Beat egg whites and salt together until foamy. Add sugar gradually, beating well after each addition, and continue beating until stiff and glossy. Beat in vanilla.

Peel bananas and slice into egg white mixture and continue beating until quite smooth.

Whip cream until stiff and fold in.

Stand 2 of the chocolate wafers up on the sides of each of 4 sherbet glasses and spoon in whipped mixture. Crush remaining wafers coarsely and sprinkle over top. Chill. (Serves 4.)

## Orange Fluff

4 medium oranges
1 cup orange juice
1/4 cup regular long-grain rice
2 tbsp. sugar
1/4 tsp. ground nutmeg
   (optional)
2/3 cup evaporated milk
   (1 small can)
1/2 tsp. lemon juice
orange sections (optional)

Peel and section oranges, drain well and chill.

Heat orange juice to boiling. Add rice, cover and simmer 20 to 25 minutes. Stir in sugar and nutmeg. Chill.

Put evaporated milk in a metal pan and set in freezer until ice crystals form around edges of milk. Put in a chilled bowl and beat until soft peaks form. Add lemon juice and continue beating until stiff peaks form. Fold into rice mixture.

Put chilled orange sections in 6 sherbet glasses. Top with rice mixture. Chill about 1 hour. Garnish with more orange sections if desired. (Serves 6.)

## Cheese Layers

1 cup cottage cheese
   (one 250 g carton)
2 tbsp. sugar
1 tsp. vanilla extract
1/2 cup graham wafer crumbs
2 tbsp. melted butter or
   margarine
1/8 tsp. ground cinnamon
fresh fruit

Press cottage cheese through a sieve. Stir in sugar and vanilla.

Combine graham wafer crumbs, butter or margarine and cinnamon. Layer cottage cheese mixture and graham wafer crumbs in parfait glasses, making as many layers as possible. Chill until serving time. Top with fruit. (Serves 2 or 3.)

## Ginger Ice Cream

2 L vanilla ice cream
6-oz. jar preserved ginger

Soften ice cream a few minutes in the refrigerator if very hard. Chill a large bowl and beaters or a large spoon.

Chop ginger very finely (you should have about 1/2 cup chopped ginger and about 1/3 cup ginger syrup).

Turn ice cream into chilled bowl and beat with electric mixer at low speed or with large spoon just until soft enough to blend with ginger. (Work quickly so ice cream softens but does not melt.) Add chopped ginger and syrup and blend well.

Spoon into a large metal pan, cover and freeze until firm. Store in plastic cartons if desired. (Makes about 2 qt.)

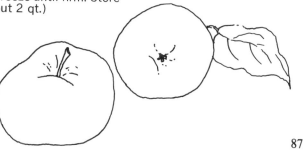

## Apple Snow

19-oz. can apple juice
2 tbsp. sugar
1 tbsp. lemon juice
1 tsp. grated lemon rind

Combine all ingredients, stirring until sugar is dissolved. Pour into an 8-inch square metal pan and freeze until firm.

At serving time, scrape off hard-frozen mixture with the edge of a spoon to make "snow." Spoon into sherbet glasses. Serve immediately. (Serves 4.)

## Spanish Cream

1 envelope (1 tbsp.)
  unflavored gelatin
2 tbsp. sugar
$1/8$ tsp. salt
2 egg yolks
2 cups milk
$1 1/2$ tsp. vanilla extract
2 egg whites
$1/4$ cup sugar
Chocolate Sauce
  (recipe follows)

Combine gelatin, 2 tbsp. sugar and salt in a saucepan. Beat egg yolks and 1 cup of the milk together with a fork and add to gelatin mixture. Cook over moderate heat, stirring constantly, until mixture just reaches the boiling point and gelatin is dissolved. Remove from heat.

Stir in remaining milk and vanilla. Chill by setting in ice water until mixture begins to hold its shape when dropped from a spoon.

Beat egg whites until foamy. Add $1/4$ cup sugar gradually and continue beating until stiff and glossy. Beat in gelatin mixture.

Pour into eight 6-oz. custard cups and chill until firm. Unmold and serve with Chocolate Sauce. (Serves 8.)

## Chocolate Sauce

6-oz. pkg. chocolate chips
$1/4$ cup water
$1/2$ cup corn syrup
$1/4$ cup light cream
1 tsp. vanilla extract

Combine chocolate chips, $1/4$ cup water and corn syrup in a heavy saucepan and heat gently until chips are melted and mixture is blended. Remove from heat and stir in cream and vanilla. Serve warm or cold. (Makes $1 1/2$ cups.)

## Lime Parfaits

Put jelly powder in a bowl. Add 1 cup boiling water and stir until jelly powder is dissolved. Cool to room temperature.

Beat cheese at high speed with a mixer until fluffy. Beat in jelly, lime juice and lemon juice gradually. Stir in grated lime rind. Set in ice water and chill, stirring often, until beginning to thicken.

Whip cream and sugar together until mixture is stiff.

Spoon half of lime mixture into 4 sherbet glasses. Top with whipped cream. Add a layer of remaining lime mixture and a sprinkling of coconut. Chill until serving time. (Serves 4.)

3-oz. pkg. lime-flavored jelly
    powder
1 cup boiling water
250 g pkg. cream cheese
    (room temperature)
2 tbsp. lime juice
2 tbsp. lemon juice
1 tsp. grated lime rind
1/2 cup whipping cream
2 tbsp. sugar
2 tbsp. coconut, lightly toasted

## Jellied Strawberries and Pineapple

Add sugar to strawberries and stir lightly. Let stand at room temperature 30 minutes. Drain well. Measure strawberry juice and add enough water to make 1 cup liquid.

Combine liquid and pineapple juice in a small saucepan and heat to boiling. Put jelly powder in a bowl and add hot liquid. Stir until jelly powder is dissolved. Stir in lemon juice and salt. Set bowl in ice water and chill, stirring occasionally, until just beginning to thicken. Fold in strawberries and pineapple tidbits. Spoon into sherbet glasses and chill until set. (Serves 6.)

1/4 cup sugar
2 cups sliced fresh strawberries
1/2 cup pineapple juice
    (drained from tidbits)
3-oz. pkg. strawberry jelly
    powder
2 tbsp. lemon juice
pinch salt
1 cup canned pineapple
    tidbits (well drained)

## Peach Crisp

Heat oven to 375°F. Butter a 1-qt. casserole.

Combine brown sugar, graham wafer crumbs, cinnamon, nutmeg and butter or margarine first with a fork then with fingers until crumbly.

Put peaches in prepared casserole. Sprinkle with lemon juice. Spread with crumbly mixture.

Bake until peaches are tender, about 25 minutes. Serve warm with cream or ice cream. (Serves 4.)

1/2 cup packed brown sugar
1/2 cup fine graham wafer
    crumbs
1/2 tsp. ground cinnamon
1/2 tsp. ground nutmeg
1/4 cup soft butter
    or margarine
2 1/2 cups sliced peaches
1 tbsp. lemon juice
pouring cream or ice cream

## Prune Puff

3 egg whites
1/3 cup sugar
dash salt
1 cup finely cut-up cooked
   prunes
1 tbsp. lemon juice
1 tsp. grated lemon rind
1/4 cup finely chopped nuts
   (optional)
1/2 recipe Custard Sauce
   (recipe p. 168)

Heat oven to 350°F. Set a pan with 1 inch hot water in it in oven while it is heating. Butter and sugar six 6-oz. custard cups.

Combine egg whites, sugar and salt in a small bowl and beat with a rotary beater until stiff. Add prunes and beat again until mixture is blended and holding its shape. Fold in lemon juice, rind and nuts.

Spoon into prepared custard cups. Set in pan of hot water in oven and bake until set, about 30 minutes. Turn out onto hot plates and serve immediately with Custard Sauce. (Serves 6.)

## Honey Apples

6 medium baking apples
1/2 cup liquid honey
1 1/2 tsp. grated lemon rind
ground nutmeg
pouring cream

Heat oven to 350°F. Have ready a baking dish just large enough to hold apples with a little space between.

Scoop out cores of apple from stem end, leaving bottom end intact (scoop to about 1/4 inch from bottom). Peel apples about 1/4 of the way down from the stem end. Set in baking dish.

Combine honey and lemon rind and spoon into cavities in apples. Sprinkle generously with nutmeg.

Cover baking dish and bake about 20 minutes. Uncover and continue baking until apples are tender, about 10 minutes more. Serve warm with pouring cream. (Serves 6.)

## Johnny Cake with Maple Syrup

1 1/3 cups sifted all-purpose
   flour
4 tsp. baking powder
1/2 tsp. salt
2/3 cup cornmeal
2/3 cup milk
1/3 cup maple syrup
1/4 cup butter or margarine,
   melted
2 eggs, beaten
maple syrup

Heat oven to 375°F. Grease a 9-inch square cake pan.

Sift flour, baking powder and salt into a mixing bowl. Add cornmeal and blend with a fork. Add milk, 1/3 cup maple syrup, butter or margarine and eggs and stir to blend. Pour into prepared pan.

Bake until a toothpick inserted in the centre comes out clean, about 25 minutes.

Cut into squares while hot and put pieces in fruit or cereal bowls. Pour maple syrup over and serve immediately. (Serves 9.)

# 3
# *Dinner*

When I was growing up in a small city everyone could get home at noon, and among the families we knew, everyone did. So dinner was at noon. Now most of us are lucky if we can get the whole family together for a meal even once in a while, let alone for noon dinner, so in many homes dinner is the evening meal.

No matter when you take your main meal, it's an important part of the day, and whether it is a fairly simple family affair or a celebration or entertaining time, careful planning and some bright ideas can make most meals both reasonably easy on the cook and something special for the diners. I have tried to include a bit of everything in the main course section, and you'll find that the dishes range from the simple and relatively inexpensive to a few that are unabashedly complicated and expensive. Soups and salads are lighter than those suggested for lunch; there is a large vegetable section, plenty of traditional and not-so-traditional desserts — and, I hope, some of those bright ideas!

## Appetizers

Ten taste treats to put your guests in the right mood. Choose a Shrimp Pâté or a Melon Frappé from among other favorites.

## Soups

Fifteen favorites— delicious but not too filling. Guaranteed to hit the right note for the dinner to come.

## Main Dishes

Seventy-one recipes to help make your reputation as a great cook. Choose a simple German-Style Pot Roast, gourmet-style Scampi in Creamy Wine Sauce or a traditional Steak and Kidney Pudding.

## Salads

Sixteen salads, slaws and dressings. Choose one to blend perfectly with any main dish you serve.

## Breads

Nine great breads— some quick, some with yeast. A range from Cheese Buns to Crusty French Stick.

## Vegetables

Thirty-four tempting recipes, using 22 different vegetables plus noodles, rice and barley, to help you prepare everyday goodness in exciting new ways.

## Desserts

Thirty-three ways to let yourself go! Puddings, pies and fruit desserts— some rich and creamy, others plain and simple and some with special sauces— every one delicious.

# Appetizers

Since most of us are unlikely to make special appetizers to start everyday family meals, these recipes are a little on the glamorous side — very nice to start company meals or family celebrations. From pâté to fruit, each should tickle the palate and pep up the appetite.

### Ham Pâté

Cut chicken livers into halves. Melt butter or margarine in a skillet over low heat and cook livers 5 minutes. Put in glass of blender and add eggs, brandy, Madeira or sherry, pepper, ginger and cloves. Buzz until smooth.

Put ham through the fine blade of the food chopper (you should have about 4 cups). Put bacon, onion and garlic through food chopper and mix with ham. Add chicken liver mixture and mix well.

Cut sausages into halves lengthwise. Heat oven to 350°F and put a pan of hot water into oven. Line a 9 × 5 × 3-inch glass loaf pan with strips of salt pork, saving some for top of pâté.

Put about 1/3 of the ham mixture into loaf pan, spreading evenly. Top with half of the sausage pieces, running in rows lengthwise. Add another 1/3 of the ham mixture and remaining sausage pieces. Top with remaining ham mixture and lay slices of salt pork over all. Cover with foil. Set in hot water in oven. Bake 3 hours.

Remove from oven and weight pâté by setting a foil-wrapped piece of heavy cardboard or another loaf pan on top and adding weights. Chill. Cut into thin slices to serve. (Makes about 25 slices.)

Note: Chill sausages very well or freeze lightly to make cutting into halves lengthwise easier.

Advance preparation: Can be made and stored in the refrigerator up to 4 days.

1/2 lb. chicken livers
2 tbsp. butter or margarine
4 eggs
1/4 cup brandy
1/4 cup Madeira or sherry
1/2 tsp. black pepper
1/4 tsp. ground ginger
pinch ground cloves
1 lb. cooked ham
1/2 lb. fat bacon
1 medium onion, cut up
2 cloves garlic
1/2 lb. pork sausages (see note)
1/2 lb. salt pork, sliced very thinly

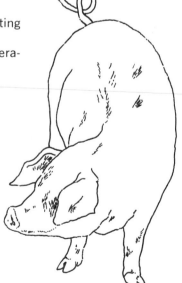

## Quick Chicken Liver Pâté

1 lb. chicken livers
*1/4 cup butter or margarine*
*1 small clove garlic, minced*
*1/4 tsp. salt*
*dash black pepper*
*3 tbsp. brandy*
*125 g pkg. cream cheese*
*(room temperature)*
*2 tbsp. mayonnaise*
*1 tbsp. Worcestershire sauce*
*1 tsp. lemon juice*
*1/2 tsp. salt*
*1/4 tsp. black pepper*
*1/4 tsp. curry powder*
*1/8 tsp. ground nutmeg*
*dash cayenne*
*1/2 cup toasted sesame seeds*
*French bread or crackers*

Wash and dry chicken livers. Trim and cut into pieces.

Heat butter or margarine in a large skillet and cook livers and garlic, stirring constantly, until livers are lightly browned but still pink inside, 3 to 4 minutes. Sprinkle with 1/4 tsp. salt and dash pepper. Remove from heat.

Lift livers out of pan with a slotted spoon and set aside. Add brandy to pan and stir to scrape up all browned bits. Pour brandy and drippings into glass of blender. Cut up cream cheese and add to blender glass along with mayonnaise, Worcestershire, lemon juice, 1/2 tsp. salt, 1/4 tsp. pepper, curry powder, nutmeg and cayenne. Buzz until mixture is smooth.

Add chicken livers a few at a time, buzzing until smooth after each addition. Refrigerate several hours.

Blend sesame seeds into pâté shortly before serving and pack the pâté into a small crock or bowl. Serve with French bread or crackers. (Makes about 2 cups.)

Advance preparation: Make ahead and refrigerate up to 3 days.

## Shrimp Pâté

*1 small clove garlic, cut in half*
*1 slice onion*
*2 whole cloves*
*1 small piece bay leaf*
*1 sprig parsley*
*4 peppercorns*
*1/2 cup dry white wine*
*1 lb. fresh shrimp*
*1/4 cup lemon juice*
*1 tbsp. grated lemon rind*
*1/8 tsp. salt*
*1/2 tsp. finely grated onion*
*1/8 tsp. ground mace*
*dash cayenne*
*1/3 cup olive oil (approx.)*
*1/2 cup butter*
*crackers*

Combine garlic, onion, cloves, bay leaf, parsley, peppercorns and wine in a medium saucepan. Bring to a boil, lower heat, cover and simmer 10 minutes. Add shrimp and enough boiling water to cover. Bring back to a boil and simmer 3 minutes.

Drain, peel and clean shrimp. Put through the fine blade of the food chopper twice. Add lemon juice, lemon rind, salt, onion, mace, cayenne and enough olive oil to make a paste, blending well with a fork. Put mixture in glass of blender and buzz until creamy. Pack in small jars or pots.

Heat butter in a small saucepan until it foams up. Remove from heat, skim off and discard foam. Pour remaining clear oil in a thin layer over pâté, discarding sediment in bottom of pan. Chill. Serve with crackers. (Makes 1 1/3 cups.)

*Note:* Butter prepared as in the last step of the recipe is clarified butter, and besides being a good sealer for pâté, as in this recipe, it is excellent for frying crumb-coated foods to give good browning and eliminate sticking.

Advance preparation: Make ahead and refrigerate up to 2 days.

## Potted Salmon

1/2 lb. fresh salmon
1 tbsp. lemon juice
1 sprig dill (optional)
1/2 lb. soft unsalted butter
1/2 tsp. salt
dash white pepper
dash cayenne
1 tbsp. chopped parsley
2 tsp. finely chopped fresh dill
   or 1 tsp. dried dill weed
1 tsp. white wine vinegar
1/2 cup butter

Set salmon on a piece of heavy aluminum foil. Turn foil up to form a dish, leaving top open. Sprinkle salmon with lemon juice and top with sprig of dill.

Bring about 1/2 inch of water to a boil in a skillet. Lower salmon on foil into water, cover and simmer 10 minutes per inch of thickness of fish. (A small steak, 1/2 inch thick, would be simmered 5 minutes.) Let fish cool in its own juice.

Skin and bone salmon and chop coarsely. Put through the fine blade of the food chopper. Mix in remaining ingredients except 1/2 cup butter. Pack into small jars or pots.

Heat 1/2 cup butter in a small saucepan until it foams up. Remove from heat, skim off and discard foam. Pour some of remaining clear oil in a thin layer over pâté, discarding sediment in bottom of pan. Chill. Serve as a spread. (Makes about 2 cups.)

Advance preparation: Make ahead and refrigerate up to 2 days.

## Eggplant Appetizer

1 lb. eggplant
1 tbsp. cooking oil
1/2 cup chopped onion
1/2 cup chopped green pepper
1/4 cup flaked coconut
dash Tabasco
2 tbsp. lemon juice
salt
crackers

Heat oven to 400°F. Oil a pie plate lightly.

Wash eggplant and put whole on pie plate. Bake until soft, 45 to 60 minutes. Cool and peel. Slice, then chop slices very finely and put into a bowl.

Heat oil in a small skillet. Add onion and green pepper and cook gently until limp but not browned, about 5 minutes. Add to eggplant. Mix in coconut, Tabasco, lemon juice and salt. Cover and chill several hours. Add salt to taste.

Serve as a spread on crackers. (Makes about 1 3/4 cups.)

## Herbed Tomato Juice

19-oz. can tomato juice
1 1/2 tbsp. tarragon wine vinegar
2 tsp. sugar
1/4 tsp. salt
1/4 tsp. dried leaf basil
1 tbsp. chopped parsley
dash black pepper
cheese crackers
parsley sprigs

Combine all ingredients except crackers and parsley sprigs in a saucepan. Bring to a boil. Simmer 5 minutes.

Pour into soup cups and top each serving with a cheese cracker garnished with a parsley sprig. Pass more cheese crackers. (Serves 4.)

94

## Peach Appetizer

3 ripe peaches, peeled and
   sliced
2 cups honeydew melon balls
1 cup orange juice
2 tbsp. lime juice
2 tbsp. liquid honey
2 tbsp. finely chopped
   preserved ginger
1 tbsp. ginger syrup
   (from preserved ginger)

Combine peach slices with melon balls in a bowl. Combine remaining ingredients and pour over fruit. Chill very well.

Spoon into sherbet glasses to serve. (Serves 6.)

## Melon Frappé

1 cup small cubes honeydew
   melon
1 cup small cubes cantaloupe
2 tbsp. lime juice
1 cup fresh orange juice
1/2 cup cranberry juice cocktail
6 ice cubes
mint sprigs

Combine all ingredients except mint sprigs in glass of blender and buzz until smooth and fluffy.

Pour into chilled champagne glasses and garnish each with a sprig of mint. Serve immediately. (Serves 6.)

## Melon Ambrosia

cantaloupe balls
honeydew melon balls
flaked coconut
1 small bottle ginger ale
mint sprigs

Alternate layers of cantaloupe and honeydew melon balls in parfait glasses with a sprinkling of flaked coconut between each layer. Chill.

Put ginger ale in a metal pan and freeze until ice crystals form around the edges. Spoon a little of the ginger ale over each serving of melon at serving time and top with a sprig of mint.

## Fruit Cocktail

1 large ripe avocado, cubed
1/2 cup cubed canned peaches
1 cup halved seeded grapes
   (see note)
1/2 cup frozen strawberries,
   thawed just enough to break
   apart
1/4 cup canned peach syrup
2 tbsp. lime juice
2 tbsp. liquid honey

Combine fruits in a bowl. Combine peach syrup, lime juice and honey and pour over fruit. Cover with transparent wrap and chill well, stirring occasionally.

Spoon into sherbet glasses to serve. (Serves 4 to 6.)

*Note:* Any grapes are good in this mixture but I like the large black ones best for looks.

# Soups

Most of these soups are quite light and so are suitable to start the heaviest meal of the day. And most are made with stock — either chicken or beef. You'll find the recipes for making stocks on page 48 in the Lunch/Supper section, and though I know they look like work, they really are quite easy to prepare. If you have a freezer, making a large batch of stock to bottle and freeze every week or so can be one of the most valuable things you do with your precious time. Delicious and different soups like these can be made in a matter of minutes once the stock is thawed. For advance preparation, will you take a minute to reread the introduction to soups on page 40.

## Asparagus-Potato Soup

1 lb. fresh or 10-oz. pkg.
   frozen asparagus
$\frac{1}{2}$ cup boiling water
2 cups diced potatoes
1 tsp. salt
$\frac{1}{4}$ tsp. black pepper
4 cups chicken stock
   (recipe p. 48)
salt and pepper
$\frac{1}{2}$ cup whipping cream
$\frac{1}{4}$ tsp. salt

Wash and trim asparagus and put in a large saucepan. Add $\frac{1}{2}$ cup boiling water, cover and cook over moderate heat until tender. (Use package instructions for frozen.) Lift asparagus out of pan, saving cooking water. Cut tips off asparagus and set aside. Cut stalks into pieces.

Cook potatoes in asparagus cooking water until very tender. Without draining, turn into glass of blender. Add asparagus stalks, 1 tsp. salt, $\frac{1}{4}$ tsp. pepper and 1 cup of the chicken stock. Buzz until smooth and return mixture to saucepan.

Add remaining chicken stock. Bring to a boil, lower heat and simmer 10 minutes, stirring often. Add salt and pepper to taste.

Whip cream and $\frac{1}{4}$ tsp. salt until stiff. Ladle soup into cups and top with cream and some asparagus tips. (Serves 6.)

## Avocado Soup

1 tbsp. cooking oil
$\frac{1}{4}$ cup finely chopped onion
1 tbsp. flour
$\frac{1}{2}$ cup chopped, peeled,
   seeded and drained tomato
   (1 medium)
$\frac{1}{8}$ tsp. salt
dash black pepper
4 cups chicken stock
   (recipe p. 48)
3 medium-size ripe avocados
$\frac{1}{3}$ cup light cream
salt and pepper
Tortilla Bits (recipe follows)

Heat oil in a large saucepan. Add onion and cook gently 3 minutes, stirring. Sprinkle in flour and continue cooking until flour is lightly browned. Add tomato and cook quickly 3 minutes, stirring. Add $\frac{1}{8}$ tsp. salt and dash pepper and stir in 3 cups of the chicken stock gradually. Cover and simmer 10 minutes.

Peel avocados and cut up into glass of blender. Add remaining 1 cup chicken stock and cream and buzz until smooth and blended. Add to hot stock and heat but do not boil. Add salt and pepper to taste.

Pour into a tureen or ladle into soup bowls to serve. Top with Tortilla Bits. (Serves 6.)

## Tortilla Bits

2 tbsp. cooking oil
3 tortillas (see note)

Heat oil in a large heavy skillet. Cut tortillas into small squares and fry in oil until crisp and golden. Lift out with a slotted spoon and drain well on paper toweling.

*Note:* Tortillas are available in cans and frozen in many supermarkets and in food specialty stores. Use 3 for the soup and fry the rest whole to serve as bread.

## Lettuce Soup

$^1/_2$ cup butter or margarine
8 cups finely shredded
  leaf lettuce
2 tbsp. finely chopped green
  onions
$^1/_4$ cup flour
2 cups light cream
4 cups chicken stock
  (recipe p. 48)
1 tsp. salt
$^1/_2$ tsp. Worcestershire sauce
salt and pepper
$^1/_4$ cup chopped chives
paper thin slices radishes

Heat butter or margarine in a large saucepan. Add lettuce and green onions and cook quickly, stirring constantly, just until lettuce is limp, about 1 minute. Sprinkle in flour and stir to blend.

Remove from heat and add cream and chicken stock all at once. Stir to blend. Return to heat and bring to a boil. Turn heat to low. Stir in salt and Worcestershire. Simmer 3 minutes. Add salt and pepper to taste.

Stir in chives and ladle into soup cups. Garnish with radish slices and serve immediately. (Serves 8.)

## Pumpkin Soup

1 tbsp. butter or margarine
1 tbsp. finely chopped onion
1 cup mashed cooked or
  canned pumpkin
$2^1/_2$ cups chicken stock
  (recipe p. 48)
1 cup whole milk or light cream
1 tbsp. flour
1 tsp. salt
dash black pepper
$^1/_4$ tsp. ground ginger
$^1/_8$ tsp. ground nutmeg
2 eggs
chopped parsley

Heat butter or margarine in a medium saucepan. Add onion and cook gently 3 minutes. Stir in pumpkin and chicken stock. Bring to a boil.

Combine $^1/_4$ cup of the milk or light cream, flour, salt, pepper, ginger and nutmeg, stirring until blended and smooth. Stir into boiling soup gradually. Cook 5 minutes over low heat, stirring constantly.

Beat remaining $^3/_4$ cup milk or light cream and eggs together in a small bowl. Stir about half of hot mixture into eggs gradually, then stir egg mixture back into soup. Cook over low heat 5 minutes, stirring constantly.

Serve garnished with parsley. (Serves 4.)

## Tomato-Onion Soup

3 tbsp. butter or margarine
2 cups finely chopped onion
1 cup thinly sliced celery
19-oz. can tomatoes
2 tbsp. chopped parsley
1 tsp. salt
$^1/_4$ tsp. black pepper
1 small bay leaf, crushed
6 cups chicken stock
  (recipe p. 48)

Melt butter or margarine in a large saucepan over low heat. Add onion and celery and stir until tender but not browned, about 5 minutes. Add tomatoes, parsley and seasonings and simmer 5 minutes. Add chicken stock, bring to a boil, reduce heat and simmer 15 minutes.

Ladle into soup bowls and serve immediately. (Serves 6.)

## Creamy Herb Soup

2 tbsp. butter or margarine
6 green onions with tops,
  finely chopped
1 cup finely shredded iceberg
  lettuce
1/2 cup finely shredded spinach
  (stems removed)
1/2 cup chopped watercress
  leaves
1/4 cup chopped parsley
1/4 cup chopped celery leaves
1/4 tsp. dried leaf thyme
1/4 tsp. dried leaf chervil
6 cups chicken stock
  (recipe p. 48)
1 cup light cream
1 tsp. salt (approx.)
1/4 tsp. pepper (approx.)
chopped chives

Heat butter or margarine in a large saucepan over moderate heat. Add green onions and cook gently, stirring constantly, 3 minutes. Add lettuce, spinach, watercress leaves, parsley and celery leaves, cover and cook over low heat 5 minutes.

Add thyme, chervil and chicken stock. Cover and simmer 30 minutes, stirring occasionally. Add cream and salt and pepper to taste. Heat but do not boil.

Serve topped with chopped chives. (Serves 6.)

## Spinach Soup

two 12-oz. pkg. frozen
  chopped spinach
8 cups chicken stock
  (recipe p. 48)
3 tbsp. butter or margarine
2 tbsp. flour
1/2 tsp. salt
1/4 tsp. black pepper
1/8 tsp. ground nutmeg
salt and pepper
2 hard-cooked eggs, sliced
  (optional)

Thaw and drain spinach. Put in glass of blender and add 1 cup of the stock. Buzz until spinach is chopped finely.

Bring remaining stock to a boil in a large saucepan. Add spinach and cook gently 5 minutes. Pour mixture into a large bowl.

Heat butter or margarine in same saucepan. Sprinkle in flour and stir to blend. Remove from heat. Blend in some of hot stock-spinach mixture gradually. Add remaining stock-spinach mixture and stir to blend.

Set over high heat and stir until boiling, thickened and smooth. Turn heat to low, add 1/2 tsp. salt, 1/4 tsp. pepper and nutmeg, cover and simmer 10 minutes. Add salt and pepper to taste.

Serve very hot in soup cups, topping each serving with slices of hard-cooked eggs. (Serves 8.)

## Celery Consommé

4 cups clarified beef stock
  (recipe p. 48)
10 large stalks celery with
  some leaves, coarsely cut up
salt and pepper

Bring stock and celery to simmering in a large saucepan over moderate heat. Lower heat and simmer until soup has a strong celery flavor, about 30 minutes. Strain, saving celery. Add salt and pepper to taste.

Cut some of the celery into very fine strips and add a little to each serving. (Serves 4.)

## Consommé Madrilène

Bring all ingredients to a boil in a large saucepan. Lower heat and simmer, uncovered, 20 minutes. Strain and serve very hot. (Serves 6.)

6 cups clarified beef stock (recipe p. 48)
2 cups fresh tomato purée or canned tomato sauce
2 tbsp. finely chopped onion
$\frac{1}{2}$ tsp. dried leaf basil

## Consommé à l'Alsacienne

Heat stock to boiling. Add sausage, lower heat and simmer 5 minutes, then add sauerkraut and simmer 5 minutes more. Serve immediately. (Serves 4.)

4 cups clarified beef stock (recipe p. 48)
1 cup thin slices wieners or any sausage that is cooked by simmering
$\frac{1}{2}$ cup canned sauerkraut, drained

## Blender Vegetable Soup

Put vegetables into glass of blender. Add all remaining ingredients. Buzz about 2 seconds (mixture should not be smooth).

Pour into a saucepan, bring to a boil, turn down heat and simmer 10 minutes. Serve immediately. (Serves 2.)

$\frac{1}{4}$ small onion, coarsely chopped
$\frac{1}{2}$ small stalk celery, coarsely chopped
1 small carrot, scraped and coarsely cut up
1 sprig parsley, coarsely chopped
$\frac{3}{4}$ cup tomato juice
$\frac{1}{2}$ cup water
1 beef bouillon cube
$\frac{1}{8}$ tsp. Worcestershire sauce
$\frac{1}{4}$ tsp. salt
dash black pepper

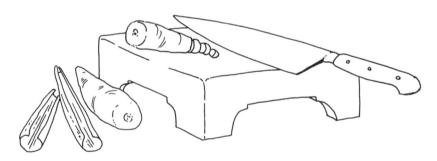

## Quick Curried Beef Soup

Combine all ingredients except lemon juice in a large saucepan and bring to a boil. Turn down heat and simmer, covered, 20 minutes. Pour into glass of blender and buzz until smooth. Return to saucepan and heat to scalding. Stir in lemon juice and serve. (Serves 6.)

two 10-oz. cans beef bouillon
$2\frac{1}{2}$ cups water
1 medium onion, sliced
1 large apple, peeled, cored and sliced
1 tsp. curry powder
2 tbsp. lemon juice

### Cream of Green Onion Soup

3 small bunches green onions (about 18)
1 cup boiling water
1/2 tsp. salt
2 tbsp. flour
2 tbsp. soft butter or margarine
1 tsp. salt
1/8 tsp. white pepper
1/8 tsp. paprika
4 cups milk
grated Parmesan cheese

Wash and trim onions, keeping as much of the green tops as possible. Cut up coarsely and put in a medium saucepan (you should have about 2 cups).

Add 1 cup boiling water and 1/2 tsp. salt. Bring to a boil over moderate heat, cover and cook until onions are tender, about 5 minutes.

Pour onions and water into glass of blender. Add flour, butter or margarine, 1 tsp. salt, pepper, paprika and 1 cup of the milk and buzz until smooth. Return mixture to saucepan, add remaining milk and heat to scalding (do not boil). Stir in 2 tbsp. Parmesan.

Ladle into soup bowls and sprinkle with more Parmesan. (Serves 4 to 6.)

### Green Pepper and Tomato Soup

3 cups slivered green peppers (2 large)
4 cups peeled, seeded and coarsely chopped tomatoes (6 medium)
1/2 cup chopped onion
2 tbsp. chopped parsley
1 cup water
1 tsp. sugar
2 tbsp. butter or margarine
1 small clove garlic, peeled and cut in half
2 tbsp. flour
2 tsp. salt
1/4 tsp. black pepper
1/2 tsp. dried leaf basil
1/4 tsp. dried leaf oregano
1 cup light cream

Put green peppers, tomatoes, onion, parsley, 1 cup water and sugar in a medium saucepan. Bring to a boil, turn down heat, cover and simmer until all vegetables are very tender. Pour into glass of blender and buzz until smooth.

Melt butter or margarine in same saucepan. Add garlic pieces and cook gently, stirring, until golden. Remove and discard garlic. Sprinkle flour into butter in pan and let bubble up. Remove from heat and stir in tomato mixture. Add seasonings.

Return to moderate heat, bring to a boil, stirring constantly, and boil gently 5 minutes. Stir in cream and heat but do not boil. Serve immediately. (Serves 6.)

### Jellied Gazpacho

3 cups liquid (19-oz. can tomato juice plus water)
2 envelopes (2 tbsp.) unflavored gelatin
2 chicken bouillon cubes
2/3 cup white vinegar
2 tsp. salt
1 tsp. paprika
1 tsp. dried leaf basil
1/4 tsp. ground cloves
1/8 tsp. Tabasco
3 cups finely chopped, peeled and seeded fresh tomatoes
1 cup finely chopped green pepper
1/2 cup finely chopped celery
1/2 cup finely chopped green onions
2 small cloves garlic, crushed
sour cream
watercress

Put 1 cup of the tomato juice-water mixture in a medium saucepan. Add gelatin. Let stand 5 minutes. Set over low heat and stir just until gelatin is dissolved. Add bouillon cubes and stir until dissolved. Remove from heat.

Stir in remaining 2 cups liquid, vinegar, salt, paprika, basil, cloves and Tabasco. Set in a bowl of ice water and chill, stirring often, until syrupy.

Combine tomatoes, green pepper, celery, green onions and garlic in a bowl. Add gelatin mixture and fold together. Cover and chill at least 1 hour.

Spoon into small soup bowls at serving time (mixture should not be stiff — just softly set). Top each serving with a small dab of sour cream and a sprig of watercress. Serve immediately. (Serves 6 to 8.)

# Main Dishes

How to corn beef at home; new uses for ground beef; old-fashioned favorites such as pot roasts, Steak and Kidney Pudding, Short Ribs and Dumplings or Jellied Veal and Pork; new-fashioned delights such as Loin of Pork with Peach Glaze, Minty Deviled Lamb Chops or Soybean-Nut Loaf; poultry for the holiday season or for family pleasure; plain and fancy fish and seafood recipes — all of these and many more are included in this freewheeling selection of dishes to make dinner memorable whether it's a stew for the simplest of family gatherings or the main dish for the get-together you plan to make the party of the year.

### Savory Sirloin Tip

Heat oven to 325°F. Set roast on a rack in a roasting pan. Combine salt, pepper, marjoram, thyme, savory and basil and rub all over meat. Roast 1 1/2 to 2 hours (140° on the meat thermometer) for rare or about 2 1/2 hours (160° on the meat thermometer) for medium, brushing often with a mixture of the wine and Worcestershire. Serve with Wine Gravy.

4-lb. beef sirloin tip roast
1/2 tsp. salt
1/8 tsp. black pepper
1/4 tsp. dried leaf marjoram
1/4 tsp. dried leaf thyme
1/4 tsp. dried leaf savory
1/4 tsp. dried leaf basil
1/2 cup dry red wine
1 tsp. Worcestershire sauce
Wine Gravy (recipe follows)

### Wine Gravy

Pour drippings from roasting pan into a saucepan. Stir in 1 cup water and wine. Bring to a boil. Shake flour and 1/2 cup cold water together in a jar with a tight lid until blended. Stir into boiling liquid gradually. Bring back to a boil, turn down heat and simmer 5 minutes. Add salt and pepper to taste.

drippings from roast
1 cup water
1 cup dry red wine
1/4 cup flour
1/2 cup water
salt and pepper

## German-Style Pot Roast

Cut pork into 1/4-inch-thick strips about 1 inch long. Put in a bowl and add finely chopped onion, salt, pepper, lemon rind and ground allspice.

Make large incisions all over the roast with the tip of a sharp knife and pack some of the pork strips mixture into each of the cuts, continuing until all the pork mixture is used. Put roast in a large casserole or bowl.

Combine vinegar, 1 cup water, sliced onions, peppercorns, cloves, whole allspice and bay leaf in a medium saucepan. Bring to a boil, pour over roast, cover tightly and refrigerate for 2 days, turning the meat occasionally.

Lift meat out of marinade and pat dry with paper toweling. Heat oil in a large heavy saucepan or Dutch oven. Add meat and brown quickly on all sides. Pour marinade over meat. Bring to a boil, cover tightly, turn down heat and simmer until meat is very tender, about 3 hours.

Lift meat out of pan and put on a hot platter. Keep warm in low oven.

Strain meat cooking liquid, pressing as much of the vegetable mixture as possible through the sieve. Skim off as much fat as possible. Return cooking liquid to pan and bring to a boil.

Shake 1/4 cup water and flour together in a small jar with a tight lid and stir into boiling liquid gradually. Turn down heat and cook, stirring occasionally, about 5 minutes. Slice the roast and serve with gravy.

Advance preparation: Cook until just done, then refrigerate and reheat when needed. The reheating will actually improve the flavor.

*1/4 lb. salt pork*
*1 medium onion, finely chopped*
*2 tsp. salt*
*1 1/2 tsp. black pepper*
*1 tsp. grated lemon rind*
*1/2 tsp. ground allspice*
*4- to 5-lb. rump roast of beef*
*2 cups tarragon wine vinegar*
*1 cup water*
*3 medium onions, sliced*
*1 tsp. peppercorns*
*8 whole cloves*
*6 whole allspice*
*1 bay leaf*
*2 tbsp. cooking oil*
*1/4 cup water*
*2 tbsp. flour*
*salt and pepper*

## Pot Roast with Kidney Beans

Heat oil in a large heavy saucepan or Dutch oven. Add meat and brown well on all sides. Add salt, pepper, chili powder, onion and 2 cups water. Cover and simmer until meat is tender, about 3 hours. Add kidney beans and their liquid and heat well.

Lift meat out onto a hot platter. Strain broth in pan. Put beans and onion on platter around meat and measure liquid. Add water to liquid, if necessary, to make 4 cups and return to pan. Bring to a boil.

Shake flour and 2/3 cup cold water together in a jar with a tight lid to blend well. Stir this mixture into boiling liquid gradually. Heat until boiling, thickened and smooth. Turn down heat and simmer 3 minutes. Serve over slices of roast.

Advance preparation: Cook meat until just tender. Do not add beans. Refrigerate and reheat when needed, adding beans after roast is heated through.

*2 tbsp. cooking oil*
*4-lb. blade roast*
*2 tsp. salt*
*1/4 tsp. black pepper*
*1 tsp. chili powder*
*1 large onion, sliced*
*2 cups water*
*14-oz. can kidney beans*
*1/3 cup flour*
*2/3 cup cold water*

### Beef in Beer

2 tbsp. cooking oil
4-lb. beef cross rib roast
2 large onions, finely chopped
1 cup beer
1 tbsp. salt
$^1/_4$ tsp. black pepper
2 tsp. dry mustard
$^1/_2$ cup water
$^1/_4$ cup flour
salt and pepper

Heat oil in a large heavy saucepan or Dutch oven. Add roast and brown slowly on all sides. Remove from pan. Pour off all but 1 tbsp. of drippings left in pan.

Heat 1 tbsp. drippings and add onion. Cook gently, stirring often, 5 minutes. Return meat to pan. Add beer, 1 tbsp. salt, $^1/_4$ tsp. pepper and mustard. Bring to a boil, turn down heat, cover tightly and simmer, turning meat occasionally, until meat is very tender, about $3^1/_2$ hours. Put meat on a hot platter and keep warm in low oven.

Remove fat from liquid in pan. To do this, pour pan liquid into a tall narrow container (a 4-cup glass measuring cup is useful for this) so fat will rise quickly to the top. Add 2 or 3 ice cubes to speed up cooling if desired. Skim off all fat.

Return liquid to pan in which roast was cooked. Bring to a boil. Shake $^1/_2$ cup water and flour together in a jar with a tight lid until smooth and stir into boiling liquid gradually. Turn down heat and cook gently, stirring often, 5 minutes. Add salt and pepper to taste. Serve with meat.

Advance preparation: Cook until just tender, then refrigerate and reheat when needed.

### Home Corned Beef

4 qt. cold water
2 cups coarse (pickling) salt
$^1/_2$ cup dark brown sugar
2 tbsp. whole mixed pickling
  spices
5 peppercorns, crushed
10 bay leaves
5 lb. brisket
4 cloves garlic, peeled
  (optional)

Combine all ingredients except meat and garlic in a large kettle. Boil hard 10 minutes, then cool.

Put meat in a large bowl, enameled pot or stoneware crock, add garlic and pour brine over. Top meat with a plate, then put weights on plate until meat is totally immersed (wrap weights in foil or plastic so they're protected from the brine). Cover container and store in a cool place 2 weeks.

Use meat immediately as directed in any corned beef recipe, or drain, wash well, cover and refrigerate up to 1 week.

### Corned Beef Dinner

Heat oven to 350°F.

Lift beef out of brine, washing it well to remove excess salt and spices. Discard brine. Put meat in a large ovenproof pot or Dutch oven and add cold water to nearly cover. Add onion, celery, peppercorns and bay leaf. Cover tightly and cook in oven until fork-tender and very moist, 3 to 3½ hours.

Slice and serve hot with the cooked vegetables and Sweet-Hot Mustard.

*Home Corned Beef*
*(recipe p. 103)*
*2 large onions, sliced*
*2 large stalks celery with leaves, cut up*
*6 peppercorns, crushed*
*1 large bay leaf*
*steamed cabbage wedges, boiled potatoes, onions, carrots and turnip*
*Sweet-Hot Mustard (recipe follows)*

### Sweet-Hot Mustard

Beat sugar, mustard, flour and eggs in a medium saucepan until smooth, then stir in vinegar and ⅓ cup water. Set over moderate heat and stir until thick. (Makes about 1 cup.)

*½ cup packed brown sugar*
*¼ cup dry mustard*
*1 tbsp. flour*
*2 eggs*
*⅓ cup white vinegar*
*⅓ cup water*

### Freezer Meatballs

Combine beef, bread crumbs, onion, eggs, milk, salt, pepper, nutmeg and Worcestershire in a large bowl. Mix well. Shape into small balls, about 1 inch in diameter (you should have about 240).

Heat oil in a large heavy skillet. Brown meatballs a few at a time in hot oil, lifting them out as they brown.

Sprinkle flour into drippings left in skillet. Stir to blend. Remove from heat and stir in consommé and 3½ cups water. Return to heat and cook until mixture boils and thickens, stirring constantly. Turn heat to low and simmer 5 minutes. Remove from heat and cool. (You should have about 7 cups.)

Divide meatballs into 4 large freezer containers (about 60 in each). Divide the gravy evenly, pouring about 1¾ cups over the meatballs in each container. Seal containers and freeze.

Thaw meatballs and use for the recipes for Curried Meatballs, Meatballs Stroganoff, Creole Meatballs or Meatballs Polynesian Style, following. One container is needed for each recipe and serves 6. You can, of course, increase the ingredients for any variation to use 2, 3 or all 4 of the cartons of meatballs.

Advance preparation: Several cartons of these made at a quiet time and popped into the freezer, then used as needed in simple yet interesting ways, is the perfect answer for those days when the cook is too rushed for much cooking.

*6 lb. ground beef*
*3 cups fine dry bread crumbs*
*1½ cups finely chopped onion*
*6 eggs*
*3 cups milk*
*4 tsp. salt*
*½ tsp. black pepper*
*½ tsp. ground nutmeg*
*1 tbsp. Worcestershire sauce*
*½ cup cooking oil*
*⅓ cup flour*
*three 10-oz. cans beef consommé*
*3½ cups water*

## Curried Meatballs

Heat butter or margarine in a large heavy saucepan. Add curry powder and cook gently 3 minutes, stirring. Add apple and stir until soft. Add tomatoes, raisins and salt. Cover and simmer 15 minutes.

Add meatballs and their gravy, cover and simmer until meatballs are very hot, about 15 minutes. Serve with rice and pass the chutney. (Serves 6.)

2 tbsp. butter or margarine
1 tbsp. curry powder
2 cups chopped, peeled apple
19-oz. can tomatoes
1/2 cup seedless raisins
1/2 tsp. salt
1 container Freezer Meatballs, thawed (recipe p. 104)
hot cooked rice
chutney

## Meatballs Stroganoff

Melt butter or margarine in a large saucepan. Add garlic and mushrooms and cook gently 3 minutes, stirring. Sprinkle in flour, salt and pepper. Stir to blend. Remove from heat and stir in 1 cup water. Return to heat and stir until thick and smooth.

Add meatballs and their gravy. Cover and simmer, stirring occasionally, until meatballs are very hot, about 15 minutes.

Stir in sour cream and heat but do not boil. Sprinkle with parsley or dill. Serve with rice. (Serves 6.)

2 tbsp. butter or margarine
1 clove garlic, minced
2 cups sliced mushrooms
2 tbsp. flour
1/2 tsp. salt
1/4 tsp. black pepper
1 cup water
1 container Freezer Meatballs, thawed (recipe p. 104)
1 cup sour cream
2 tbsp. snipped parsley or fresh dill
hot cooked rice

## Creole Meatballs

Heat oil in a large heavy saucepan or Dutch oven. Crumble in bay leaf. Add parsley, celery leaves and green pepper and cook gently 5 minutes, stirring. Add rice and stir until rice browns lightly. Add salt, Tabasco, cayenne, tomatoes, tomato sauce and 1 cup water. Cover and cook gently until rice is tender and most of liquid is absorbed, about 30 minutes.

Add meatballs and their gravy and simmer until meatballs are very hot, about 15 minutes. (Serves 6.)

3 tbsp. olive oil
1 bay leaf
1/4 cup finely chopped parsley
1 tbsp. snipped celery leaves
1 cup chopped green pepper
1 cup regular long-grain rice
1 1/2 tsp. salt
1/2 tsp. Tabasco
1/8 tsp. cayenne
19-oz. can tomatoes
7 1/2-oz. can tomato sauce
1 cup water
1 container Freezer Meatballs, thawed (recipe p. 104)

## Meatballs Polynesian Style

Heat oil in a large heavy saucepan. Add garlic and cook gently 2 minutes, stirring. Add chicken stock and meatballs and their gravy. Cover and simmer until meatballs are very hot, about 15 minutes.

Add green pepper and pineapple pieces. Cover again and simmer 5 minutes (green pepper must be crisp).

Mix cornstarch and sugar thoroughly in a small bowl. Stir in pineapple juice gradually, blending until smooth. Stir in vinegar and soya sauce. Stir this mixture into boiling liquid in saucepan. Stir until thickened, clear and smooth. Add tomato pieces and serve immediately with rice. (Serves 6.)

1 tbsp. cooking oil
1 clove garlic, crushed
$1/2$ cup chicken stock
  (recipe p. 48)
1 container Freezer Meatballs,
  thawed (recipe p. 104)
2 large green peppers, cut in
  1-inch squares
1 cup drained pineapple
  chunks
3 tbsp. cornstarch
$1/4$ cup sugar
$1/2$ cup pineapple juice
  (drained from chunks)
$1/2$ cup cider vinegar
3 tbsp. soya sauce
1 large tomato, peeled, seeded
  and coarsely chopped
hot cooked rice

## Hamburger Pie

Combine bread cubes and consommé in a large bowl.

Heat oil in a large heavy skillet. Add beef and onion and cook gently, stirring and breaking meat apart, just until meat loses its pink color. Remove from heat and add to bread cube mixture along with salt, pepper, thyme, nutmeg and Worcestershire. Blend well.

Heat oven to 375°F. Have ready a 9-inch pie pan.

Prepare pastry, adding cheese, paprika, mustard and cayenne to dry ingredients before adding the liquid. Roll out half of the pastry and use to line pie pan. Pile in meat mixture.

Roll out remaining pastry and use to top pie. Beat egg yolk and 1 tbsp. water together with a fork and brush top of pie (not edge) with mixture. Cut slashes in top crust to allow steam to escape. Cover edge of pie with a narrow strip of aluminum foil to keep it from getting too brown.

Bake until pastry is golden and filling is bubbling well, about 45 minutes. Serve hot or cold. (Serves 6.)

$1^1/2$ cups $1/4$-inch bread cubes
  (use day-old bread)
10-oz. can beef consommé
2 tbsp. cooking oil
$1^1/2$ lb. ground beef
1 small onion, chopped
1 tsp. salt
$1/2$ tsp. black pepper
$1/4$ tsp. dried leaf thyme
$1/8$ tsp. ground nutmeg
2 tsp. Worcestershire sauce
pastry for 2-crust 9-inch pie
  (recipe p. 172)
$1/2$ cup finely grated old
  Cheddar cheese
$1/2$ tsp. paprika
$1/4$ tsp. dry mustard
dash cayenne
1 egg yolk
1 tbsp. cold water

## Porcupine Beef Loaf

Heat oven to 325°F. Grease a 13 × 9 × 2-inch glass baking dish.

Combine beef, rice, onion, salt, pepper, mustard, oregano, thyme and Worcestershire. Blend well. Shape into an oval loaf and put into prepared baking dish. Pour beef stock around loaf. Cover lightly with aluminum foil and bake 2 hours.

Lift loaf out onto a hot platter and keep hot. Measure liquid in baking pan and add water, if necessary, to make 2 cups. Heat this liquid to boiling.

Shake 1/4 cup water and flour together in a small jar with a tight lid. Stir into boiling liquid gradually. Cook until boiling, thickened and smooth. Turn heat to low and boil gently 2 minutes. Serve as gravy with thick slices of meat loaf. (Serves 6.)

1 1/2 lb. ground beef
1/2 cup regular long-grain rice
1/2 cup chopped onion
1 1/2 tsp. salt
1/4 tsp. black pepper
1 tsp. dry mustard
1/2 tsp. dried leaf oregano
1/2 tsp. dried leaf thyme
1 tsp. Worcestershire sauce
2 cups beef stock or 2 beef bouillon cubes dissolved in 2 cups boiling water
1/4 cup cold water
2 tbsp. flour

## Beef Strips in Onion Sauce

Cut beef into thin strips across the grain. Mix 2 tbsp. flour, 1/4 tsp. salt, paprika and dash pepper in a flat dish. Toss meat strips in mixture.

Heat 2 tbsp. of the butter or margarine in a large heavy skillet over high heat. Add beef strips and cook quickly until lightly browned. Lift out with a slotted spoon and reduce heat to moderate.

Add remaining 2 tbsp. butter or margarine to skillet. Add onion, green pepper and garlic and stir 3 minutes.

Sprinkle in 1 1/2 tbsp. flour and stir to blend. Remove from heat and stir in consommé, 1 cup water, 1 tsp. salt, 1/4 tsp. pepper and savory. Return to heat and bring to a boil, stirring constantly.

Add meat strips, reduce heat, cover and simmer until meat is beginning to get tender, about 30 minutes. Add kidney beans and simmer 15 minutes more. Add salt and pepper to taste and serve with noodles. (Serves 4.)

1/2 lb. top round of beef
2 tbsp. flour
1/4 tsp. salt
1/4 tsp. paprika
dash black pepper
1/4 cup butter or margarine
2 large Spanish onions, chopped (about 3 1/2 cups)
1 large green pepper, chopped
1 clove garlic, minced
1 1/2 tbsp. flour
10-oz. can beef consommé
1 cup water
1 tsp. salt
1/4 tsp. black pepper
1/2 tsp. dried leaf savory
19-oz. can kidney beans, drained
salt and pepper
hot buttered noodles

107

## Steak and Kidney Pudding

2 lb. round steak, cut 1 inch
  thick
3 or 4 lamb kidneys
3 tbsp. flour
1 tsp. salt
1/4 tsp. black pepper
1/2 tsp. dried leaf thyme
1/2 tsp. paprika
Suet Pastry (recipe follows)

Trim fat from steak and cut into thin strips about 3 inches long. Remove fat from kidneys and pull off thin membranes. Cut kidneys into halves lengthwise and cut out core and tubes with kitchen shears. Slice kidneys thinly.

Combine flour and seasonings and dip meat and kidney in this mixture to coat lightly.

Grease a 2-qt. ceramic dish well and line with 3/4 of the pastry, letting it hang over the edge at least 1/2 inch. Add layers of meat and kidney.

Roll out remaining pastry a little larger than the top of the dish. Add boiling water to nearly cover meat. Add top crust and seal to bottom crust well, turning both under and crimping. Cut slashes in top crust to allow steam to escape.

Cover dish tightly with aluminum foil and set on a rack in a large kettle. Pour boiling water to halfway up outside of dish. Bring to a boil, reduce heat, cover kettle and boil gently 4 hours. Keep water boiling at all times and add more as needed to keep level halfway up side of dish. Serve hot. (Serves 6.)

## Suet Pastry

2 3/4 cups sifted all-purpose
  flour
1 tsp. baking powder
1 tsp. salt
1 cup ground suet
1 1/3 cups cold water (approx.)

Sift flour, baking powder and salt together into a bowl. Add suet and toss together. Add enough of the water to form a moderately stiff dough, mixing lightly with a fork. Shape into a round, roll out on a floured board and use for Steak and Kidney Pudding as directed.

## Groundnut Stew

2 lb. boneless beef chuck,
  cut in 1-inch cubes
2 cups water
2 tsp. salt
1/4 tsp. black pepper
2 medium onions, peeled and
  coarsely cut up
2 medium tomatoes, peeled
  and coarsely cut up
2 tbsp. cooking oil
1 cup unsalted peanuts,
  coarsely chopped
hot cooked rice
orange sections, shredded
  coconut, pineapple chunks,
  fried onion rings (optional)

Put meat in a large saucepan or Dutch oven. Add 2 cups water, salt and pepper. Cover and simmer until meat is tender, about 1 3/4 hours.

While meat is cooking, put onions and tomatoes in glass of blender and buzz until smooth (if you don't have a blender, chop very finely).

Put oil in a large heavy skillet and add onion-tomato mixture. Set over high heat and cook quickly, stirring, 3 minutes. Turn heat to moderate. Add meat mixture and peanuts and cook, uncovered, until sauce thickens, about 20 minutes.

Spoon over rice to serve. Pass small bowls of orange sections, coconut, pineapple chunks and onion rings to add to the dish if desired. (Serves 4.)

Advance preparation: Cook meat as directed until tender and refrigerate until ready to complete stew.

## Short Ribs and Dumplings

3 lb. beef short ribs, cut up
1 cup ketchup
1 cup water
2 tbsp. prepared horseradish
1 large bay leaf, crumbled
1 tbsp. prepared mustard
1 tbsp. white vinegar
1 tbsp. Worcestershire sauce
dash Tabasco
1 tsp. salt
$1/4$ tsp. black pepper
2 medium onions,
    finely chopped
Dumplings (recipe follows)

Trim all outer fat from pieces of short ribs.

Combine ketchup, 1 cup water, horseradish, bay leaf, mustard, vinegar, Worcestershire, Tabasco, salt and pepper in a large shallow baking dish. Add short ribs and turn them over to coat well with sauce. Sprinkle with onion.

Cover and refrigerate several hours or overnight, turning meat occasionally.

Put ribs and marinade in a large heavy saucepan or Dutch oven. Bring to a boil, turn down heat, cover and simmer until meat is very tender, about $1^1/2$ hours. Chill. Lift off and discard fat.

Heat meat and sauce to boiling, turn heat to moderate so sauce is at a slow boil. Drop dumplings by heaping tablespoonfuls on top of meat rather than in liquid (if dumplings are in liquid they tend to become heavy because they soak up liquid). You should have 12 dumplings. Cover pan and boil gently 20 minutes.

Lift dumplings out of saucepan with a slotted spoon and place them around the outside of a hot platter. Pile short ribs in centre of platter. Serve immediately. (Serves 6.)

Advance preparation: Cook ribs as directed down to the point where they are chilled and fat removed. Keep refrigerated until needed, then heat and add dumplings.

## Dumplings

2 cups sifted all-purpose flour
4 tsp. baking powder
1 tsp. salt
1 tbsp. shortening
$1/4$ cup finely chopped parsley
$1^1/4$ cups milk

Sift flour, baking powder and salt together into a medium bowl. Add shortening and cut in finely with a pastry blender. Add parsley and toss with a fork to blend. Add milk and stir with fork just until dry ingredients are dampened (dough should be soft and quite sticky).

## Ranch Ribs

3 to 4 lb. beef spareribs
    (see note)
salt and pepper
10-oz. bottle chili sauce
1 tbsp. Worcestershire sauce
3 drops Tabasco
1 cup water
$1/4$ cup white vinegar
1 tbsp. sugar
1 tsp. salt
1 tsp. celery seeds

Heat oven to 450°F.

Put ribs in a single layer in a roasting pan, sprinkle with salt and pepper and bake 30 minutes. Turn heat to 350°F and continue baking 30 minutes more.

Put ribs into a 13 × 9 × 2-inch baking dish, discarding fat. Combine remaining ingredients in a saucepan and bring to a boil. Pour over ribs.

Bake at 350°F until meat is very tender, about 45 minutes more. Turn ribs every 15 minutes. (Serves 4.)

Note: Have butcher cut ribs into 3-inch lengths and separate into individual ribs.

Advance preparation: Bake ribs for first hour as directed. Put into baking dish and cover with remaining ingredients. Cover and refrigerate until needed, then bake remaining 45 minutes.

## Jellied Tongue

3-lb. fresh beef tongue
1 medium onion, cut up
1 large carrot, cut up
1 large stalk celery with leaves, cut up
several sprigs parsley
1 small bay leaf
6 peppercorns
2 tsp. salt
2 envelopes (2 tbsp.) unflavored gelatin
1 tsp. salt
1/4 tsp. black pepper
1 tbsp. prepared horseradish mustard
1 tbsp. lemon juice
1 tsp. Worcestershire sauce
2 hard-cooked eggs, chopped
1/4 cup finely chopped sweet pickle
1/4 cup finely chopped celery
1/4 cup mayonnaise

Put tongue in a large kettle. Add onion, carrot, cut-up celery, parsley, bay leaf, peppercorns and 2 tsp. salt. Cover with boiling water. Cover and simmer until tongue is tender, about 3 hours.

Lift tongue out of liquid. Let cool just until it can be handled. Skin and trim by removing roots, small bones, gristle and fat. Return to cooking liquid and let cool.

Lift out tongue when it is cool. Strain stock and measure out 2 cups. Heat 1 1/2 cups of the stock to just boiling. Cool remaining 1/2 cup stock.

Cut 6 thin slices of tongue to be used to garnish bottom of pan. Chop remaining tongue fairly finely. (You should have 2 to 2 1/2 cups.)

Add gelatin to the 1/2 cup cold stock and let stand 5 minutes. Add to the 1 1/2 cups hot stock and stir until gelatin is dissolved. Stir in 1 tsp. salt and pepper. Blend mustard with lemon juice and Worcestershire and stir into gelatin mixture.

Set in ice water and chill until mixture is just beginning to thicken. Fold in remaining ingredients and chopped tongue.

Lay slices of tongue on the bottom of a 9 × 5 × 3-inch glass loaf pan. Spoon in gelatin mixture carefully. Chill until set. Cut into thick slices to serve. (Serves 6.)

## Liver and Bacon Patties

2 medium potatoes, peeled and quartered
2 slices bacon
1 lb. beef liver
1 small onion, peeled and quartered
1 tsp. salt
1/8 tsp. black pepper
1/8 tsp. ground nutmeg
3 tbsp. flour
1 egg, slightly beaten
2 tbsp. butter or margarine (approx.)

Put potatoes in a saucepan and cover with boiling water. Cover pan and boil until the tip of a sharp knife penetrates easily 1/2 inch into potatoes, about 5 minutes. Drain immediately and cool until they can be handled. Grate finely.

Fry bacon in a large heavy skillet until crisp. Drain and save fat. Put bacon through the fine blade of the food chopper with liver and onion. Mix in potatoes and remaining ingredients except butter or margarine.

Heat about 1 tbsp. of the bacon fat and the butter or margarine in skillet over moderate heat. Drop liver mixture by large spoonfuls into hot fat and cook, turning once, until well browned, about 1 minute each side. Add more fat as needed. Keep hot in low oven until all are done. (Makes about 12.)

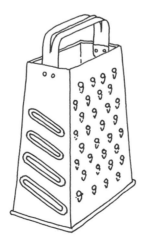

## Blanquette of Veal

Put meat in a large heavy saucepan. Add 4 cups water, carrots, onions, parsley, celery, leek, bay leaf, garlic, peppercorns, thyme and salt. Bring to a boil. Turn down heat, cover and simmer until veal is very tender, 1 to 1½ hours.

Lift meat, carrots and onions out onto a hot platter with a slotted spoon. Keep hot in low oven. Strain broth left in pan. Discard ingredients in strainer and return broth to saucepan. Boil hard until reduced to about half the volume.

Cream 2 tbsp. butter or margarine with flour, then add bit by bit to boiling broth, stirring constantly. Simmer 3 minutes.

Heat 2 tbsp. butter or margarine in a large skillet. Add whole mushrooms and cook quickly, stirring, until lightly browned.

Combine cream and egg yolks, beating together with a fork to blend. Stir into simmering broth gradually and heat, stirring, just until mixture returns to the boiling point (do not boil). Pour over meat and vegetables.

Garnish platter with mushrooms. Serve with rice or boiled potatoes. (Serves 6.)

2 lb. shoulder or leg of veal, cut in 1½-inch cubes
4 cups cold water
3 carrots, cut in large pieces
12 small silver onions, peeled
3 sprigs parsley, coarsely chopped
1 large stalk celery, cut in large pieces
1 leek (white and pale green parts only), sliced
1 bay leaf
1 clove garlic, crushed
¼ tsp. peppercorns
¼ tsp. dried leaf thyme
2 tsp. salt
2 tbsp. butter or margarine
2 tbsp. flour
2 tbsp. butter or margarine
½ lb. (1 pt.) fresh mushrooms, washed and trimmed
1 cup light cream
2 egg yolks
rice or boiled potatoes

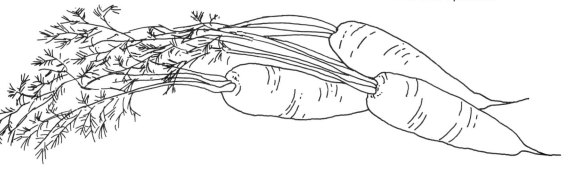

## Jellied Veal and Pork

Put veal shank and pork hocks in a large kettle. Cover with boiling water. Add bay leaf, salt, celery salt, peppercorns, onion and parsley. Bring to a boil, lower heat, cover and simmer about 2 hours.

Lift meat out of stock. Strain stock and chill until fat comes to the surface. Discard fat. Boil stock down to 2 cups. Cool but do not chill.

Take meat from bones and pull into rather small pieces. Combine with vinegar, celery and green pepper.

Put a very thin layer of the meat stock in the bottom of a 9 × 5 × 3-inch glass loaf pan. Add egg slices, making an attractive arrangement. Chill until egg slices are held in place but jellied mixture is still sticky.

Add meat mixture to remaining meat stock. Chill by setting in ice water just until stock begins to thicken. Pour over egg layer and chill several hours or overnight.

Unmold at serving time and cut into thick slices. (Serves 8.)

2 to 2½ lb. veal shank, cut up
1 to 1½ lb. pork hocks, cut up
1 bay leaf
2 tsp. salt
1 tsp. celery salt
4 peppercorns
1 thick slice onion
6 sprigs parsley
2 tbsp. white vinegar
1 cup finely chopped celery
½ cup finely chopped green pepper
1 hard-cooked egg, sliced

## Veal and Mushrooms

1 1/2 lb. thin veal cutlets
2 tbsp. bottled French dressing
1/4 cup cooking oil
1 small onion, sliced
2 tbsp. flour
salt and pepper
2 tbsp. finely chopped green
  pepper
1 1/2 cups chicken stock or
  1 chicken bouillon cube
  dissolved in 1 1/2 cups
  boiling water
2 tbsp. butter or margarine
1/2 lb. (1 pt.) fresh mushrooms,
  sliced
1/4 cup sliced stuffed olives

Coat veal cutlets with French dressing and let stand 15 minutes.

Heat oil in a large heavy skillet. Add cutlets and brown lightly. Push to one side of pan and add onion to other side and cook gently 3 minutes. Spread meat out in pan again and sprinkle with flour. Brown lightly again. Sprinkle with salt and pepper. Add green pepper and chicken stock. Cover tightly and cook gently until veal is very tender, about 5 minutes a side.

While veal is cooking, heat butter or margarine in another skillet. Add mushrooms and cook quickly 3 minutes, stirring. Remove from heat.

Put veal on a hot platter. Add mushrooms and olives to liquid left in pan. Stir and heat well. Pour over veal. Serve immediately. (Serves 4.)

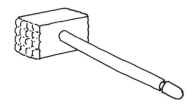

## Veal Piccate

3/4 to 1 lb. veal escalopes,
  (see note)
salt and pepper
1 tbsp. lemon juice
flour
2 tbsp. butter
3 tbsp. Marsala wine
2 tbsp. veal or chicken stock

Season prepared veal with salt and pepper and drizzle lemon juice over. Dust pieces lightly with flour.

Heat butter in a large heavy skillet. Fry pieces of veal quickly until lightly browned, about 1 minute a side. Put on a hot platter.

Add Marsala and stock to pan. Drop veal back into pan and heat. Serve immediately. (Serves 2.)

*Note:* Escalopes should be cut about 1/4 inch thick (they are usually cut from the leg). For this recipe they should be trimmed of all fat and sinew, then pounded between 2 sheets of waxed paper with a mallet, the side of a cleaver or a rolling pin to make as thin as possible, 1/16 to 1/8 inch thick. The thin pieces of veal should then be cut into strips 4 inches long by 1 1/2 inches wide.

## Old-Fashioned Veal and Pork Loaf

1 1/2 lb. ground veal
1 1/2 lb. ground pork
1 cup fine dry bread crumbs
2 cloves garlic, minced
1/4 cup grated onion
1/2 cup chopped parsley
2 eggs, lightly beaten
1 tsp. dried leaf thyme
2 tsp. salt
1/2 tsp. black pepper
1/2 lb. bacon

Heat oven to 375°F. Have ready a 9 × 5 × 3-inch glass loaf pan.

Combine all ingredients except bacon, blending well.

Line bottom of loaf pan with half of the bacon. Turn meat mixture into pan, spread evenly and pack down lightly. Top with remaining bacon.

Bake 1 1/2 hours. Cut into thick slices to serve. (Serves 8.)

## Veal and Pork Pie

Heat oil in a large heavy saucepan or Dutch oven. Add veal and pork and brown well on all sides. Sprinkle salt, pepper, celery salt, garlic salt, thyme, marjoram and bay leaf over meat. Add 4½ cups boiling water.

Stick 1 clove in each onion and add to meat. Bring to a boil, turn down heat, cover tightly and simmer until meat is beginning to get tender, about 1 hour.

Add carrots and potatoes and continue simmering 30 minutes. Add beans and simmer until everything is tender, about 30 minutes more.

Shake ½ cup water and flour together in a small jar with a tight lid until blended. Add to hot liquid in pan gradually, stirring constantly. Cook until boiling, thickened and smooth. Pour mixture into a 14 × 10 × 2-inch baking dish. Cool.

Heat oven to 425°F.

While meat mixture cools, make Cheese Biscuit Dough and roll it slightly larger than top of baking dish. Lift carefully and lay over top of meat. Seal well to edges of pan. Cut a large vent in the top to allow steam to escape.

Beat egg yolk and 1 tbsp. water together and brush over top of dough. Bake until crust is well browned and meat mixture is bubbling, about 20 minutes. (Serves 8.)

Advance preparation: Make meat mixture and put in baking dish. Cover and refrigerate. Bring to room temperature and add cheese biscuit topping when needed.

3 tbsp. cooking oil
¾ lb. cubed veal shoulder
¾ lb. cubed lean pork
3 tsp. salt
¼ tsp. black pepper
1 tsp. celery salt
¼ tsp. garlic salt
¼ tsp. dried leaf thyme
⅛ tsp. dried leaf marjoram
1 small bay leaf, crumbled
4½ cups boiling water
6 whole cloves
6 small whole onions
1½ cups sliced carrots
2½ cups 1-inch cubes
   potatoes
1½ cups cut-up green beans
½ cup cold water
¼ cup flour
Cheese Biscuit Dough
   (recipe follows)
1 egg yolk
1 tbsp. cold water

## Cheese Biscuit Dough

Sift flour, baking powder, salt and celery seeds into a bowl. Add shortening and cut in finely. Stir in cheese with a fork.

Stir in with a fork enough of the milk to make a soft, puffy dough that is easy to handle. Turn out onto a floured board and knead gently 12 times. Roll and use to top meat pie as directed in recipe.

3 cups sifted all-purpose flour
5½ tsp. baking powder
1½ tsp. salt
1 tsp. celery seeds
6 tbsp. shortening
¾ cup grated old Cheddar
   cheese
1 cup plus 2 tbsp. milk
   (approx.)

## Loin of Pork with Peach Glaze

3¹/₂- to 4-lb. loin of pork roast
1 tbsp. olive oil
2 tsp. dried leaf marjoram
14-oz. can peach halves
¹/₄ cup sugar
¹/₂ tsp. dry mustard
1 tsp. paprika
2 tsp. cornstarch
2 tbsp. white vinegar
chili sauce or hot pepper relish

Heat oven to 325°F. Put roast, resting on bones, in a small roasting pan. Rub fat side of roast with olive oil and sprinkle with marjoram. Roast 1¹/₂ hours.

Score fat on roast and continue roasting until meat thermometer registers 170°F to 185°F (another 1 to 1¹/₂ hours or 35 to 40 minutes a pound total cooking time).

Make glaze while roast is cooking. Drain and dry peach halves well, saving liquid. Combine sugar, mustard, paprika and cornstarch in a small saucepan. Stir in ¹/₂ cup of the juice drained from peaches gradually, blending until smooth. Stir in vinegar. Set over high heat and bring to a boil, stirring constantly. Cook until thick and clear.

Put peach halves in a small baking pan and fill centre of each with some chili sauce or hot pepper relish.

Drain almost all fat from pan when roast is done. Spread roast with glaze. Put roast and peach halves in oven until roast is glazed and peaches are hot, about 15 minutes. Baste roast several times. Put on platter and garnish with peach halves.

## Pot-Roasted Pork Shoulder

2 tbsp. cooking oil
4 lb. shoulder of pork
3 small carrots, scraped and coarsely cut up
3 cloves garlic, minced
4 small onions, peeled and sliced
1 tsp. salt
¹/₈ tsp. black pepper
1 tsp. dried leaf thyme
¹/₂ cup water
1 cup boiling water
1 beef bouillon cube
salt and pepper

Heat oil in a large heavy saucepan or Dutch oven. Add roast and brown slowly on all sides. Add carrots, garlic, onions, 1 tsp. salt, ¹/₈ tsp. pepper, thyme and ¹/₂ cup water. Cover tightly and simmer until meat is very tender, about 2¹/₂ hours. Put roast on a hot platter and keep hot in low oven.

Add 1 cup boiling water and bouillon cube to liquid and vegetables in pan and stir until cube is dissolved. Remove fat from liquid. To do this, pour the pan liquid into a tall narrow container (a 4-cup glass measuring cup is useful for this) so fat will rise quickly to the top. Add 2 or 3 ice cubes to speed up cooling if desired. Skim off all fat.

Buzz liquid and vegetables in glass of blender a little at a time until smooth (vegetables will thicken gravy). Return to pan in which roast was cooked. Heat to boiling. Add salt and pepper to taste. Serve with meat.

Advance preparation: Cook meat until tender. Refrigerate in cooking pan, then reheat and make gravy when needed.

## Sweet and Sour Pork Tenderloin Bits

Combine vinegar, sugar, ketchup, Worcestershire and 1 tsp. salt in a small saucepan. Bring to a boil.

Mix 1 1/2 tsp. cornstarch into 1/4 cup water until smooth. Gradually stir into boiling mixture. Continue stirring until clear and slightly thickened. Remove from heat and set aside.

Cut each piece of frenched pork tenderloin into 4 pieces. Put in a bowl and sprinkle with 1/4 tsp. salt. Combine 1 tbsp. water and 1 tbsp. cornstarch until smooth. Pour over meat and mix until pieces are coated. Let stand 15 minutes.

Heat garlic in about 1/4-inch cooking oil in a large heavy skillet. (An electric skillet set at 350°F is fine.) Discard garlic.

Put 2 tbsp. of the cornstarch on a plate or waxed paper and roll pieces of meat in it to coat all sides, adding remaining cornstarch if needed.

Add about half the meat to hot oil and cook 5 to 7 minutes, turning pieces with tongs as they brown. When cooked through and golden brown on both sides, lift out and drain on paper toweling. Repeat with remaining meat.

Drain all but 1 tbsp. of the oil from pan. Add green onion, green pepper and ginger and stir over high heat 2 minutes. Add sauce you set aside and pork pieces and heat just long enough for meat to be heated through again. Serve immediately with rice. (Serves 3.)

*Note:* Buy a whole piece of pork tenderloin if you prefer, cut it into 2-inch-long pieces and flatten them as thinly as possible by pounding with the flat of a cleaver or with a rolling pin.

1/3 cup white vinegar
1/3 cup sugar
1/4 cup ketchup
1 tbsp. Worcestershire sauce
1 tsp. salt
1 1/2 tsp. cornstarch
1/4 cup water
1 lb. pork tenderloin, frenched (see note)
1/4 tsp. salt
1 tbsp. water
1 tbsp. cornstarch
1 clove garlic, peeled and cut in half
cooking oil
3 tbsp. cornstarch (approx.)
1 large green onion, cut in 1-inch lengths
1 small green pepper, seeded and cut in 1-inch squares
2 tbsp. very thin slices preserved ginger
hot cooked rice

## Pork Chops in Cider

Heat oven to 350°F. Have ready a 13 × 9 × 2-inch-baking dish.

Trim excess fat from chops. Put a little of this fat in a heavy skillet and heat until pan is well greased. Discard all fat. Add butter or margarine to skillet.

Combine flour, salt, pepper, paprika, marjoram and basil in a flat dish (a pie plate is good). Dip chops in mixture to coat both sides. Put in skillet and brown slowly on both sides. Put into baking dish in a single layer as they brown.

Add a little more butter or margarine to skillet if necessary and add onion. Cook just until limp but not browned. Spoon over chops. Pour cider or apple juice over all.

Cover (use aluminum foil if baking dish has no cover) and bake until chops are very tender, 45 to 60 minutes. (Serves 6.)

Advance preparation: Make down to point of cooking and adding onion. Refrigerate, then add cider or apple juice and bake when needed.

6 thick pork chops
2 tbsp. butter or margarine (approx.)
1/4 cup flour
1 tsp. salt
1/4 tsp. black pepper
1/4 tsp. paprika
pinch dried leaf marjoram
pinch dried leaf basil
2 cups chopped onion
2 cups dry cider or apple juice

## Pork Chops with Onion Sauce

Combine $1/2$ tsp. salt, $1/8$ tsp. pepper and cloves and rub mixture over outside of pork chops. Heat oil, garlic and bay leaf in a large heavy skillet. Discard garlic. Add chops and brown well on both sides. Cover tightly and cook slowly until very tender, about 30 minutes for 1-inch chops.

While chops are cooking, melt butter or margarine in a medium saucepan. Heat until butter or margarine is lightly browned. Add flour, stir to blend and cook until lightly browned. Add onion, parsley, $1/2$ tsp. salt and $1/8$ tsp. pepper and stir to blend. Gradually blend in beef stock. Simmer 20 minutes.

Put chops onto a hot serving platter when they are done and keep hot in low oven. Drain any fat from skillet and add $1/2$ cup boiling water to skillet. Bring to a boil, scraping up any browned bits. Add to sauce along with vinegar and mustard. Pour over chops and serve immediately. (Serves 6.)

*$1/2$ tsp. salt*
*$1/8$ tsp. black pepper*
*dash ground cloves*
*6 large pork chops*
*2 tbsp. cooking oil*
*1 clove garlic, peeled and cut in half*
*1 small bay leaf, crumbled*
*3 tbsp. butter or margarine*
*$1/4$ cup flour*
*3 medium onions, finely chopped (about $1 1/2$ cups)*
*2 tbsp. chopped parsley*
*$1/2$ tsp. salt*
*$1/8$ tsp. black pepper*
*$1 1/2$ cups beef stock (recipe p. 48)*
*$1/2$ cup boiling water*
*1 tsp. red wine vinegar*
*1 tsp. prepared mustard*

## Pork Hocks and Bean Stew

Put pork hocks, salt, pepper, garlic and bay leaf in a large saucepan or Dutch oven. Add enough of the 7 cups boiling water to cover. Bring to a boil, turn down heat, cover and simmer $1 1/2$ hours. Chill. Lift off and discard fat.

Rinse beans and discard any discolored ones. Put in a large saucepan and add 8 cups boiling water. Bring to a boil and boil 2 minutes. Remove from heat, cover and let soak 1 hour. Drain.

Bring pork hocks and their liquid back to a boil. Add beans. Bring to a boil, turn down heat, cover and simmer 30 minutes.

Stick cloves into one of the onions and add onions and carrots to pork hock-bean mixture. Cover and simmer until meat is tender and vegetables are almost tender, about 45 minutes. Add lemon juice and simmer 15 minutes more.

Lift pork hocks out of mixture. Remove and discard skin, fat and bones, leaving meat in bite-size pieces. Return meat to saucepan and heat well. Serve with plenty of French bread to soak up cooking liquid. (Serves 6.)

*Note:* Pork hocks may be done in 2 hours. If you find meat is beginning to fall off the bones at the time you are about to add onions and carrots, you can take them out, strip off meat and put it back in stew shortly before serving.

Advance preparation: Make completely, refrigerate, then reheat slowly when needed.

*4 lb. pork hocks*
*2 tbsp. salt*
*$1/4$ tsp. black pepper*
*2 cloves garlic, crushed*
*1 small bay leaf*
*7 cups boiling water (approx.)*
*16-oz. pkg. dry pea beans (about $2 1/2$ cups)*
*8 cups boiling water*
*4 whole cloves*
*12 small white onions*
*6 medium carrots, cut in chunks*
*2 tbsp. lemon juice*
*French bread*

## Pork Loaf Oriental

Heat oven to 350°F. Grease a 9 × 5 × 3-inch glass loaf pan.

Combine all ingredients except Vegetable Sauce, blending well. Turn into prepared pan and bake 1½ hours. Make Vegetable Sauce near the end of meat loaf cooking time.

Cut loaf into thick slices to serve and pass the Vegetable Sauce. (Serves 6.)

1½ lb. ground pork
1½ cups soft bread crumbs
1 cup milk
¼ cup thinly sliced green
   onions
¼ cup toasted chopped
   walnuts
½ tsp. salt
¼ tsp. black pepper
2 tbsp. soya sauce
¼ tsp. ground ginger
1 egg, lightly beaten
Vegetable Sauce
   (recipe follows)

## Vegetable Sauce

Bring chicken stock to a boil in a medium saucepan. Add carrots and cook 5 minutes. Add peas and cook until vegetables are tender-crisp, about 5 minutes more. Stir in sugar, vinegar and soya sauce and bring to a boil.

Stir cornstarch into ¼ cup water, blending until smooth. Add to boiling vegetables gradually, stirring constantly. Turn heat to low and cook gently 1 minute. (Makes about 3 cups.)

1 cup chicken stock or
   1 chicken bouillon cube
   dissolved in 1 cup boiling
   water
2 cups thin slices carrots
12-oz. pkg. frozen peas
¼ cup sugar
¼ cup white vinegar
3 tbsp. soya sauce
1 tbsp. cornstarch
¼ cup cold water

## Chilied Pork Balls

Combine tomatoes, ¼ cup onion, 2 tsp. salt, sugar, ¼ tsp. garlic salt, ¼ tsp. pepper, Tabasco, chili powder and oregano in a large saucepan. Bring to a boil, turn down heat, cover and simmer 30 minutes.

Combine pork, beef, 1 tbsp. onion, ¼ tsp. pepper, ¼ tsp. garlic salt, parsley, 1 tsp. salt, bread crumbs, cheese and eggs. Shape into meatballs about 1½ inches in diameter.

Heat oil in a heavy skillet and brown meatballs well on all sides. Add more oil if needed.

Add meatballs to tomato sauce after it has simmered the 30 minutes. Cover and continue simmering 45 minutes more. Serve over rice. (Serves 6.)

Advance preparation: Make and brown meatballs. Make tomato sauce. Refrigerate both, then reheat sauce and add meatballs and simmer as directed.

28-oz. can tomatoes
¼ cup chopped onion
2 tsp. salt
1 tsp. sugar
¼ tsp. garlic salt
¼ tsp. black pepper
¼ tsp. Tabasco
1 tbsp. chili powder
1 tsp. dried leaf oregano
1 lb. ground lean pork
½ lb. ground beef
1 tbsp. finely chopped onion
¼ tsp. black pepper
¼ tsp. garlic salt
2 tbsp. chopped parsley
1 tsp. salt
1 cup fine dry bread crumbs
¾ cup grated old Cheddar
   cheese
2 eggs, beaten
2 tbsp. cooking oil (approx.)
hot cooked rice

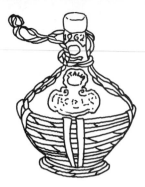

## English-Style Boiled Lamb

Mix vinegar, 2 tsp. salt, 1/4 tsp. pepper, thyme, bay leaves, parsley and onion in a large glass or pottery baking dish. Add lamb, cover and refrigerate 24 hours. Turn occasionally.

Lift lamb out of marinade. Discard bay leaves and parsley sprigs and measure marinade, adding enough water to make 1 cup liquid.

Heat butter or margarine and oil in a large Dutch oven. Add mushrooms and carrots and stir 5 minutes. Add lamb, 1 cup liquid and wine. Bring to a boil, reduce heat, cover and simmer until lamb is very tender, about 2 1/2 hours. Turn occasionally.

Put roast on a hot platter and keep hot in low oven. Remove fat from liquid left in pan. To do this, pour the pan liquid into a tall narrow container (a 4-cup glass measuring cup is useful for this) so fat will rise quickly to the top. Add 2 or 3 ice cubes to speed up cooling if desired. Skim off all fat.

Buzz liquid and vegetables in glass of blender a little at a time. Return blended mixture to pan and boil hard, uncovered, until reduced to about 1 1/2 cups.

Combine 1/4 cup water and cornstarch, blending until mixture is smooth. Stir into boiling liquid gradually. Boil until thick and clear. Add jelly and stir until jelly is melted. Stir in lemon juice and add salt and pepper to taste. Pass as sauce with meat.

*Note:* If you have difficulty getting a boned leg or shoulder, try this recipe with a bone-in upper leg of lamb from the frozen meat counter. It's delicious.

1/2 cup red wine vinegar
2 tsp. salt
1/4 tsp. black pepper
1 tsp. dried leaf thyme
2 bay leaves
2 sprigs parsley
1/4 cup finely chopped onion
4 lb. boned leg or shoulder of lamb (see note)
2 tbsp. butter or margarine
1 tbsp. cooking oil
4 cups sliced fresh mushrooms
1 cup finely chopped carrots
1 1/4 cups dry red wine
1/4 cup water
1 tbsp. cornstarch
1/2 cup red currant jelly
1 tbsp. lemon juice
salt and pepper

## Mock Venison

Combine wine, oil, onion, garlic, parsley, rosemary, cloves, juniper berries, salt, pepper and bay leaf in a deep bowl. Trim excess fat from lamb and put lamb in bowl, turn over, cover and let stand in refrigerator 24 hours, turning meat often.

Heat oven to 325°F.

Lift meat out of marinade and drain well. Put, resting on bones, in a shallow roasting pan. Cook to an internal temperature of 150°F for medium or 175°F for well-done. Allow about 20 minutes per pound for medium and 30 to 40 minutes per pound for well-done. Strain marinade and baste meat with it often during roasting.

Cream butter or margarine and flour together to blend well. Heat remaining marinade to boiling and stir butter-flour mixture bit by bit into boiling liquid, using only enough so that liquid is slightly thickened.

Serve marinade as sauce with sliced meat. Red currant jelly and cooked wild rice make good accompaniments.

2 cups dry red wine
1/2 cup cooking oil
1 medium onion, minced
3 cloves garlic, minced
1/4 cup chopped parsley
1/4 tsp. dried leaf rosemary
2 whole cloves
4 juniper berries
2 tsp. salt
1 tsp. coarse black pepper
1 bay leaf, crumbled
4 lb. leg of lamb
1/3 cup butter or margarine
2 tbsp. flour
red currant jelly (optional)
cooked wild rice (optional)

## Minty Deviled Lamb Chops

6 double loin lamb chops
2 tbsp. Worcestershire sauce
2 tbsp. butter or margarine
2 tbsp. lemon juice
2 tbsp. white vermouth
grating fresh black pepper
1/2 cup mint jelly
1 tbsp. white vinegar

Trim excess fat from chops. Put them in a shallow glass or pottery dish.

Heat Worcestershire, butter or margarine, lemon juice, vermouth and pepper in a small saucepan just until butter melts. Pour over chops. Turn chops and let stand at room temperature 30 minutes, turning once or twice.

Put chops on a rack in broiler pan and broil low in oven (put oven rack just above centre of oven) until done, about 15 minutes a side. Check whether done by cutting into meat near bone with the point of a knife.

Heat marinade in a small saucepan shortly before serving time. Add jelly and vinegar and continue heating gently until jelly is melted. Serve hot over chops. (Serves 6.)

## Lamb Chops with Potatoes

4 shoulder lamb chops
2 tbsp. butter or margarine
  (approx.)
2 medium onions, finely
  chopped
1 clove garlic, finely chopped
1/2 tsp. salt
1/8 tsp. black pepper
1 small bay leaf
1 cup chicken stock or
  1 chicken bouillon cube
  dissolved in 1 cup
  boiling water
3 large baking potatoes
1/2 tsp. salt
1/8 tsp. black pepper
2 tbsp. chopped parsley
1 tbsp. fine dry bread crumbs
2 tbsp. butter or margarine

Trim all excess fat from chops. Heat 2 tbsp. butter or margarine in a large heavy skillet. Add chops and brown on both sides. Put in a single layer in a 12 × 7 × 2-inch baking dish as they brown.

Heat oven to 350°F.

Cook onion and garlic in same skillet, adding a little more butter or margarine if needed. Spoon mixture on top of chops. Sprinkle with 1/2 tsp. salt and 1/8 tsp. pepper. Break bay leaf into 4 pieces and put a piece on top of each chop. Add chicken stock to baking dish and cover tightly with aluminum foil. Bake 30 minutes.

Peel and slice potatoes very thinly. Remove baking dish from oven and spread potatoes over chops. Sprinkle with 1/2 tsp. salt and 1/8 tsp. pepper. Cover and bake 30 minutes more.

Remove from oven. Combine parsley and bread crumbs and sprinkle over potatoes. Dot with 2 tbsp. butter or margarine. Cover and bake until chops are very tender, about 15 minutes more.

Remove foil and put dish under broiler for a minute or two to lightly brown top of potatoes. Serve immediately. (Serves 4.)

Advance preparation: Make down to point where potatoes are to be added, then cool and refrigerate. Add potatoes and complete when needed.

## Lamb Pie

Heat oven to 350°F. Butter a 2½-qt. casserole.

Combine flour and paprika in a flat dish (a pie plate is good) and roll cubes of lamb in mixture.

Heat oil in a large saucepan or Dutch oven. Add lamb pieces and brown well on all sides. Add 1½ cups boiling water, bouillon cubes, onion, ¼ cup parsley, peppercorns, bay leaf, 1½ tsp. salt, marjoram and lemon. Cover tightly and simmer until meat is beginning to get tender, about 1½ hours. Add beans and carrots and simmer until everything is tender, about 30 minutes more. Put in prepared casserole.

Beat potatoes, butter or margarine, eggs, 1 tsp. salt and pepper together until fluffy. Beat in ½ cup parsley. Drop by large spoonfuls on top of meat.

Bake until meat mixture is bubbling well and top is lightly browned, about 20 minutes. (Serves 6.)

Advance preparation: Brown and simmer meat, adding vegetables as directed but cooking only 20 minutes. Reheat meat and vegetables when needed, put in casserole and complete.

¼ cup flour
2 tsp. paprika
2 lb. lamb shoulder, cubed
¼ cup cooking oil
1½ cups boiling water
2 chicken bouillon cubes
2 large onions, chopped
¼ cup chopped parsley
4 peppercorns
small piece bay leaf
1½ tsp. salt
½ tsp. dried leaf marjoram
½ lemon, sliced paper thin
½ lb. green beans, cut in
   1-inch pieces
2 large carrots, sliced
3 cups hot mashed potatoes
¼ cup soft butter or margarine
2 eggs
1 tsp. salt
½ tsp. black pepper
½ cup chopped parsley

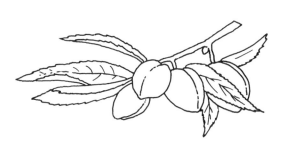

## Lamb and Rice Indian Style

Put lamb cubes in a large saucepan or Dutch oven. Add 6 cups water and salt.

Tie 1 chopped onion, garlic, ginger root, 5 cloves, 1 cardamom seed and coriander and anise seeds in a small cheesecloth bag and add to meat. Bring to a boil, turn down heat, cover tightly and simmer until lamb is tender, 1 to 1½ hours.

Drain off stock and set aside for use later. Discard bag of seasonings.

Add oil to meat in saucepan along with the other chopped onion and stir until meat and onion are lightly browned. Add rice and stir until rice is lightly browned.

Add 3½ cups of the stock and the remaining spices, cover tightly and simmer until rice is tender and liquid is absorbed, about 25 minutes. Add milk and butter or margarine and stir lightly with a fork.

Serve immediately on a large platter, sprinkled with almonds and raisins. (Serves 6.)

Advance preparation: Brown and simmer lamb cubes until tender. Drain and refrigerate both lamb and stock until ready to complete recipe.

2 lb. shoulder of lamb, cut in
   1-inch cubes
6 cups cold water
2 tsp. salt
1 medium onion, chopped
1 clove garlic, peeled and cut
   in half
1-inch piece dried ginger root,
   cut up
5 whole cloves
1 cardamom seed
1 tsp. coriander seeds
1 tsp. anise seeds
2 tbsp. cooking oil
1 medium onion, chopped
1½ cups regular long-grain rice
8 whole cloves
3 cardamom seeds
½ tsp. cumin seeds
½ cup milk
2 tbsp. butter or margarine
½ cup slivered toasted
   almonds
½ cup raisins

## Lamb Loaf with Onion Sauce

4 cups soft bread crumbs
$1/2$ cup milk
2 eggs
2 lb. ground lamb
2 tbsp. soft butter or margarine
3 tsp. salt
$1/2$ tsp. black pepper
$1/2$ cup finely chopped parsley
Onion Sauce (recipe follows)

Heat oven to 350°F. Grease a 9 × 5 × 3-inch glass loaf pan.

Put bread crumbs in a large bowl. Add milk and stir until milk is absorbed by bread. Add all remaining ingredients except Onion Sauce and blend lightly with a fork.

Spoon into prepared pan. Bake $1^1/2$ hours.

Drain liquid from pan carefully and turn loaf out onto a hot platter. Cut into thick slices and serve with Onion Sauce. (Serves 6.)

## Onion Sauce

$1^1/2$ cups finely chopped onion
$1/4$ tsp. salt
3 tbsp. butter or margarine
1 tbsp. flour
1 cup milk
$1/2$ tsp. salt
$1/8$ tsp. black pepper
$1/4$ tsp. sugar
pinch ground nutmeg
$1/4$ cup heavy cream
1 tbsp. butter or margarine

Put chopped onion and $1/4$ tsp. salt in a bowl and cover completely with boiling water. Let stand 3 minutes, then drain very well.

Heat 2 tbsp. of the butter or margarine in a heavy saucepan. Add onion, cover and cook gently, stirring often, until onion is limp but not browned, about 5 minutes.

Melt remaining 1 tbsp. butter or margarine in another saucepan. Sprinkle in flour and let bubble up. Remove from heat and add milk all at once. Stir to blend.

Add $1/2$ tsp. salt, pepper, sugar and nutmeg. Return to moderate heat and cook, stirring, until boiling, thickened and smooth. Add onion. Cover tightly and simmer, stirring often, until onion is very tender, about 30 minutes.

Press mixture through a sieve or buzz, half at a time, in glass of blender. Return to saucepan and heat well. Stir in cream and 1 tbsp. butter or margarine. Serve hot with Lamb Loaf. (Makes about 2 cups.)

## Persian Meat Loaf

$1^1/2$ lb. ground lamb
1 slice day-old white bread
1 large onion, finely chopped
$1/4$ cup finely chopped green onions
$1/4$ cup finely chopped parsley
$1/4$ cup finely chopped celery leaves
1 tsp. salt
$1/2$ tsp. black pepper
$1/4$ tsp. ground cinnamon
2 eggs
$1/4$ cup tomato paste
1 tbsp. lemon juice

Heat oven to 350°F. Grease a 9 × 5 × 3-inch glass loaf pan.

Put lamb in a large bowl. Soak bread in enough water to cover 2 minutes. Squeeze out and discard water. Break bread up into meat, add remaining ingredients and mix well.

Pack meat mixture into prepared pan. Bake 1 hour and 10 minutes. Drain loaf, cover and chill. Slice thinly to serve. (Serves 6.)

## Rabbit à l'Orange

Combine flour, paprika, salt and pepper in a flat dish (a pie plate is good). Roll rabbit pieces in mixture to coat all sides. Heat butter or margarine and oil in a large skillet and brown rabbit lightly. Put meat in a shallow baking dish in a single layer.

Heat oven to 350°F.

Combine remaining ingredients except wine in a small saucepan. Bring to a boil, lower heat and simmer 10 minutes. Stir in wine and pour over rabbit.

Bake rabbit, basting often, until very tender, about 1½ hours. (Serves 3 or 4.)

1/4 cup flour
3/4 tsp. paprika
1/4 tsp. salt
1/8 tsp. black pepper
3½-lb. rabbit, cut up
2 tbsp. butter or margarine
2 tbsp. cooking oil
2 medium onions, thinly sliced
3/4 cup orange juice
1½ tsp. grated orange rind
1/2 tsp. dried leaf thyme
1/2 tsp. salt
pinch black pepper
3/4 cup dry white wine

## Almond-Stuffed Capon

Heat oven to 300°F.

Put almonds on a large baking sheet and toast in oven, stirring often, until just beginning to brown, about 15 minutes. Add bread cubes to baking sheet and continue toasting until bread cubes are golden, about 10 minutes. Put almonds and bread cubes in a large bowl. Add 1 tsp. salt, poultry seasoning, marjoram, nutmeg, 1/4 tsp. pepper and parsley.

Heat 1/2 cup butter or margarine in a large heavy skillet. Fry capon liver gently just until it loses its pink color. Lift out of pan with a slotted spoon and set aside.

Add onion and celery to butter or margarine in skillet and cook gently, stirring, 5 minutes. Add to bread-almond mixture. Chop capon liver and add. Toss together lightly with a fork.

Sprinkle inside of capon with salt and pepper. Stuff loosely with bread-almond mixture and skewer openings closed. Tie legs and wings close to body of bird. Set on rack. Brush all over with melted butter or margarine. Cover with a loose tent of aluminum foil.

Heat oven to 325°F. Roast until drumstick moves easily, 3½ to 4 hours. Remove foil for last hour of roasting to let capon brown well. Baste often. Serve with Wine Gravy.

Advance preparation: Make stuffing as directed but do not stuff bird. Refrigerate when cool and stuff bird just before cooking time.

1 cup coarsely chopped
   blanched almonds
3 cups 1/4-inch bread cubes
1 tsp. salt
1/2 tsp. poultry seasoning
1/4 tsp. dried leaf marjoram
pinch ground nutmeg
1/4 tsp. black pepper
1/4 cup chopped parsley
1/2 cup butter or margarine
capon liver
1/4 cup chopped onion
3/4 cup chopped celery
6-lb. capon
salt and pepper
melted butter or margarine
Wine Gravy (recipe follows)

## Wine Gravy

Heat drippings in a saucepan. Sprinkle in flour and let bubble up, stirring constantly. Remove from heat and add chicken stock all at once. Stir to blend.

Return to moderate heat and stir until boiling, thickened and smooth. Add salt and pepper to taste. Stir in vermouth and heat but do not boil. Stir in parsley just before serving. (Makes about 3 cups.)

1/4 cup capon drippings
1/4 cup flour
3 cups chicken stock
   (recipe p. 48)
1 tsp. salt (approx.)
1/4 tsp. black pepper (approx.)
1/4 cup white vermouth
2 tbsp. chopped parsley

## Cornish Game Hens Bonne Femme

Combine $1/2$ cup soft butter or margarine, 2 tbsp. chopped parsley, $1/2$ tsp. salt, pepper and finely chopped mushrooms, blending well. Put a tablespoonful of mixture inside each washed and dried hen. Truss birds. Rub outside of birds with 2 tbsp. butter or margarine.

Cut salt pork into small strips. Pour boiling water over strips in a small saucepan. Bring to a boil, turn down heat and simmer 10 minutes. Drain and dry well on paper toweling.

Put half the salt pork in each of 2 large Dutch ovens. Heat until pork is browned and pans are well greased. Lift out pork with a slotted spoon and set aside.

Brown birds in fat left in pans, turning carefully with 2 wooden spoons so as not to break skin. Put on a platter as they brown. Discard fat in Dutch ovens.

Pour boiling water over onions and simmer 5 minutes. Drain. Cover carrots with cold water, bring to a boil and drain immediately. Trim and wash 1 lb. mushrooms, leaving them whole if they are small, cutting into halves if large.

Heat 3 tbsp. butter or margarine in each of the Dutch ovens. Return bits of pork to pans, dividing them evenly. Add half the mushrooms to each pan and cook quickly until lightly browned. Lift out mushrooms and set aside until needed.

Add 4 game hens to each pan with breast side up. Add half of onions and half of carrots and 1 cup wine to each pan.

Make 2 *bouquets garnis* by tying in each of 2 pieces of cheesecloth 2 sprigs parsley, 1 bunch celery leaves, $1/2$ small bay leaf and $1/4$ tsp. thyme.

Add one of these *bouquets garnis* to each pan. Lay a sheet of aluminum foil closely over hens in each pan, then cover pans tightly. Bring to a boil, turn down heat and simmer 30 minutes. Uncover and turn birds twice during this 30 minute cooking.

Add mushrooms and continue cooking, covered, 15 minutes. Sprinkle 1 tsp. salt over birds in each pan. Divide peas between 2 pans. Cover and cook until everything is tender, about 10 minutes.

Drizzle with $1/4$ cup melted butter or margarine. Sprinkle with chopped parsley. Serve immediately. (Serves 8.)

*$1/2$ cup soft butter or margarine*
*2 tbsp. finely chopped parsley*
*$1/2$ tsp. salt*
*$1/8$ tsp. black pepper*
*$1/4$ cup finely chopped fresh mushrooms*
*8 frozen game hens (12 to 16 oz. each), thawed*
*2 tbsp. butter or margarine*
*$1/4$ lb. salt pork*
*24 small white onions*
*32 tiny new carrots (or use strips of large carrots)*
*1 lb. (2 pt.) small whole fresh mushrooms*
*6 tbsp. butter or margarine*
*2 cups dry white wine*
*4 sprigs parsley*
*2 bunches celery leaves*
*1 small bay leaf, broken in half*
*$1/2$ tsp. dried leaf thyme*
*2 tsp. salt*
*2 lb. fresh peas, shelled*
*$1/4$ cup melted butter or margarine*
*chopped parsley*

### Scandinavian Roast Goose

12-oz. pkg. pitted prunes
giblets
10- to 12-lb. goose
1 tbsp. salt
black pepper
2 lb. apples, peeled, cored
   and quartered
6 tbsp. cold water
$^1/_4$ cup flour
2 or 3 tart apples, cored and
   sliced in $^1/_2$-inch-thick rings
salt and pepper
2 tbsp. butter or margarine
2 tbsp. brown sugar
cooked pitted prunes

Soak 12-oz. pkg. prunes in boiling water to cover until prunes are plump, about 30 minutes. Drain and cut into halves.

Simmer giblets in boiling salted water to cover until tender, about $1^1/_2$ hours. Drain, saving broth, and chop giblets finely. Refrigerate both broth and giblets to use for gravy.

Heat oven to 425°F.

Remove all fat from inside goose. Rub inside and out with 1 tbsp. salt. Sprinkle inside generously with pepper. Stuff with apple and prune pieces. Truss as usual.

Put on a rack in a roasting pan. Roast 30 minutes. Remove from oven and reduce oven temperature to 325°F. Drain all fat from roasting pan.

Return goose to oven and continue roasting, allowing about 25 minutes a pound total cooking time. Remove fat from pan as it accumulates. Turn goose a few times after the first hour of roasting, finishing by roasting it 15 minutes back side up. Spoon 3 tbsp. of the cold water over goose at beginning of this 15 minute roasting. Turn breast side up and spoon remaining 3 tbsp. cold water over goose. Roast 10 minutes more. (Scandinavians suggest this water treatment to crisp the skin.)

Check drumstick — if it moves easily, goose is done. Turn off oven and leave bird standing 15 minutes with door partly open to make carving easier.

Put goose on a hot platter. Drain almost all fat from pan. Stir flour into fat left in pan and let bubble up and brown lightly, stirring constantly. Remove from heat and stir in 3 cups of the giblet broth. Return to heat and stir until boiling.

Add enough of remaining giblet broth or hot water to make a thin gravy. Turn down heat and simmer 5 minutes. Add chopped giblets. Heat and add salt and pepper to taste.

Fry apple rings lightly in butter or margarine in a heavy skillet, turning once. Sprinkle rings with brown sugar and centre them with cooked prunes. Use to garnish platter. (The fruit in the goose may absorb too much fat to be edible.) Serve immediately with giblet gravy.

## Coq au Vin

Cover cubes of salt pork with boiling water and let stand 5 minutes. Drain and dry on paper toweling.

Heat a large heavy saucepan or Dutch oven and add pork bits. Fry until golden brown and crisp. Lift out with a slotted spoon and drain on paper toweling.

Add ¼ cup butter or margarine to pan and heat. Add chicken pieces, a few at a time, and brown lightly. Remove as they brown.

Drain fat from pan into a small container after all chicken is browned. Return chicken pieces to pan, pour brandy over and flame by lighting brandy with a long match. When flame dies out remove chicken from pan again and drain off and save any drippings left in pan.

Return 2 tbsp. of the fat drained off earlier to pan and heat. Add onions and cook, turning often, until lightly browned. Return chicken pieces and brandy drippings to pan. Add wine, chicken stock and seasonings. Cover and simmer until chicken is tender, 30 to 45 minutes.

While chicken is cooking, fry slices of French bread in a heavy skillet in 2 tbsp. butter or margarine until golden.

Wash mushrooms and remove stems (save for another dish). Dry caps well on paper toweling. Heat 2 tbsp. butter or margarine in a heavy skillet. Add mushroom caps and cook over high heat, stirring, until lightly browned. Sprinkle lightly with salt, pepper and lemon juice. Add to chicken and cook 5 minutes.

Put chicken pieces, onions and mushrooms on a large hot platter and keep hot in low oven. Boil broth left in pan hard until reduced to about half the volume. Combine ⅓ cup water and flour, blending until smooth. Stir into boiling broth gradually. Turn down heat and cook gently, stirring, 3 minutes.

Pour sauce over chicken and vegetables. Garnish platter with fried bread and sprinkle salt pork bits over all. (Serves 6 to 8.)

6 oz. salt pork, cut in very small cubes
¼ cup butter or margarine
two 2½-lb. chickens, cut up
¼ cup brandy
18 small silver onions, peeled
2 cups dry red wine
2 cups chicken stock (recipe p. 48)
2 cloves garlic, crushed
1 tsp. salt
6 peppercorns
1 bay leaf
½ tsp. dried leaf thyme
6 to 8 small slices French bread, cut 1 inch thick
2 tbsp. butter or margarine
½ lb. (1 pt.) fresh mushrooms
2 tbsp. butter or margarine
salt and pepper
1 tsp. lemon juice
⅓ cup cold water
¼ cup flour

## Old-Fashioned Pressed Chicken

Put chickens in a large kettle. Add all remaining ingredients. Bring to a boil, lower heat, cover and simmer until chicken is very tender, about 1½ hours.

Remove chicken from kettle and cool. Strain chicken stock, return to kettle and boil hard, uncovered, until reduced to about half the volume.

Take meat off bones and break it up into small pieces. Add to reduced chicken stock and simmer 5 minutes.

Set a large glass loaf pan, at least 9 × 5 × 3 inches, in another pan. (Lower pan will catch any overflow.) Pour chicken mixture into loaf pan. (If you have too much, make another small loaf, but pan should be filled solidly right to top with chicken.)

Cut a piece of heavy cardboard just the size of the inside of the loaf pan. Wrap it in heavy aluminum foil. Set it on top of chicken and weight it (use cans of food, a brick, an iron or anything heavy wrapped in foil).

Chill several hours or overnight. Cut into thick slices to serve. (Serves 8 to 12.)

three 3½-lb. chickens, cut up
8 cups boiling water
2 tbsp. salt
1 large carrot, cut up
1 cup coarsely chopped celery with leaves
12 sprigs parsley
¾ tsp. dried leaf savory
1 medium onion, peeled and sliced

## Chicken Cutlets

**3 whole chicken breasts,**
   **cut in half to make 6 sides**
**2 tbsp. flour**
**$1/2$ tsp. paprika**
**$1/2$ tsp. salt**
**$1/8$ tsp. black pepper**
**$1/4$ cup butter or cooking oil**
**1 cup light cream**
**2 tbsp. dry sherry**
**$1/2$ tsp. grated lemon rind**
**$1 1/2$ tsp. lemon juice**
**$1/2$ cup grated Gruyère cheese**
**$1/4$ cup chopped parsley**

Bone and skin chicken pieces. Put each of the 6 thick pieces of chicken between 2 sheets of waxed paper, skinned side up, and pound with a rolling pin to make chicken pieces a little larger and thinner.

Combine flour, paprika, salt and pepper on a piece of waxed paper. Dip chicken pieces in mixture to coat both sides.

Heat butter or oil in a large heavy skillet. Cook chicken pieces in hot fat until they are dark golden brown and tender, 5 to 7 minutes a side.

Push chicken pieces to one side of skillet and sprinkle any flour left over from coating chicken into drippings in skillet. Stir to blend well. Stir in cream gradually.

Add sherry, lemon rind and lemon juice and stir to blend well. Sprinkle cheese over chicken pieces. Cover skillet and heat until cheese melts, about 2 minutes.

Put chicken pieces on a hot serving platter and pour the sauce over. Sprinkle with parsley and serve immediately. (Serves 3 to 6.)

Advance preparation: Bone, skin and flatten chicken pieces and refrigerate with waxed paper between until needed.

## Stuffed Chicken Breast

**1 large whole chicken breast,**
   **cut in half**
**2 tbsp. butter or margarine**
**1 tbsp. finely chopped onion**
**1 tbsp. finely chopped celery**
   **leaves**
**2 cups day-old bread cubes**
**$1/4$ tsp. salt**
**dash black pepper**
**1 tsp. dried leaf parsley**
**$1/2$ tsp. poultry seasoning**
**pinch dried leaf marjoram**
**salt and pepper**
**paprika**
**2 tbsp. melted butter or**
   **margarine**

Bone and skin chicken pieces. Put both of the thick pieces of chicken between 2 sheets of waxed paper, skinned side up, and pound with a rolling pin to make chicken pieces a little larger and thinner.

Heat oven to 350°F. Butter a shallow baking dish just large enough to hold 1 chicken piece. Put chicken piece in dish, skinned side down.

Heat 2 tbsp. butter or margarine in a small skillet over moderate heat. Add onion and celery leaves and stir 3 minutes. Add half of the bread cubes and continue stirring until cubes are coated with butter or margarine and lightly browned. Add to remaining bread cubes along with $1/4$ tsp. salt, dash pepper, parsley, poultry seasoning and marjoram.

Toss stuffing together, then spread on chicken piece in baking dish. Lay the other piece of chicken on top, skinned side up. Press edges of pieces together to seal. Sprinkle lightly with salt and pepper and generously with paprika. Pour melted butter or margarine over all.

Bake chicken 30 minutes, then turn it and sprinkle with more salt, pepper and paprika. Add a little more melted butter or margarine if pan is dry. Continue baking until very tender, about 30 minutes, basting often with drippings in pan or extra butter or margarine. Cut into halves to serve. (Serves 2.)

Advance preparation: Bone, skin and flatten chicken pieces. Refrigerate with waxed paper between until needed. Prepare stuffing and refrigerate.

## Chicken in a Chemise

Cream 1 cup butter or margarine and cheese together well. Add flour and $1/2$ tsp. salt and mix with a fork until blended. Gather into a ball, wrap in waxed paper and chill.

Bone and skin chicken pieces. Put each of the 8 thick pieces of chicken between 2 sheets of waxed paper, skinned side up, and pound with a rolling pin to make chicken pieces a little larger and thinner.

Lay out chicken pieces, skinned side down. Sprinkle lightly with salt and pepper.

Wash shrimp and put in a small saucepan. Add wine, bring to a boil, turn down heat and simmer 5 minutes. Strain, setting wine aside for sauce. Shell, devein and chop shrimp.

Heat 3 tbsp. butter or margarine in a medium saucepan over high heat. Add onions and mushrooms and stir 3 minutes. Reduce heat to moderate and sprinkle in flour, $1/2$ tsp. salt, $1/8$ tsp. pepper and tarragon. Stir to blend. Remove from heat and stir in reserved wine. Return to heat and stir until boiling, thickened and smooth. Stir in parsley and remove from heat. Add 2 tbsp. of mixture to shrimp, blending well.

Divide shrimp mixture evenly among chicken pieces (a heaping tablespoonful each), placing it toward one end. Fold other end over stuffing and press around edges to seal meat to itself.

Heat $1/4$ cup butter or margarine in a large skillet over moderate heat and add chicken pieces. Cook until lightly browned, about 2 minutes a side. Cool.

Heat oven to 425°F. Have ready a large cookie sheet.

Divide cream cheese pastry into 8 equal pieces and roll each piece into a thin oval large enough to wrap around a piece of chicken to make a turnover. After wrapping each, crimp pastry edges to seal. Put on cookie sheet.

Beat egg yolk and 1 tsp. water together with a fork and brush over each turnover (not on edges). Prick tops. Bake until well browned, 15 to 20 minutes.

While turnovers are baking, heat remainder of onion-mushroom mixture and stir in cream. Serve chicken hot, topped with this sauce. (Serves 8.)

1 cup soft butter or margarine
250 g pkg. cream cheese
  (room temperature)
$1^3/4$ cups sifted all-purpose
  flour
$1/2$ tsp. salt
4 medium-size whole chicken
  breasts, cut in half to make
  8 sides
salt and pepper
$1/2$ lb. raw shrimp
1 cup dry white wine
3 tbsp. butter or margarine
3 green onions, finely chopped
8 large mushrooms, finely
  chopped
3 tbsp. flour
$1/2$ tsp. salt
$1/8$ tsp. black pepper
pinch dried leaf tarragon
$1/4$ cup finely chopped parsley
$1/4$ cup butter or margarine
1 egg yolk
1 tsp. water
$1/2$ cup light cream

## Spicy Chicken Wings

3 lb. large chicken wings
1/4 cup red wine vinegar
4 tsp. sugar
2 tsp. dry mustard
2 tsp. chili powder
2 tsp. salt
1 tsp. black pepper
1/8 tsp. crushed dried red pepper
pinch dried leaf tarragon
2 cups water
2 tbsp. Worcestershire sauce
dash Tabasco
2 tbsp. very finely chopped onion
2 cloves garlic, crushed
1/4 cup butter or margarine

Wash chicken wings and separate them at the joints, making 3 pieces from each wing.

Put wing tips in the freezer to add to soup kettle next time you are brewing up stock. This leaves 2 pieces from each wing (The wings I use are frozen and quite large. About 16 chicken wings will make the 3 lb. called for in this recipe, so I end up with about 32 pieces.)

Combine vinegar, sugar, mustard, chili powder, salt, pepper, red pepper and tarragon in a medium saucepan and blend until smooth. Stir in 2 cups water, Worcestershire, Tabasco, onion and garlic. Bring to a boil, turn down heat and simmer 5 minutes. Cool.

Put chicken wing pieces in a baking dish large enough to hold them in a single layer, at least 13 × 9 × 2 inches, and pour the spicy mixture over. Let stand at room temperature 1 hour, turning often.

Heat oven to 400°F.

Lift chicken pieces out of marinade, shaking off any excess. Drain marinade from baking dish into a saucepan. Wipe out baking dish and put butter or margarine in dish. Set in oven until butter or margarine is melted.

Remove from oven and put chicken pieces into dish in a single layer. Return dish to oven and bake 25 minutes. Turn chicken pieces and bake until chicken is very tender and lightly browned, about 15 minutes more.

Heat marinade when chicken is ready for serving and put a little of the spicy mixture in 6 small dishes. Serve 4 or 5 pieces of the chicken and some of the dipping sauce to each person. (Serves 6.)

Advance preparation: Separate wings and put them in marinade. Refrigerate up to 24 hours, turning pieces occasionally.

## Honey-Garlic Wings

1/2 cup liquid honey
1/4 cup lemon juice
1/2 cup water
3 tbsp. ketchup
2 cloves garlic, crushed
1 tsp. salt
1 tsp. ground ginger
3 lb. chicken wings
1/4 cup butter or margarine

Heat honey, lemon juice, 1/2 cup water, ketchup, garlic, salt and ginger just to boiling. Pour into a 13 × 9 × 2-inch baking dish.

Separate chicken wings at the joints, making 3 pieces from each wing. Put wing tips in a bag and freeze to add to soup kettle. Add remaining pieces to baking pan, turning them over in marinade. Let stand several hours, turning pieces often.

Heat oven to 400°F.

Lift chicken from marinade, shaking pieces to remove excess liquid, and set aside. Pour marinade into a small saucepan.

Put butter or margarine in drained pan and set in oven until butter or margarine is melted. Put wings in pan, turning them over in butter or margarine, then bake 25 minutes. Turn pieces and bake until tender, about 20 minutes more. Heat marinade and use as a dip. (Serves 4 to 6.)

## Hawaiian Wings

Heat oven to 400°F. Put butter or margarine in a 13 × 9 × 2-inch baking dish and set in oven to melt.

Separate chicken wings at the joints, making 3 pieces from each wing. Put wing tips in a bag and freeze to add to soup kettle.

Combine ketchup and garlic. Brush mixture on separated wings, then roll pieces in bread crumbs to coat all sides. Put in baking dish, turning them over in butter or margarine. Bake 30 minutes.

Remove pan from oven and turn chicken pieces. Drain pineapple, measuring juice. If necessary, add water to make ³/₄ cup liquid. Combine with molasses, lemon juice, ginger and Worcestershire and pour over wings.

Bake until chicken is very tender, about 30 minutes, adding pineapple chunks for last 5 minutes. Serve with rice. (Serves 4 to 6.)

Advance preparation: Separate wings and refrigerate until they are needed.

¹/₃ cup butter or margarine
³/₄ cup ketchup
1 small clove garlic, crushed
3 lb. chicken wings
1 cup fine dry bread crumbs (approx.)
14-oz. can unsweetened pineapple chunks
¹/₃ cup molasses
1 tbsp. lemon juice
¹/₂ tsp. ground ginger
1 tbsp. Worcestershire sauce
hot cooked rice

## Salmon and Cucumber Sauce

Combine 2 cups water, wine, bay leaf and peppercorns in a large skillet. Bring to a boil and add salmon steaks. Return liquid to just under the boil, turn down heat, cover and simmer 5 minutes.

Turn steaks, cover again and simmer 5 minutes. (If steaks are less than 1 inch thick, cook them less time. The rule is 10 minutes cooking for each inch of thickness. Steaks are done when they turn a pale, opaque pink and flake easily with a fork.)

Lift steaks out of water and drain well. Put on a plate, sprinkle lightly with salt and chill.

Combine remaining ingredients except lettuce and lemon wedges. Blend well and chill.

Put a steak on a bed of lettuce on each of 4 plates at serving time. Garnish with lemon wedges and top with a little of the cucumber mixture. (Serves 4.)

*Note:* You can replace wine and water used for poaching the salmon with 3 cups water and 2 tbsp. lemon juice.

2 cups water
1 cup dry white wine (see note)
small piece bay leaf
4 peppercorns
4 salmon steaks, 1 inch thick
salt
1 cup coarsely grated unpeeled cucumber, drained and dried on paper toweling
¹/₂ cup plain yogurt
¹/₄ cup mayonnaise
1 tbsp. finely chopped parsley
2 tsp. grated onion
2 tsp. white vinegar
¹/₂ tsp. salt
dash black pepper
lettuce
lemon wedges

## Salmon Steaks with Vermouth Sauce

1 cup white vermouth
$1/4$ tsp. salt
6 small salmon steaks
4 egg yolks, lightly beaten
$2/3$ cup very cold butter
1 tbsp. light cream
paprika (optional)

Heat vermouth to simmering in a large skillet. Add salt. Put salmon steaks in pan in a single layer, cover and simmer until fish is done, about 10 minutes. Lift out salmon steaks and put on a serving dish that can go under the broiler. Keep fish hot.

Boil liquid in pan very hard until reduced to half the volume. Turn heat to low. Beat half of hot liquid into egg yolks gradually. Return mixture to pan.

Add half of butter and cook over lowest heat until butter melts. Add remaining butter and cream and stir over low heat until butter melts and sauce is thick.

Pour sauce over salmon steaks, sprinkle with paprika and broil until lightly browned, 1 to 2 minutes. (Serves 6.)

## Broiled Ocean Perch

2 lb. frozen ocean perch
salt
$1/2$ cup butter or margarine
1 tsp. paprika
$1/2$ tsp. black pepper
2 tbsp. finely chopped chives
2 tbsp. finely chopped parsley
$1/4$ tsp. dried leaf tarragon
2 tsp. lemon juice

Thaw fish enough so pieces can be separated.

Heat broiler. Oil a large broiler pan.

Lay fish pieces, skin side down, on broiler pan. Sprinkle lightly with salt.

Cream butter or margarine. Stir in paprika, pepper, chives, parsley, tarragon and lemon juice, blending well. Spread mixture over pieces of fish.

Broil 6 to 8 inches from heat just until fish flakes easily with a fork, about 6 minutes. Do not turn. Serve immediately. (Serves 6.)

## Broiled Mackerel

two 1-lb. mackerel
3 tbsp. butter or margarine, melted
salt and pepper
lemon wedges
Mustard Sauce (recipe follows)

Have fish heads removed and fish cleaned and split. Rinse fish and pat dry with paper toweling.

Oil a broiler pan. Spread fish open and put on pan, skin side down. Brush generously with melted butter or margarine. Put close to hot broiler and broil about 6 minutes, brushing once more with melted butter or margarine. Fish is done when it flakes easily with a fork. Sprinkle with salt and pepper.

Put fish on a hot platter or on 2 dinner plates and garnish with lemon wedges. Pass the Mustard Sauce. (Serves 2.)

## Mustard Sauce

2 tbsp. butter or margarine
$1^{1}/2$ tbsp. flour
$1/4$ tsp. salt
$1/8$ tsp. black pepper
$2/3$ cup milk
2 tsp. chopped parsley
$1^{1}/2$ tsp. Dijon mustard
dash Tabasco

Melt butter or margarine in a small saucepan. Sprinkle in flour, salt and pepper. Stir to blend. Remove from heat and stir in milk all at once. Return to heat and stir until boiling, thickened and smooth. Stir in parsley, mustard and Tabasco. Keep warm to serve with fish. (Makes about $2/3$ cup.)

## Herbed Fillets

1 cup soda biscuit crumbs
  (see note)
1/2 tsp. salt
1/4 tsp. black pepper
1 tbsp. chopped parsley
1/4 tsp. dried leaf tarragon or
  1 tbsp. chopped fresh dill
1/2 cup milk
1/3 cup flour
1/2 tsp. paprika
6 fresh fillets of sole
1/4 cup butter or margarine
3 tbsp. cooking oil

Combine soda biscuit crumbs, salt, pepper, parsley and tarragon or dill in a flat dish (a pie plate is good). Put milk in another flat dish and blend flour and paprika in a third flat dish.

Wash fish and dip each piece first in flour mixture, then in milk and finally in crumbs to coat both sides well.

Heat butter or margarine and oil in a large skillet. Add fish and fry quickly just until well browned on both sides. Serve immediately. (Serves 6.)

Note: Do not roll the biscuits to make the crumbs. Just crush them with the hand so they aren't too fine. I find if they are a little coarser than fine bread crumbs they lift the fish from the pan during frying and act as insulation so the fish cooks through without being overcooked.

## Fillets of Sole Jeannine

1 lb. fresh or frozen fillets
  of sole
salt and pepper
1 tbsp. butter or margarine
1 tsp. curry powder
1 tbsp. finely chopped green
  onion
1 cup sliced mushrooms
1 tbsp. flour
1/2 tsp. salt
1/4 tsp. black pepper
2 large tomatoes, peeled,
  seeded and chopped
1 cup dry white wine
1 cup light cream, heated
  to scalding
2/3 cup fine dry bread crumbs
2/3 cup grated Swiss cheese

Thaw fish if necessary until the fillets can be separated easily.

Heat oven to 350°F. Butter a 12 × 7 × 2-inch baking dish.

Lay fish fillets in baking dish in a single layer. Sprinkle lightly with salt and pepper.

Heat butter or margarine in a medium saucepan. Add curry powder and cook gently 3 minutes, stirring. Add green onion and mushrooms and continue stirring 3 minutes more.

Sprinkle in flour, 1/2 tsp. salt and 1/4 tsp. pepper and stir to blend. Remove from heat. Add tomatoes and wine. Stir to blend. Set over moderate heat and cook, stirring, until slightly thickened and tomatoes have cooked into a sauce. Continue cooking slowly, stirring often, until quite thick. Stir in hot cream. Pour over fish.

Cover baking dish with aluminum foil and bake until fish flakes easily with a fork, 15 to 20 minutes. Remove baking dish from oven and uncover. Turn on broiler.

Combine bread crumbs and cheese and sprinkle over all. Slip under broiler to brown lightly (watch carefully so crumbs don't burn). Serve immediately. (Serves 4.)

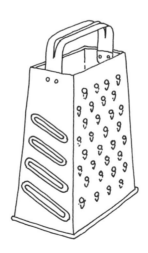

## Mediterranean Fish Pie

Wash fish and dry well. Cut into pieces about 1 inch wide by 1½ inches long. Combine flour, salt and pepper in a flat dish (a pie plate is good) and roll fish in this mixture to coat all sides.

Heat ¼ cup olive oil in a large heavy skillet. Fry fish pieces quickly until very lightly browned but still firm, about 3 minutes. Lift out fish pieces as they are ready.

Add 2 tbsp. olive oil to skillet after all fish has been taken out. Add onion and cook 3 minutes, stirring constantly.

Add tomatoes and garlic and stir 5 minutes. Add spinach, parsley, olives, salt, pepper, tarragon and lemon juice, cover pan and cook quickly 1 minute. Uncover and stir until spinach is limp, about 2 minutes more. Cool.

Line a 9-inch pie pan with half the pastry. Put pieces of fish in pastry-lined pan and spoon tomato mixture over. Top with remaining pastry. Seal and flute edge.

Heat oven to 425°F.

Beat egg yolk and 1 tbsp. water together lightly with a fork and brush over top crust (not on edge). Cut slashes in top of pie to allow steam to escape. Put a strip of aluminum foil around pie to cover fluted pastry edge and keep it from browning too much.

Bake until pie is well browned on top and bottom, about 1 hour. Serve hot. (Serves 6.)

2 lb. halibut steaks,
cut 1 inch thick
¼ cup flour
½ tsp. salt
dash black pepper
¼ cup olive oil
2 tbsp. olive oil
2 medium onions, thinly sliced
4 large tomatoes, peeled,
seeded and chopped
1 clove garlic, crushed
10-oz. bag fresh spinach,
washed and torn up
¼ cup finely chopped parsley
¼ cup sliced stuffed olives
1½ tsp. salt
¼ tsp. black pepper
⅛ tsp. dried leaf tarragon
(optional)
1 tbsp. lemon juice
pastry for 2-crust 9-inch pie
(recipe p. 172)
1 egg yolk
1 tbsp. water

## Cod in Milk

Cut fish into serving-size pieces. Heat milk, salt, bay leaf, peppercorns and clove to boiling in a large skillet. Add fish pieces and bring to simmering. Lower heat, cover and simmer until fish flakes easily with a fork, about 5 minutes. Lift fish out with an egg turner and put on a hot platter. Keep warm.

Melt butter or margarine in a small saucepan over low heat. Add 1 tbsp. of the green onions and stir 3 minutes. Sprinkle in flour and pepper and stir to blend. Remove from heat. Stir in fish cooking liquid.

Return pan to heat and stir sauce until boiling, thickened and smooth. Stir in lemon juice. Pour over fish and sprinkle with remaining green onions. Serve immediately. (Serves 3.)

1 lb. cod fillets
1¼ cups skim milk
½ tsp. salt
small piece bay leaf
3 peppercorns
1 whole clove
2 tbsp. butter or margarine
2 tbsp. chopped green onions
2 tbsp. flour
⅛ tsp. black pepper
1 tsp. lemon juice

## Indian Ocean Fish Curry

2 lb. fillets of any firm white fish (cod or haddock are fine)
1/4 cup cooking oil
1 onion, chopped
2 cloves garlic, peeled and finely chopped
1/4 tsp. crushed dried red pepper
1 tsp. ground coriander
1/2 tsp. chili powder
1/2 tsp. ground turmeric
1/2 tsp. crushed mustard seeds
1 cup Coconut Milk (recipe follows)
1 tsp. rice flour
2 tbsp. lemon juice
hot cooked rice

Wash fish and cut into 1 1/2-inch squares. Dry well on paper toweling.

Heat oil in a large heavy skillet. Add onion and garlic and cook gently 3 minutes, stirring. Add red pepper, coriander, chili powder, turmeric and mustard seeds.

Put a little of the 1 cup coconut milk in a small dish. Add rice flour and stir to blend.

Add remaining coconut milk to skillet, bring to a boil and stir in rice flour mixture gradually. Add lemon juice. Stir until slightly thickened. Add fish pieces and spoon sauce over fish. Cover and simmer until fish is tender, about 5 minutes. Serve with rice. (Serves 4.)

## Coconut Milk

1 small coconut
2 cups boiling water

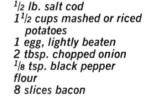

Heat oven to 350°F.

Put coconut in oven and heat 30 minutes. Cool. Punch in eyes of coconut with a screwdriver or ice pick and drain. (Save the liquid to drink later.) Break coconut and loosen meat. Peel brown skin off meat and cut meat into small pieces. Put coconut a little at a time into glass of blender and buzz until grated.

Put grated coconut in a bowl and add 2 cups boiling water. Cover tightly and let stand until lukewarm, about 30 minutes.

Line a sieve with several thicknesses of cheesecloth and pour in the coconut mixture. Twist cheesecloth to squeeze out all liquid. This liquid is the coconut milk called for in many curry recipes. Discard coconut.

Measure out the 1 cup coconut milk needed for fish curry recipe and refrigerate remainder to use for another curry.

## Cod Cakes

1/2 lb. salt cod
1 1/2 cups mashed or riced potatoes
1 egg, lightly beaten
2 tbsp. chopped onion
1/8 tsp. black pepper
flour
8 slices bacon

Soak salt cod overnight in cold water. Drain, add fresh water and bring to a boil over high heat. Lower heat and simmer 15 minutes. Drain and flake fish.

Combine potatoes, egg, onion and pepper. Blend in flaked fish with a fork. Shape mixture into 4 thick cakes. Dip in flour to coat both sides.

Fry bacon until crisp. Lift out of pan and keep warm. Drain all but about 2 tbsp. of bacon fat from pan. Fry cakes until golden brown on both sides and very hot, adding more bacon fat if needed. Serve with bacon. (Serves 4.)

## Shrimp and Scallop Curry

Heat butter or margarine in a medium saucepan over low heat. Add onion and curry powder and cook gently 5 minutes, stirring often. Sprinkle in flour and stir 2 minutes.

Remove from heat, add cream and stir to blend. Add bouillon cube and return to moderate heat. Bring to a boil and stir in cayenne and chutney. Lower heat and simmer 5 minutes. Set pan aside.

Shortly before serving time, heat wine to boiling in a medium saucepan. Add scallops, cover, lower heat and simmer 3 minutes. Add shrimp, cover and simmer 5 minutes more. Stir in curry mixture and lemon juice. Heat and taste, adding more salt or lemon juice if needed. Sprinkle in parsley. Serve over rice. (Serves 4.)

*2 tbsp. butter or margarine*
*1 small onion, chopped*
*1 to 2 tbsp. curry powder*
*1 tbsp. flour*
*2/3 cup light cream*
*1 chicken bouillon cube*
*dash cayenne*
*1 tbsp. chopped fruit from chutney*
*1/2 cup dry white wine*
*1 lb. scallops, cut in half if very large*
*1/2 lb. medium shrimp, shelled and deveined*
*2 tsp. lemon juice*
*2 tbsp. chopped parsley*
*hot cooked rice*

## Scampi in Creamy Wine Sauce

Combine flour, 1/2 tsp. salt and grating of pepper and roll scampi in mixture. Heat butter or margarine in a heavy skillet over moderate heat. Add scampi and cook gently 5 minutes, turning often. Sprinkle in any flour left from coating scampi, stirring to blend.

Remove from heat and stir in cream and wine. Add parsley and tarragon, return to heat and cook until sauce is thick. Add salt and pepper to taste. Serve immediately on rice. (Serves 3.)

*3 tbsp. flour*
*1/2 tsp. salt*
*good grating fresh black pepper*
*1 lb. medium scampi, thawed and shelled, with back vein removed*
*1/4 cup butter or margarine*
*3/4 cup light cream*
*2 tbsp. dry white wine*
*2 tbsp. chopped parsley*
*1/4 tsp. dried leaf tarragon*
*salt and pepper*
*hot cooked rice*

## Baked Vegetable Loaf

Cook potatoes and carrots in a small amount of boiling water until barely tender. Drain, saving cooking water. Measure cooking liquid and add water, if necessary, to make 1/2 cup. Bring this liquid to a boil, remove from heat, add bouillon cube and stir until cube is dissolved.

Heat oven to 350°F. Grease a 9 × 5 × 3-inch glass loaf pan.

Combine all ingredients except Mushroom Sauce and spoon into prepared pan. Bake until set, about 1 hour. Cut into thick slices to serve. Top slices with Mushroom Sauce. (Serves 4.)

*1 1/2 cups diced raw potatoes*
*2 cups diced raw carrots*
*1 vegetable or beef bouillon cube*
*1/4 cup finely chopped green pepper*
*1/4 cup finely chopped onion*
*1 cup toasted wheat germ*
*1/4 cup melted butter or margarine*
*2 eggs, lightly beaten*
*1 tsp. salt*
*1/4 tsp. black pepper*
*1/2 tsp. dried leaf savory*
*Mushroom Sauce (recipe follows)*

## Mushroom Sauce

1/4 cup butter or margarine
1/2 lb. (1 pt.) fresh
 mushrooms, sliced
2 tbsp. flour
1 1/2 cups milk
1 tsp. salt
1/4 tsp. black pepper

Heat butter or margarine in a saucepan. Add mushrooms and cook gently 3 minutes, stirring. Sprinkle in flour and stir to blend. Remove from heat and add milk all at once. Add salt and pepper and stir to blend. Return to heat and cook, stirring constantly, until boiling, thickened and smooth. Turn heat to low and continue stirring 5 minutes. (Makes about 2 cups.)

## Soybean-Nut Loaf

2 cups soybeans
1 cup cooked brown rice
1/4 cup toasted wheat germ
1 cup Tomato Sauce
 (recipe follows)
1 cup finely chopped celery
1/2 small onion, chopped
1/2 small clove garlic, crushed
 (optional)
1/2 cup chopped peanuts or
 almonds
1 tsp. salt
1/4 tsp. black pepper
1/2 tsp. dried leaf savory

Wash and look over beans. Cover with cold water and bring to a boil. Boil 2 minutes. Let stand 1 hour.

Bring beans and soaking water to a boil, turn down heat, cover and simmer until very tender, about 3 hours. Add water if necessary during cooking. Drain.

Heat oven to 350°F. Put a pan of hot water in oven.

Mash beans very well and combine with remaining ingredients. Put in a 9 × 5 × 3-inch glass loaf pan and cover with aluminum foil. Set in pan of hot water in oven and bake 45 minutes. Uncover and bake 30 minutes more. Serve with remaining sauce. (Serves 6 to 8.)

Advance preparation: Cook and mash beans and prepare Tomato Sauce. Refrigerate until ready to complete loaf.

## Tomato Sauce

28-oz. can tomatoes
1 tbsp. cooking oil
1/2 cup chopped onion
1/2 cup chopped green pepper
1 tsp. sugar
1 tsp. salt
1/8 tsp. black pepper
1 tsp. dried leaf basil
1/4 tsp. dried leaf savory

Drain tomatoes, saving juice, and chop pulp finely.

Heat oil in a medium saucepan. Add onion and green pepper and cook gently, stirring, 3 minutes. Add saved tomato juice and all remaining ingredients except tomato pieces.

Cook gently, uncovered, until quite thick. Stir in tomato pieces. (Makes 2 1/2 to 3 cups.)

## Split Pea Loaf

1 lb. green split peas
1 medium onion, chopped
6 cups cold water
1 1/2 tsp. salt
1/4 tsp. black pepper
1/2 tsp. dried leaf marjoram
dash ground nutmeg
1/3 cup wheat germ
2 eggs, beaten
Tomato Sauce
 (see Soybean-Nut Loaf)

Put peas in a large saucepan with onion and 6 cups water. Bring to a boil, lower heat, cover and simmer until peas are tender, about 1 1/4 hours. Drain, saving water to add to a soup stock.

Heat oven to 350°F. Grease a 9 × 5 × 3-inch glass loaf pan.

Buzz pea mixture in glass of blender until smooth, adding 1/4 cup of cooking water if peas are too dry to blend. Combine with remaining ingredients except sauce. Pour into prepared pan and bake until set in the middle, about 1 1/4 hours. Cool a few minutes, turn out and cut into thick slices to serve. Pass the Tomato Sauce. (Serves 6.)

Advance preparation: Cook and mash peas and prepare Tomato Sauce. Refrigerate until ready to complete loaf.

## Stuffed Cabbage Leaves

1/2 cup brown rice
2 tbsp. cooking oil
1/2 lb. (1 pt.) mushrooms, sliced
1 medium onion, finely chopped
1 1/2 tsp. seasoned salt
1/4 tsp. black pepper
1/2 tsp. dried leaf marjoram
1 large head cabbage
1/4 cup grated Parmesan cheese
14-oz. can tomato sauce
1 tbsp. lemon juice
1/4 cup brown sugar
1 cup water
1/2 tsp. salt
1/4 tsp. black pepper

Cook rice as directed on package.

Heat oil in a large heavy skillet (do not use a black iron one). Add mushrooms and onion and stir 3 minutes. Remove from heat. Add seasoned salt, 1/4 tsp. pepper, marjoram and rice. Stir to blend.

Cut core out of cabbage and pour boiling water into cavity until outer leaves separate from centre easily. Remove 6 of the very large outside leaves, put them in a bowl, cover with boiling water and let stand until leaves are limp enough to roll easily.

Stir Parmesan into rice mixture and divide this mixture evenly among the 6 cabbage leaves. Fold in the sides of the leaves, then roll them so filling is completely enclosed.

Grate or cut very finely enough of the remaining cabbage to make 4 cups. Put it in skillet used to cook mushroom mixture. Add tomato sauce, lemon juice, brown sugar, 1 cup water, salt and 1/4 tsp. pepper and stir over low heat to blend well. Bring to a boil, turn heat down again and add cabbage rolls to sauce.

Cover and simmer until cabbage rolls are hot and tender, about 25 minutes. (Serves 3 to 6.)

Advance preparation: Stuff cabbage leaves and make sauce as directed and refrigerate separately until ready to complete dish. Then reheat sauce, add cabbage rolls and simmer the 25 minutes.

## Lentil and Barley Stew

1/2 lb. dried lentils
4 cups cold water (or saved vegetable cooking water)
1 cup pearl barley
2 tbsp. cooking oil
2 large onions, diced
2 large carrots, scraped and diced
2 potatoes, peeled and diced
1 cup diced celery
1/2 cup diced turnip
28-oz. can tomatoes
2 tsp. salt
1/8 tsp. black pepper
1/2 tsp. dried leaf thyme
1 small bay leaf

Cover lentils with 4 cups cold water or vegetable cooking water in a saucepan. Bring to a boil and boil 2 minutes. Remove from heat and let stand 1 hour.

Rinse barley under cold water.

Heat oil in a large Dutch oven. Add onion and stir 3 minutes. Add lentils, their water, barley and remaining ingredients. Bring to a boil, turn down heat, cover and simmer until everything is very tender, about 2 hours. Stir often and add more water if needed to keep mixture from sticking. (It should be thick.)

Good served with crusty bread and salad. (Serves 6.)

Advance preparation: Make completely, refrigerate and reheat slowly at serving time.

# Salads

Salad may be served with, before or after the main course at dinner. It all depends on your taste. I like salad with the meal if the meal is steak. Otherwise I prefer it after the main dish as a sort of delicious palate clearer. One reason for not serving it with the meal is that wine and salad don't mix. So if wine is on the menu, serve the salad either before or after the wine has been enjoyed.

The salads served with the main meal of the day should be on the light side, and you'll find easy and good dressings here for the usual greens, as well as some salad combinations that make an interesting change from the usual.

## Mimosa Salad

Heat butter or margarine and 2 tbsp. oil in a large heavy skillet. Add garlic and cook gently 1 minute, stirring. Add bread cubes and stir until golden. Lift out bread cubes with a slotted spoon and drain on paper toweling. Discard garlic pieces.

Put salad greens in a large salad bowl. Grind pepper generously over greens and sprinkle lavishly with paprika. Toss very lightly. Add enough of the $1/3$ cup oil so that all the leaves are shiny but there is no excess in the bottom of the bowl. Toss lightly. Add vinegar and toss again lightly.

Toss bread cubes, watercress and $1/2$ tsp. salt with greens. Add more salt and pepper to taste. Press hard-cooked eggs through a sieve all over top of salad. (Serves 6 to 8.)

Advance preparation: Wash greens and store in a plastic bag in the refrigerator with paper toweling between layers. Prepare croutons and cook eggs.

3 tbsp. butter or margarine
2 tbsp. olive oil
2 cloves garlic, peeled and cut in half
3 slices day-old bread, cut in $1/4$-inch cubes
8 cups torn-up mixed salad greens
grating fresh black pepper
paprika (optional)
$1/3$ cup olive oil (approx.)
2 tbsp. red wine vinegar
$1/2$ cup chopped watercress leaves
$1/2$ tsp. salt
salt and pepper
2 hard-cooked eggs

## Red Cabbage Slaw

Cook bacon until crisp in a large skillet. Drain and crumble. Drain most of fat from skillet.

Add cabbage and wine to same skillet. Cook over high heat until cabbage is just limp and wine has nearly cooked away. Put cabbage in a bowl. Add bacon bits, green onions, salt, pepper, sugar, oil and vinegar. Toss to blend well. Serve at room temperature. (Serves 3.)

Advance preparation: This can be made several hours ahead.

3 strips bacon
4 cups finely shredded red cabbage
$1/4$ cup dry white wine
$1/4$ cup thinly sliced green onions
$1/2$ tsp. salt
$1/4$ tsp. black pepper
$1/2$ tsp. sugar
2 tbsp. olive oil
1 tbsp. red wine vinegar

## Lettuce-Pickle Slaw

Slice lettuce coarsely shortly before serving time. Put in a large bowl. Combine remaining ingredients and pour over. Toss thoroughly. Serve immediately. (Serves 6.)

1 medium head iceberg lettuce
1/2 cup mayonnaise
2/3 cup undrained sweet pickle relish
1/4 tsp. seasoned salt
dash black pepper

## Turnip Salad

Combine all vegetables in a medium bowl. Sprinkle lightly with salt and pepper. Combine mayonnaise, French dressing and mustard, add to vegetables and toss lightly. Pile in a lettuce-lined bowl. (Serves 4 to 6.)

Advance preparation: Combine vegetables and cover with transparent wrap. Refrigerate up to 6 hours, then make dressing and combine with vegetables to serve.

2 cups finely grated raw turnip
1 cup finely shredded cabbage
1 cup finely grated carrots
1 cup sliced fresh mushrooms
1/4 cup diced green pepper
1/4 cup diced celery
1 tbsp. grated onion
salt and pepper
1/2 cup mayonnaise
1/4 cup bottled French dressing
1 tsp. prepared mustard
lettuce

## Cheesy Waldorf Salad

Toss all ingredients except lettuce together lightly with a spoon, using only enough of the mayonnaise to coat the ingredients well. Serve in lettuce cups. Very good with cold chicken. (Serves 4 to 6.)

2 1/2 cups cubed unpeeled apple
1 tbsp. lemon juice
1 cup chopped celery
1 cup seeded red grape halves
1 cup 1/4-inch cubes Edam or Gouda cheese
1/2 cup coarsely chopped walnuts
1/3 cup mayonnaise (approx.)
lettuce

## Tomato-Yogurt Salad

Put chopped tomatoes in a sieve and let drain well.

Combine remaining ingredients except lettuce. Fold in tomatoes. Spoon over lettuce wedges. (Serves 6.)

3 medium tomatoes, peeled and finely chopped
1 tbsp. finely chopped parsley
1 tbsp. finely grated onion
1/2 tsp. salt
dash black pepper
1 tsp. Worcestershire sauce
1 tbsp. vinegar
2/3 cup plain yogurt (one 175 g carton)
6 lettuce wedges

## Cucumber and Yogurt

Slice cucumber as thinly as possible (you can peel it or not as you prefer). Put slices in a bowl and sprinkle with 1 tsp. salt. Let stand a few minutes.

Combine yogurt, dill, onion and pepper. Drain cucumber slices, pressing them firmly with the back of a spoon to press out all excess liquid. Return to bowl and add yogurt mixture. Mix lightly. Add salt to taste. Chill. Spoon onto lettuce to serve. (Serves 6.)

1 English cucumber or 2 medium-size regular cucumbers
1 tsp. salt
1 cup plain yogurt
1 tbsp. chopped fresh dill
1 tbsp. finely chopped green onion
dash black pepper
salt
lettuce

## Hot Spinach-Macaroni Salad

Fry bacon until crisp. Add onion to pan and stir until transparent but not browned. Combine flour, sugar, salt and pepper. Stir in vinegar and blend until smooth. Add to bacon mixture with 1$^1$/$_2$ cups water and stir until slightly thickened. Keep hot.

Cook macaroni in plenty of boiling salted water until just tender, about 7 minutes, then drain. Combine hot macaroni, spinach, celery, pickle and pimento and mix well in a large bowl. Pour hot bacon mixture over all and toss to blend. Serve immediately. (Serves 8.)

$^1$/$_2$ lb. bacon, cut in small pieces
1 medium onion, finely chopped
$^1$/$_4$ cup flour
$^1$/$_4$ cup sugar
1 tsp. salt
$^1$/$_4$ tsp. black pepper
$^3$/$_4$ cup white vinegar
1$^1$/$_2$ cups water
500 g pkg. elbow macaroni
two 10-oz. bags spinach, torn up
1 cup chopped celery
$^1$/$_2$ cup chopped dill pickle
2 tbsp. chopped pimento

## Blender Gazpacho Salad

Drain tomatoes, saving liquid and pressing pulp gently to squeeze out excess juice. Measure liquid and add water, if necessary, to make 1$^1$/$_2$ cups. Soak gelatin in $^1$/$_2$ cup of the tomato liquid 5 minutes. Heat remaining tomato liquid to boiling. Add gelatin and stir until gelatin is dissolved. Chill in ice water until beginning to thicken.

Cut up tomato pulp, onion, cucumber and green pepper coarsely. Put them, along with garlic and parsley, a bit at a time into glass of blender and buzz until smooth. Combine blended mixture with vinegar, lemon juice, Tabasco, salt and pepper. Stir into slightly thickened gelatin mixture.

Spoon into individual molds and chill until set. Unmold on lettuce at serving time. Top with a small spoonful of sour cream and a sprinkling of chives if desired. (Serves 6.)

28-oz. can tomatoes
2 envelopes (2 tbsp.) unflavored gelatin
1 medium onion, peeled
1 medium cucumber, peeled
1 medium green pepper, seeded
1 small clove garlic, peeled
$^1$/$_4$ cup coarsely chopped parsley
1 tbsp. red wine vinegar
1 tbsp. lemon juice
dash Tabasco
1$^1$/$_2$ tsp. salt
$^1$/$_8$ tsp. black pepper
lettuce
sour cream (optional)
chopped chives (optional)

139

## Eggs in Jelly

Soak gelatin in ½ cup cold water in a small dish 5 minutes. Set dish in a pan of hot water and heat until gelatin is dissolved. Stir into mayonnaise. Add celery, green pepper, pickle relish, lemon juice, salt, pepper and eggs. Stir slightly to blend and spoon into 8 individual molds. Chill until firm. Unmold at serving time. (Serves 8.)

2 envelopes (2 tbsp.)
   unflavored gelatin
½ cup cold water
2 cups mayonnaise
1 cup finely chopped celery
¼ cup finely chopped green
   pepper
¼ cup well-drained sweet
   pickle relish
2 tbsp. lemon juice
1½ tsp. salt
dash black pepper
8 diced hard-cooked eggs

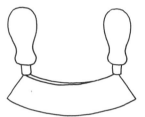

## Jellied Slaw

Combine gelatin and sugar in a medium saucepan, stirring to blend well. Stir in vinegar and lemon juice. Add 2 cups boiling water and salt. Set over low heat and stir until gelatin is completely dissolved. Set pan in ice water and chill until gelatin begins to set. Stir in vegetables.

Pour into a 6-cup mold and chill until set. Unmold on lettuce at serving time. Pass the mayonnaise. (Serves 6.)

2 envelopes (2 tbsp.)
   unflavored gelatin
¼ cup sugar
¼ cup white vinegar
2 tbsp. lemon juice
2 cups boiling water
1 tsp. salt
1½ cups coarsely grated red
   cabbage
1½ cups coarsely grated
   green cabbage
1 green pepper, diced
¼ cup diced pimento
lettuce
mayonnaise

## Cranberry Salad Mold

Soak gelatin in ½ cup water 5 minutes. Heat cranberry juice to boiling, remove from heat and add gelatin. Stir until gelatin is dissolved. Stir in pineapple and its juice and port.

Peel and slice avocado and put slices in the bottom of a 6-cup mold. Add enough of the liquid from the cranberry mixture to just cover avocado slices. Chill until firm but still sticky on top.

Once avocado layer is ready, chill remaining cranberry mixture until beginning to thicken by setting in ice water. Fold in apple and celery. Pour over avocado layer. Chill until firm. Unmold on lettuce. (Serves 8.)

2 envelopes (2 tbsp.)
   unflavored gelatin
½ cup water
2 cups cranberry juice cocktail
14-oz. can pineapple tidbits
¼ cup port wine
1 medium ripe avocado
1 cup peeled, chopped apple
½ cup chopped celery
lettuce

### Tomato Mayonnaise

1 medium tomato
1 cup thick mayonnaise
1 tbsp. finely chopped dill
  pickle
1 tsp. finely chopped parsley
$1/2$ tsp. finely snipped chives
$1/4$ tsp. finely chopped fresh or
  pinch dried leaf basil
$1/4$ tsp. finely chopped
  anchovies

Peel and seed tomato. Chop very finely and dry on paper toweling. Mix all ingredients shortly before serving time and chill until used. Good for any vegetable salad. (Makes about 1 cup.)

### Sesame Dressing

$1/3$ cup olive oil
1 clove garlic, peeled and cut
  in half
1 tbsp. sesame seeds
2 tbsp. red wine vinegar
$1/4$ tsp. salt
dash black pepper

Heat oil in a small skillet. Add garlic and sesame seeds and heat gently, stirring, until seeds are lightly browned. Discard garlic. Cool seeds. Put seeds and oil into a small jar with a tight lid. Add remaining ingredients and shake to blend well. Perfect for fresh greens or sliced tomatoes. (Makes $1/2$ cup.)

### Soy Dressing

$1/2$ cup tomato juice
2 tbsp. soya sauce
1 tbsp. lemon juice
1 tbsp. red wine vinegar
1 tbsp. water
2 tsp. Dijon mustard
$1/4$ tsp. dried leaf chervil
2 tbsp. chopped parsley

Combine all ingredients in a jar with a tight lid. Shake to blend well. Toss with fresh greens for a really good low calorie salad. (Makes $3/4$ cup.)

### Lime-Honey Dressing

$1/4$ tsp. grated lime rind
$1/3$ cup lime juice
2 tbsp. liquid honey
$1/4$ tsp. salt
$3/4$ cup salad oil
$1/2$ tsp. paprika
$3/4$ tsp. prepared mustard
$1/2$ tsp. seasoned salt

Combine all ingredients in a jar with a tight lid. Shake to blend well. Shake again before serving over any fruit salad. (Makes about 1 cup.)

# *Breads*

While bread is no longer always on the table at dinner time, there are occasions when crusty French bread or hot rolls seem called for to round out the meal. Here are some especially nice dinner rolls made with yeast, some biscuits and suggestions for making French bread very special. All of the rolls and biscuits will reheat well, so they can be baked ahead, wrapped in aluminum foil, frozen, then reheated in a 400° F oven for about 15 minutes.

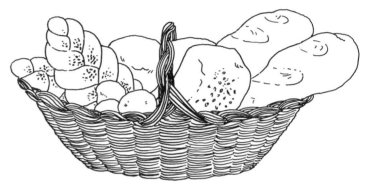

### Whole Wheat Rolls

*1 cup boiling water*
*¹/₂ cup soft shortening*
*2 tsp. salt*
*¹/₂ cup sugar*
*2 tsp. sugar*
*1 cup warm water*
*2 pkg. dry yeast*
*2 eggs, beaten*
*7 cups whole wheat flour*
  *(approx.)*
*melted butter or margarine*

Combine 1 cup boiling water, shortening, salt and ¹/₂ cup sugar in a large bowl. Cool to lukewarm.

Add 2 tsp. sugar to 1 cup warm water and stir until dissolved. Sprinkle yeast over and let stand 10 minutes. Stir well. Stir into first mixture along with eggs. Add half of the flour and beat hard with a wooden spoon to blend well. Add enough of remaining flour to make a firm but not stiff dough, mixing first with a spoon, then with your hand.

Turn out onto a floured board and knead until smooth and elastic, about 5 minutes. Round up, put in a greased bowl, turn over once to grease top of dough, cover with a damp cloth and let rise in a warm place until double, about 1 hour.

Grease two 9-inch round layer cake pans or 8-inch square cake pans.

Punch dough down. Pinch off bits of dough about ¹/₃ the size you want the finished rolls to be. Shape them into balls and put them into prepared pans, leaving a little space between. Let rise until a little more than double in size, about 30 minutes.

Heat oven to 400°F. Bake until well browned, 20 to 25 minutes. Brush tops with melted butter or margarine. Serve warm or cold. (Makes about 2¹/₂ dozen.)

Advance preparation: This is a good dough to keep in the refrigerator so you can bake a few rolls at a time. Cover dough with transparent wrap after it has risen and been punched down and store in the refrigerator up to 5 days, punching down occasionally if necessary. To bake, take off the amount of dough you need, let it warm up a little, then shape and bake as directed.

## Cheese Buns

1/2 cup warm water
1 tbsp. sugar
2 pkg. dry yeast
1/2 cup soft butter or
   margarine
2 tbsp. sugar
1 tsp. salt
1/2 tsp. dry mustard
1/2 cup milk, scalded
3 eggs, lightly beaten
1 cup finely grated old
   Cheddar cheese
4 1/2 cups sifted all-purpose
   flour
1 egg white
2 tsp. cold water
celery seeds, poppy seeds or
   sesame seeds

Measure warm water into a large mixing bowl. Add 1 tbsp. sugar and stir until sugar is dissolved. Sprinkle yeast over and let stand 10 minutes. Stir well.

Add butter or margarine, 2 tbsp. sugar, salt and mustard to hot milk and stir until butter or margarine is melted. Cool to warm if necessary and stir into yeast. Stir in eggs and cheese. Add half of the flour and beat with a wooden spoon until well blended. Add remaining flour (dough will be fairly stiff) and mix well with hand. Turn out onto a floured board and knead until smooth and elastic.

Put dough in a greased bowl, cover with a damp cloth and let rise in a warm place until double, about 1 hour. Punch down and let rise again until nearly double, about 30 minutes.

Grease two 9-inch round layer cake pans or 8-inch square cake pans. Shape dough into 18 round buns and put in prepared pans.

Beat egg white and 2 tsp. cold water together lightly with a fork and brush over tops of buns. Sprinkle with celery seeds, poppy seeds or sesame seeds. Let rise until double, about 45 minutes.

Heat oven to 375°F. Bake buns until they are well browned and sound hollow when tapped on top, about 15 minutes. Serve warm. (Makes 1 1/2 dozen.)

## Freeze and Bake Rolls

3/4 cup warm water
1 tsp. sugar
1 pkg. dry yeast
1/4 cup sugar
2 tsp. salt
1/4 cup soft shortening
3/4 cup milk, scalded
4 cups sifted all-purpose flour
melted butter or margarine

Measure water into a mixing bowl. Add 1 tsp. sugar and stir to dissolve. Sprinkle yeast over and let stand 10 minutes. Stir well.

Add 1/4 cup sugar, salt and shortening to hot milk. Stir until shortening is melted, then cool to lukewarm. Stir into yeast mixture. Add half of the flour and beat with a wooden spoon until smooth. Stir in remaining flour (dough will be quite soft).

Turn out onto a floured board and knead until smooth and elastic, kneading in more flour if needed to make the dough easy to handle but not stiff.

Put in a greased bowl and let rise until double, about 1 1/2 hours. Punch dough down and divide into 24 equal parts. Shape each of these pieces into a ball and put on a greased cookie sheet. Or divide each piece of dough into 3 and shape each little piece into a ball and put 3 of them into each of 24 greased muffin cups to make cloverleaf rolls.

Brush tops of rolls with melted butter or margarine and let rise until double, about 45 minutes.

Heat oven to 275°F. Bake rolls about 25 minutes (they should be set but only *very* lightly browned). Cool in pans 20 minutes, then remove from pans and finish cooling on cake racks.

Put in plastic bags and freeze until needed. Heat oven to 400°F when you want to serve rolls. Put them on cookie sheets and heat until well browned and hot, 10 to 12 minutes. (Makes 2 dozen.)

*Note:* If you want to use the rolls within a couple of days, they can be put in plastic bags and refrigerated rather than frozen.

## Seeded Batter Buns

1 1/2 cups warm water
2 tsp. sugar
2 pkg. dry yeast
3 3/4 cups sifted all-purpose
   flour
1/4 cup sugar
1 1/2 tsp. salt
1/3 cup soft shortening
1 egg
sesame seeds

Measure water into a large mixer bowl. Add 2 tsp. sugar and stir to dissolve. Sprinkle yeast over and let stand 10 minutes, then stir well. Add 2 cups of the flour, 1/4 cup sugar, salt, shortening and egg.

Blend at low speed on the mixer, then beat 2 minutes at medium speed on the mixer. Add remaining flour and beat by hand until well blended.

Cover with a damp cloth and let rise in a warm place until double, about 45 minutes.

Grease 18 large muffin cups. Sprinkle generously with sesame seeds and shake around to coat cups.

Stir batter down and spoon into prepared muffin cups, filling about half full. Sprinkle tops with more sesame seeds. Let rise until batter fills muffin cups, about 30 minutes.

Heat oven to 425°F. Bake buns until well browned, about 10 minutes. Serve warm. (Makes 1 1/2 dozen.)

## Butter Biscuits

4 1/2 cups sifted all-purpose
   flour
8 tsp. baking powder
1 1/2 tsp. salt
1 1/3 cups unsalted butter
4 eggs, lightly beaten
1 1/3 cups milk

Heat oven to 475°F. Have ready ungreased cookie sheets.

Sift flour, baking powder and salt together into a large bowl. Add butter and cut in coarsely. Make a well in the dry ingredients and add eggs and milk. Mix lightly with a fork just until dry ingredients are dampened (dough will be quite soft). Turn out onto a floured board and knead lightly until smooth, about 12 times.

Roll into an oblong about 16 × 12 inches, fold in three by overlapping 12-inch sides over middle, then fold in three again by overlapping short sides over middle. Repeat this rolling and folding once more, then roll dough out 3/4 inch thick. Cut into 2-inch rounds with a floured cutter and put on cookie sheets. Bake until golden, about 8 minutes. Serve hot. (Makes about 3 dozen.)

Advance preparation: Bake and store, wrapped in aluminum foil. Reheat on cookie sheets 5 minutes in 425°F oven.

## Herbed Biscuits

1 1/2 cups sifted all-purpose
   flour
2 tsp. baking powder
3/4 tsp. salt
1/4 tsp. dry mustard
1/4 tsp. paprika
dash cayenne
1/4 tsp. dried leaf thyme
3 tbsp. shortening
3/4 cup milk (approx.)

Heat oven to 450°F. Have ready a cookie sheet.

Sift flour, baking powder, salt, mustard, paprika and cayenne into a bowl. Add thyme and mix through flour mixture lightly with a fork.

Add shortening and cut in finely. Stir in enough of the milk with a fork to make a dough that is soft and puffy but easy to handle.

Turn out onto a lightly floured board and knead lightly about 12 times to smooth up. Pat or roll into a round 1/2 inch thick. Cut into 6 wedges.

Put on ungreased cookie sheet and bake until nicely browned, about 12 minutes. Serve hot. (Makes 6 large.)

## Herb Popovers

Heat oven to 425° F. Grease six 6-oz. custard cups well.

Sift flour, salt, paprika, mustard, sage and nutmeg together into a bowl. Add eggs and milk and beat together with a rotary beater just until smooth. Stir in parsley and Parmesan.

Pour into prepared custard cups, filling about half full.

Bake until popped and dark golden brown, 40 to 45 minutes. Serve hot with butter or margarine. (Makes 6.)

*1 cup sifted all-purpose flour*
*1/2 tsp. salt*
*1/4 tsp. paprika*
*1/4 tsp. dry mustard*
*1/4 tsp. rubbed sage*
*pinch ground nutmeg*
*2 eggs*
*1 cup milk*
*2 tbsp. finely chopped parsley*
*1/4 cup grated Parmesan cheese*
*butter or margarine*

## Savory French Bread

Heat oven to 350°F.

Cut French bread into 1-inch slices on the diagonal, cutting down to but not through bottom crust.

Cream remaining ingredients together until well blended. Spread between slices of bread. Wrap in foil.

Heat bread in oven until very hot and crusty, about 20 minutes.

*1 small loaf French bread*
*1/2 cup soft butter or margarine*
*1 tbsp. chopped parsley*
*1 tsp. lemon juice*
*1/2 tsp. dried leaf rosemary*
*1/2 tsp. paprika*

## Crusty French Stick

Cut French bread into halves crosswise, then cut again length-wise to make 4 long pieces.

Spread cut sides thickly with soft butter or margarine. Sprinkle lightly with paprika, garlic salt, sesame seeds and Parmesan. Put on an ungreased cookie sheet.

Heat broiler at serving time. Put bread low under broiler (put oven shelf 6 or 7 inches from heat) and broil just until edges of bread are golden.

Cut into 2-inch-wide pieces on the diagonal and serve hot.

*Note:* The long thin French loaf is sometimes called a French stick or, more correctly, a baguette. If you can't get this bread, any good French bread will do.

*1 very long thin French bread (see note)*
*soft butter or margarine*
*paprika*
*garlic salt*
*sesame seeds*
*grated Parmesan cheese*

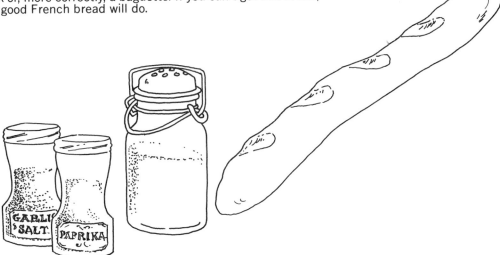

# *Vegetables*

When dinner needs to be on the table in no time flat, the easiest thing to do for a vegetable is to simply open a package or a can and heat. Vegetables, in all their variety, deserve better than that. While both canned and frozen vegetables are fine, they are even better if they are combined with a little something to give them a whole new personality. And though some fresh vegetables need little more than a light cooking and a dab of butter, even they can stand perking up at times. A trace of herbs, a sprinkling of cheese or a light sauce can make your vegetables the perfect complement to your good meal.

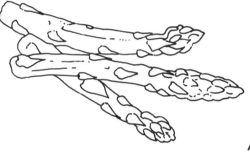

### Asparagus Indian Style

1¹/₂ lb. fresh asparagus
3 tbsp. cooking oil
¹/₄ tsp. mustard seeds
¹/₂ tsp. salt
4 cardamom seeds
2 peppercorns
1 cup cooked rice

Wash asparagus and snap off tough ends. Cut stalks into 1-inch pieces on the diagonal, leaving tips whole.

Heat oil in a large heavy skillet. Add mustard seeds and cook gently, stirring, until they begin to pop. Add asparagus and salt, cover and cook over moderate heat, shaking pan often, until asparagus is tender-crisp, 5 to 8 minutes.

Crush cardamom seeds and peppercorns in a mortar or by putting them in the bowl of a spoon and pressing hard with the bowl of another spoon. Add crushed spices and rice to pan. Toss together over moderate heat until everything is hot, about 3 minutes. Serve immediately. (Serves 4.)

### Yellow Beans Spanish Style

2 lb. yellow beans
4 slices bacon, diced
1 medium onion, chopped
1 cup bottled chili sauce
¹/₂ tsp. salt
¹/₄ tsp. ground allspice
¹/₄ cup grated Parmesan cheese

Wash and trim beans and cut into pieces about 1¹/₂ inches long on the diagonal. Cook in a small amount of boiling water until just tender, about 8 minutes. Drain, saving cooking liquid. Measure liquid and add water, if necessary, to make ¹/₄ cup.

Fry bacon until crisp. Lift out of pan with a slotted spoon and drain on paper toweling. Drain all but about 1¹/₂ tbsp. fat from pan. Add onion to bacon fat and cook gently, stirring, until transparent. Add chili sauce, the ¹/₄ cup liquid, salt and allspice. Simmer 3 minutes. Pour over beans, toss lightly and heat well.

Turn into a serving dish. Sprinkle with Parmesan and bacon bits. (Serves 6.)

## Sesame Green Beans

Blend vinegar, soya sauce and cornstarch in a small dish.

Put peanut oil, sesame seeds and salt in a wok and heat, stirring constantly, just until sesame seeds begin to brown lightly (this takes only about a second, so watch carefully or seeds will burn). Add beans immediately. Add 1/4 cup water, cover and cook over moderate heat 2 minutes.

Push beans up sides of wok and stir vinegar mixture into boiling liquid. Boil until clear, then toss all together. Serve immediately. (Serves 2 or 3.)

2 tsp. red wine vinegar
1 tsp. soya sauce
1 tsp. cornstarch
2 tbsp. peanut oil
1 tbsp. sesame seeds
1/4 tsp. salt
10-oz. pkg. frozen French-style green beans, thawed
1/4 cup water

## Herbed Lima Beans

Heat oil in a medium saucepan. Add onion and garlic and cook gently 3 minutes. Chop any large pieces of tomato and add tomatoes and their liquid to the saucepan. Add marjoram, cover and simmer 2 minutes. Add lima beans, cover and cook until beans are tender, about 12 minutes.

Sprinkle in parsley, salt and pepper and stir to blend. Serve in individual dishes. (Serves 4.)

2 tbsp. cooking oil
1 small onion, finely chopped
1 clove garlic, finely chopped
1 cup canned tomatoes with juice
1/2 tsp. dried leaf marjoram
12-oz. pkg. frozen lima beans
1 tbsp. chopped parsley
1/2 tsp. salt
1/8 tsp. black pepper

## Ginger Beets

Combine sugar, cornstarch, salt and pepper thoroughly in the top of a double boiler. Stir in vinegar, 1/2 cup water, ginger and lemon rind, blending until smooth. Set over direct heat and cook, stirring constantly, until boiling, thickened and smooth.

Set top of double boiler over boiling water in lower part of boiler and add beets. Stir to blend sauce through beets. Add butter or margarine, cover and heat over boiling water, stirring occasionally, until beets are very hot, about 10 minutes. (Serves 6.)

Advance preparation: Canned beets are fine.

1/4 cup sugar
2 tbsp. cornstarch
1/2 tsp. salt
1/8 tsp. black pepper
1/2 cup white vinegar
1/2 cup water
1 1/2 tsp. grated fresh ginger
1 tsp. grated lemon rind
4 cups cubed cooked beets (about 2 lb.)
2 tbsp. butter or margarine

## Stir-Fried Broccoli

Cut flowers off broccoli, leaving enough stem to hold bunches together. Separate into small sections or cut any large sections into halves lengthwise. Slice stems about 1/4 inch thick on the diagonal. Cut enough to make about 3 1/2 cups of vegetable.

Drop broccoli into a large amount of boiling salted water and cook, uncovered, until barely tender, about 3 minutes. Drain. Chill by rinsing with cold water. Drain again.

Heat a large heavy skillet or wok over very high heat. Add oil and heat until it ripples when pan is tipped. Add ginger and garlic and stir quickly just until very lightly browned. Add broccoli, 1 tbsp. water, sugar and salt. Turn quickly with a wooden spoon to just heat broccoli through, 1 to 2 minutes.

Turn out into a hot serving dish and sprinkle with nuts if desired. (Serves 3.)

1 to 1 1/2 lb. broccoli
1 tbsp. cooking oil (approx.)
2 tsp. finely chopped fresh ginger
1 clove garlic, finely chopped
1 tbsp. water
1 tsp. sugar
1/2 tsp. salt
toasted chopped nuts (optional)

## Scalloped Cabbage

1 tbsp. butter or margarine
1 clove garlic, crushed
5 cups coarsely cut cabbage
2 tbsp. butter or margarine
2 tbsp. flour
2 cups milk
1 1/2 tsp. salt
1/4 tsp. black pepper
1/2 tsp. celery seeds
1 cup grated old Cheddar
  cheese
1/2 cup fine dry bread crumbs
2 tbsp. butter or margarine

Heat oven to 400°F. Cream together 1 tbsp. butter or margarine and garlic and use mixture to butter a 1 1/2-qt. casserole generously.

Cover cabbage with boiling water in a large saucepan. Cover and cook 5 minutes. Drain.

Melt 2 tbsp. butter or margarine in a saucepan. Sprinkle in flour, stir to blend and let bubble up. Remove from heat and add milk all at once. Stir to blend and return to moderate heat. Cook, stirring constantly, until boiling, thickened and smooth. Stir in salt, pepper, celery seeds and cheese. Continue cooking gently, stirring, until cheese is melted.

Layer cabbage and cheese sauce in prepared casserole, beginning and ending with a layer of sauce. Sprinkle with crumbs and dot with butter or margarine.

Bake until top is browned and sauce is bubbling, 15 to 20 minutes. (Serves 4 to 6.)

Advance preparation: Make completely but do not bake. Refrigerate, then bring to room temperature before heating.

## Fried Chinese Cabbage

1 bunch Chinese cabbage
  (about 1 lb.)
2 tbsp. cooking oil
2 thin slices fresh ginger
  (about 3/4 inch in diameter)
1 tsp. salt
1/2 tsp. sugar
1/4 cup water

Wash Chinese cabbage and cut into 1-inch pieces, keeping the green leafy part separate from the white stems.

Heat oil to very hot in a large heavy skillet or wok. Add stem part of cabbage and ginger. Cook over high heat 1 minute, stirring briskly. Add leaf part of cabbage and continue stirring 30 seconds. Add salt, sugar and 1/4 cup water, cover tightly and cook over high heat 1 minute. Discard ginger slices. Serve immediately. (Serves 4.)

## Savory Carrots

3 cups sliced carrots
1 small onion, sliced
1/2 cup diced green pepper
2 tbsp. butter or margarine
salt and pepper

Cook carrots in a small amount of boiling salted water 10 minutes. Drain.

Cook onion and green pepper in butter or margarine until onion is transparent. Add carrots and salt and pepper to taste. Cover and cook gently until tender, about 5 minutes. (Serves 4.)

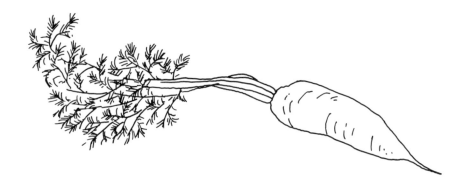

### Creamed Cauliflower and Peas

1 medium cauliflower
1 cup boiling water
1 tsp. salt
1 1/2 cups frozen peas
3 tbsp. butter or margarine
1/2 cup chopped onion
3 tbsp. flour
1/2 tsp. salt
1/8 tsp. black pepper
1/8 tsp. paprika
1 cup light cream
1 tbsp. lemon juice
2 tbsp. butter or margarine
1/2 cup fine dry bread crumbs

Butter a 2-qt. baking dish.

Trim and wash cauliflower and separate into flowerets (you should have about 5 cups). Put in a saucepan and add 1 cup boiling water and 1 tsp. salt. Cover and cook until almost tender, about 7 minutes. Add peas and cook until vegetables are tender, about 3 minutes. Drain, saving 3/4 cup of the liquid. Set vegetables aside.

Melt 3 tbsp. butter or margarine in same saucepan. Add onion and cook gently, stirring, 3 minutes. Sprinkle in flour, 1/2 tsp. salt, pepper and paprika and stir to blend. Remove from heat. Stir in cream and the 3/4 cup cooking liquid. Return to heat and cook, stirring constantly, until boiling, thickened and smooth. Stir in lemon juice.

Add vegetables and stir gently until blended with sauce. Turn into prepared baking dish.

Melt 2 tbsp. butter or margarine in a small saucepan. Add bread crumbs and toss together with a fork.

Sprinkle over vegetables and slip low under broiler to brown lightly. Serve immediately. (Serves 6.)

### Celery Amandine

1/4 cup butter or margarine
2/3 cup slivered blanched
  almonds
2 chicken bouillon cubes
8 cups diagonally sliced celery
  (1/4-inch slices)
2 tbsp. grated onion
1 tsp. sugar
1/4 tsp. black pepper
1/4 tsp. garlic powder
1/4 tsp. ground ginger

Heat butter or margarine in a large heavy skillet. Add almonds and cook gently, stirring, until lightly browned. Crumble bouillon cubes into mixture and add all remaining ingredients, stirring to blend. Cover and cook, stirring occasionally, until celery is just tender-crisp, about 7 minutes. Serve immediately. (Serves 8.)

### Celery Victor

1 clove garlic
2/3 cup olive or salad oil
3 hearts of celery
2 cups chicken stock
  (recipe p. 48)
1/3 cup red wine vinegar
1/2 tsp. salt
1/8 tsp. black pepper
watercress or lettuce
6 flat anchovies or 6 tomato
  wedges or 6 slices
  hard-cooked egg

Peel garlic, cut into halves and add to oil. Let stand 2 to 3 hours.

Wash celery hearts without separating pieces. Trim around the root but do not cut it off (it serves to hold the stalks together). Trim away all large leaves (only small centre leaves should be left). Cut each heart into halves lengthwise. Lay in a large skillet.

Add chicken stock and bring to a boil. Turn down heat, cover and simmer until celery is just tender, about 12 minutes.

Lift celery out of broth carefully (the broth will make a nice bowl of soup) and put in a single layer in a shallow baking dish.

Remove garlic from oil. Combine oil, vinegar, salt and pepper and pour over celery. Cover and chill, turning celery occasionally.

Lift celery out of marinade and serve on a bed of watercress or lettuce. Garnish each serving with an anchovy, a tomato wedge or an egg slice. (Serves 6.)

## Curried Creamed Corn

Heat butter or margarine in a large heavy skillet. Add onions and curry powder and cook gently, stirring, 3 minutes. Add corn and tomatoes and heat, stirring constantly.

Stir salt, pepper, cornstarch and sugar into cream, blending until smooth. Stir into vegetables. Heat, stirring, just until very hot and slightly thickened. Serve immediately. (Serves 6.)

Advance preparation: Cook corn on the cob in boiling water 5 minutes. Drain, cool and cut corn from cobs. In an emergency, use canned whole kernel corn.

2 tbsp. butter or margarine
$^1/_2$ cup chopped green onions
1 tsp. curry powder
3 cups fresh cooked corn (cut from cobs)
2 medium tomatoes, peeled, seeded and chopped
1 tsp. salt
$^1/_8$ tsp. black pepper
1 tsp. cornstarch
$^1/_2$ tsp. sugar
$^1/_2$ cup heavy cream

## Indian Corn

Fry bacon until crisp in a large heavy saucepan or Dutch oven. Lift out bacon, drain, cool and crumble. Set aside.

Add butter or margarine to fat left in pan and stir in rice, corn, salt, pepper, anise seeds and sugar. Cook gently, stirring, until rice is golden brown.

Put cabbage on top of rice mixture and pour in 3 cups boiling water (do not stir). Bring to a boil, turn heat to low, cover tightly and simmer 20 minutes.

Remove cover, add bacon bits and stir lightly with a fork. Continue simmering, uncovered, until all liquid disappears but mixture is still moist, about 10 minutes.

Especially good served with chicken. (Serves 8.)

5 strips bacon
2 tbsp. butter or margarine
1 cup regular long-grain rice
12-oz. can whole kernel corn, drained
1 tsp. salt
$^1/_4$ tsp. black pepper
$^1/_4$ tsp. anise seeds (optional)
2 tbsp. sugar
3 cups finely shredded cabbage ($^1/_2$ small)
3 cups boiling water

## Cucumbers in Cream

Peel and cut cucumbers into thin slices. Heat butter or margarine in a large heavy skillet. Add radishes. Cover pan tightly and cook over high heat 1 minute, shaking the pan constantly. Remove cover, add cucumber and cook over high heat, turning slices carefully, until vegetables are tender-crisp, about 2 minutes.

Remove from heat. Quickly stir in sour cream, salt and pepper. Serve immediately. (Serves 3 or 4.)

2 medium cucumbers
2 tbsp. butter or margarine
$^1/_2$ cup thinly sliced radishes
$^1/_4$ cup sour cream
$^1/_2$ tsp. salt
grating fresh black pepper

## Butter-Steamed Leeks

Heat butter or margarine over high heat in a large heavy skillet (use an electric skillet if you like). Add leeks and $^1/_4$ cup water. Stir and cover tightly. Cook at high heat, stirring frequently and adding a little more water if necessary, until leeks are just tender, about 3 minutes. Sprinkle lightly with salt and pepper, add bacon and toss with a fork. Serve immediately. (Serves 4.)

2 tbsp. butter or margarine
3 cups thinly sliced leeks (white and pale green parts only)
$^1/_4$ cup water (approx.)
salt and pepper
4 slices bacon, cooked, drained and crumbled

## Creamed Radishes

2 slices bacon
3 cups sliced radishes
1 tbsp. bacon fat or butter
1 tbsp. flour
1 cup milk
$^1/_2$ tsp. salt
dash black pepper
chopped parsley

Fry bacon crisp, then drain and crumble. Measure out the 1 tbsp. bacon fat called for.

Cook radishes in a small amount of boiling salted water just until tender-crisp, about 1 minute (do not overcook or radishes will lose their color). Drain.

Heat bacon fat or butter in a medium saucepan. Sprinkle in flour and stir to blend. Remove from heat. Add milk all at once and stir to blend. Stir in salt and pepper. Return to heat and stir until boiling and slightly thickened. Turn heat to low and simmer 1 minute.

Stir in bacon bits and radishes. Heat for 1 minute. Serve immediately, sprinkled with parsley. (Serves 3 or 4.)

## Peas in Brown Butter Sauce

$^1/_4$ cup butter
1 chicken bouillon cube
$^3/_4$ cup boiling water
$^1/_4$ tsp. dried leaf savory
2 tsp. cornstarch
$^1/_4$ cup cold water
1 tbsp. lemon juice
two 12-oz. pkg. frozen peas
salt and pepper

Heat butter slowly in a medium saucepan, stirring often, until dark golden brown. Remove from heat. Dissolve bouillon cube in $^3/_4$ cup boiling water and stir into butter. Add savory. Return to heat and bring to a boil. Stir cornstarch and $^1/_4$ cup cold water together until smooth. Stir into boiling mixture gradually. Stir in lemon juice. Keep hot.

Cook peas according to package directions, using the minimum time suggested. Drain. Add to brown butter mixture. Add salt and pepper to taste. Serve immediately. (Serves 6.)

## Scalloped Peas and Onions

2 tbsp. butter or margarine
2 cups sliced onion
10-oz. can cream of celery
  soup
$^1/_4$ cup milk
$^1/_4$ tsp. salt
$^1/_8$ tsp. black pepper
$^1/_2$ tsp. dried leaf savory
1 tbsp. chopped parsley
12-oz. pkg. frozen peas
$^1/_4$ cup fine dry bread crumbs
1 tbsp. butter or margarine,
  melted

Heat oven to 350°F. Butter a 9 × 6 × 1$^1/_2$-inch baking dish.

Heat 2 tbsp. butter or margarine in a saucepan. Add onion and cook gently, stirring, until onion is limp, about 5 minutes. Add soup, milk, salt, pepper, savory and parsley and heat.

Spread frozen peas in prepared baking dish. Pour soup mixture over. Toss bread crumbs and 1 tbsp. melted butter or margarine together with a fork and sprinkle over all. Bake until peas are tender, about 30 minutes. (Serves 6.)

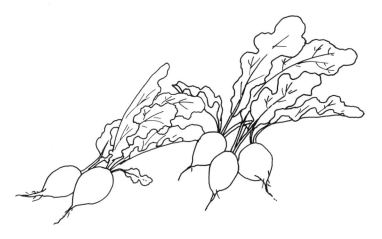

## Puffy Baked Potatoes

6 baking potatoes
2 tbsp. butter or margarine
1/2 cup hot milk
1 tsp. salt
1/4 tsp. black pepper
pinch ground nutmeg
1 egg yolk
2 egg whites
1/2 cup finely grated Swiss
  cheese
1 egg yolk
1 tbsp. water

Bake potatoes at 400°F until tender. Remove from oven and set oven at 425°F.

Cut a thin slice from the top of each potato and discard. Scoop potato pulp out into a bowl with a teaspoon, being careful not to break potato skins.

Mash potato pulp very well (use an electric mixer if you have one). Add butter or margarine, milk, salt, pepper, nutmeg and 1 egg yolk. Whip until fluffy.

Beat egg whites until stiff. Fold into potato mixture along with cheese.

Pile mixture back into potato skins. Beat remaining egg yolk and 1 tbsp. water together with a fork and brush some of this mixture over each potato.

Set potatoes in a pan and bake until very hot and nicely browned, about 15 minutes. (Serves 6.)

Advance preparation: Make but do not bake until just before serving time.

## Potato Cakes

2 tbsp. finely chopped onion
1 tbsp. bacon fat
4 cups hot mashed potatoes
  (about 8 medium)
1/4 cup soft butter or
  margarine
2 tsp. salt
1/8 tsp. black pepper
2 eggs
flour
bacon fat

Fry onion in 1 tbsp. bacon fat until transparent, about 3 minutes. Whip potatoes, butter or margarine, salt and pepper until fluffy. Add eggs and beat again to blend thoroughly. Blend in onion.

Shape into 8 large thick cakes and dip each side into flour to coat well.

Heat bacon fat in a heavy skillet and brown cakes well on both sides. (Makes 8.)

## Kugley

olive oil
6 slices bacon, cut in small
  pieces
6 large potatoes
3 small onions
3 eggs
3 tbsp. flour
2/3 cup evaporated milk
  (1 small can)
1 1/2 tsp. salt
1/8 tsp. black pepper

Heat oven to 400°F. Grease a 12 x 7 1/2 x 2-inch glass baking dish with olive oil.

Fry bacon until cooked through but not crisp. Do not drain.

Grate potatoes and onions on fine grater. Beat eggs, flour, milk, salt and pepper together with a fork in a large bowl. Add potatoes, onions and bacon with drippings. Blend lightly with a fork. Put in prepared baking dish.

Bake 1 hour. Cut into squares and serve very hot. (Serves 6.)

## Potatoes with Dill

Scrub potatoes and cook in their jackets until tender. Drain, cool and peel.

Heat lard or bacon fat in a large saucepan. Add onion and cook gently until onion is limp. Sprinkle in flour, salt and pepper and stir to blend. Continue cooking over moderate heat, stirring, until lightly browned. Remove from heat.

Dissolve bouillon cube in $1^{1}/_{2}$ cups boiling water and add to flour mixture all at once. Add dill and parsley. Stir to blend. Return to moderate heat and cook, stirring constantly, until boiling, thickened and smooth. Add dill pickle.

Slice potatoes into mixture. Heat gently until everything is hot. Add sour cream and heat but do not boil. Serve immediately. (Serves 6 to 8.)

Advance preparation: Cook potatoes. Make sauce down to point where dill pickle is to be added, then cover and store in the refrigerator. Shortly before serving time, heat sauce slowly, then add dill pickle and potatoes and continue as directed.

8 medium potatoes
2 tbsp. lard or bacon fat
1 tbsp. minced onion
$^{1}/_{4}$ cup flour
$^{1}/_{2}$ tsp. salt
$^{1}/_{4}$ tsp. black pepper
1 beef bouillon cube
$1^{1}/_{2}$ cups boiling water
1 tsp. fresh snipped or $^{1}/_{2}$ tsp. dried dill weed
$^{1}/_{4}$ cup chopped parsley
1 cup thinly sliced dill pickle
$^{1}/_{2}$ cup sour cream

## Pumpkin and Corn

Fry bacon until crisp. Lift out of pan and drain on paper toweling. Fry onion and garlic gently in bacon fat in pan 3 minutes. Add green pepper and pumpkin cubes and continue cooking gently, stirring, 5 minutes.

Stir in tomatoes, beans, corn and seasonings. Cover pan and simmer until pumpkin cubes are tender, 20 to 25 minutes.

Crumble bacon and sprinkle over vegetables before serving. (Serves 6.)

4 slices bacon
$^{1}/_{2}$ cup chopped onion
1 clove garlic, minced
1 green pepper, finely chopped
3 cups $^{3}/_{4}$-inch cubes peeled, seeded pumpkin
19-oz. can tomatoes
1 cup 1-inch pieces green beans
12-oz. pkg. frozen whole kernel corn
2 tsp. salt
$^{1}/_{8}$ tsp. black pepper

## Baked Tomatoes with Herbed Corn

Heat oven to 375°F. Butter a baking dish just large enough to hold the tomatoes, about 8 × 6 × 2 inches.

Cut and discard a slice from tops of tomatoes and scoop out centres, leaving a wall about $^{1}/_{4}$ inch thick (save centres to add to casseroles or soups). Invert tomatoes on paper toweling to drain.

Heat butter or margarine in a medium saucepan. Add onion and corn and cook gently, stirring constantly, 5 minutes. Remove from heat. Add salt, pepper, thyme, anise seeds and parsley.

Put tomatoes in prepared baking dish and spoon corn mixture into hollowed-out centres.

Bake until tomatoes are tender and filling is heated through, 20 to 25 minutes. (Serves 4.)

4 large tomatoes
3 tbsp. butter or margarine
$^{1}/_{2}$ cup finely chopped Spanish onion
2 cups fresh corn (cut from cobs)
$^{1}/_{2}$ tsp. salt
dash black pepper
pinch dried leaf thyme
pinch anise seeds
2 tbsp. finely chopped parsley

## Turnip and Apples

Peel rutabaga and cut into thin strips. Core apples but do not peel. Cut into ½-inch slices crosswise.

Melt butter or margarine in a heavy skillet. Add apple slices and brown lightly on one side. Turn. Sprinkle with turnip strips, then with sugar and salt. Cover tightly and cook gently until turnip is tender, shaking the pan often, 10 to 15 minutes. (Serves 4.)

1 medium rutabaga (yellow turnip)
2 medium apples
3 tbsp. butter or margarine
2 tbsp. sugar
1 tsp. salt

## Turnip Pudding

Peel and cut rutabagas into ¼-inch cubes (you should have about 12 cups). Put into a large saucepan and add 1½ tsp. salt. Add boiling water to cover. Bring back to a boil, cover, turn down heat and simmer until rutabaga is very tender, 15 to 20 minutes.

Heat oven to 350°F. Butter a 2½-qt. casserole generously.

Drain rutabaga and press through a sieve or food mill into a bowl, or mash until very smooth.

Combine bread crumbs and cream in a large bowl. Let stand 5 minutes. Stir in nutmeg, 1 tsp. salt and eggs. Add rutabaga and blend well.

Spoon mixture into prepared casserole and dot with butter or margarine. Bake until hot and lightly browned, about 1 hour. (Serves 8.)

Advance preparation: Make but do not bake until needed.

2 large rutabagas (yellow turnips)
1½ tsp. salt
⅓ cup fine dry bread crumbs
⅓ cup heavy cream
½ tsp. ground nutmeg
1 tsp. salt
3 eggs, beaten
2 tbsp. butter or margarine

## Zucchini Fritters

Choose zucchini just large enough to make 2 servings each. Wash zucchini, cut off and discard ends and slice into ½-inch pieces. Sprinkle with salt and let stand 15 minutes. Dry on paper toweling.

Combine flour, egg, milk and butter or margarine to make a smooth batter.

Pour about ¼ inch of oil into an electric skillet. Set skillet control for 375°F. Dip slices of zucchini in batter when oil is hot. Shake to remove excess batter and drop slices into hot oil. Brown on one side, turn with a pancake turner and brown on second side (this will take only a few minutes). Drain on paper toweling. Serve immediately. (Serves 6.)

Advance preparation: It is possible to make these ahead of time and reheat them with quite good results. Fry, being careful not to overcook. Drain, then put on a cookie sheet. To reheat just before serving, put in a 450°F oven for about 3 minutes.

3 small zucchini
salt
1 cup sifted all-purpose flour
1 egg, beaten
¾ cup milk
1 tbsp. butter or margarine, melted
cooking oil

## Savory Noodles

1 cup cream-style cottage cheese
$1/3$ cup crumbled blue cheese
1 cup sour cream
$1/2$ cup thinly sliced green onions
1 clove garlic, crushed
1 tsp. Worcestershire sauce
12-oz. pkg. medium noodles
chopped parsley

Combine cottage cheese, blue cheese, sour cream, onions, garlic and Worcestershire in the top of a double boiler. Set over simmering water, cover and heat, stirring occasionally, until very hot.

Cook noodles in plenty of boiling salted water until just tender, about 6 minutes. Drain and return to cooking pan. Add hot cheese mixture and toss all together lightly with a fork. Serve, sprinkled with chopped parsley. Good with ham or chicken. (Serves 6.)

## Green Noodles and Mushrooms

2 tbsp. butter or margarine
$1/4$ lb. fresh mushrooms, thinly sliced
salt and pepper
3 oz. green noodles (see note)
1 tbsp. chopped parsley

Heat 1 tbsp. of the butter or margarine in a heavy skillet. Add mushrooms and cook quickly until lightly browned. Sprinkle with salt and pepper.

Cook noodles in boiling salted water until just tender, about 5 minutes. Drain. Add remaining 1 tbsp. butter or margarine, parsley and mushrooms and toss all together with a fork. Serve immediately. (Serves 2.)

*Note:* Green noodles are colored with spinach and are available in delicatessens and other food specialty stores. If they aren't available, use regular egg noodles.

## Fettucine

375 g pkg. medium noodles
$1/2$ cup unsalted butter, cut in small pieces
1 cup freshly grated Parmesan cheese
1 cup light cream
$1/4$ tsp. pepper

Cook noodles in plenty of boiling salted water until just tender, about 7 minutes. Drain and return to pan. Set over lowest heat, add remaining ingredients and stir gently just until butter, Parmesan and cream melt into a smooth sauce that coats the noodles. Serve immediately. (Serves 6.)

## Nutty Brown Rice

2 tbsp. butter or margarine
1 cup chopped onion
1 cup chopped celery
1 clove garlic, crushed
1 cup uncooked brown rice
2 1/2 cups chicken stock
  (recipe p. 48)
1 tsp. seasoned salt
dash black pepper
1 cup chopped lightly toasted
  pecans

Heat oven to 350°F. Butter a 1 1/2-qt. casserole.

Melt butter or margarine in a large saucepan over moderate heat. Add onion, celery and garlic and stir 5 minutes. Mix in rice, chicken stock, seasoned salt and pepper. Pour into prepared casserole, cover and bake 1 hour.

Uncover, add nuts and stir lightly with a fork. Bake, uncovered, until liquid is absorbed but rice is still moist, about 15 minutes. Good with poultry. (Serves 6.)

Advance preparation: Make but do not bake until needed.

## Barley and Peas

2 tbsp. cooking oil
1 medium onion, chopped
1/2 cup green split peas
19-oz. can tomato juice
1/2 cup water
1/2 cup pearl barley
1 1/2 tsp. salt
1/4 tsp. black pepper
1 tsp. fennel seeds
1/4 cup chopped parsley
1/2 cup hulled sunflower seeds
2 tbsp. cooking oil
1/2 lb. (1 pt.) fresh
  mushrooms, sliced

Heat 2 tbsp. oil in a large saucepan over moderate heat. Add onion and stir 3 minutes. Add peas, tomato juice and 1/2 cup water. Bring to a boil, reduce heat, cover and simmer 15 minutes.

Add barley, salt, pepper and fennel seeds. Cover and simmer until peas and barley are tender and most of liquid is absorbed, about 50 minutes. Add parsley and sunflower seeds and heat gently 5 minutes, stirring once or twice.

Heat 2 tbsp. oil and fry mushrooms over high heat 3 minutes, stirring constantly. Add to peas and barley mixture, tossing with a fork. Serve immediately. (Serves 4.)

Advance preparation: Make dish down to point where peas and barley are cooked. Reheat over low heat and complete preparation shortly before serving time.

## Barley and Celery

1/4 cup butter or margarine
2 medium onions, chopped
2 cups sliced celery
3 chicken bouillon cubes
2 cups boiling water
1 1/4 cups pearl barley
10-oz. can mushroom pieces
1 tsp. salt
1/4 tsp. black pepper

Heat oven to 350°F. Have ready a 2-qt. casserole.

Melt butter or margarine in a skillet. Add onion and celery and cook gently, stirring, 5 minutes. Remove from heat.

Put bouillon cubes in casserole. Add 2 cups boiling water and stir until cubes are dissolved. Stir in barley, mushrooms and their liquid, salt, pepper and onion-celery mixture. Cover tightly.

Bake until barley is tender and liquid is absorbed, about 1 hour. (Serves 6.)

Advance preparation: Make, bake and refrigerate until needed. Add a small amount of water and heat in a 350°F oven, covered, until very hot, about 25 minutes.

# Desserts

It seems strange, doesn't it, that the largest meal of the day is often followed by the richest dessert. On the other hand, it would be a little ridiculous to serve a heavy steamed pudding or a glamorous cheesecake after a sandwich lunch. Perhaps we should follow the custom of many Europeans. They enjoy their desserts, whipped cream and all, with coffee during the afternoon, rather than after a big meal.

However, we North Americans do like a bit of sweet after our dinner, so here are suggestions for delicious desserts ranging from light fruit-based ones through puddings and pies to wonderful frozen treats.

### Pineapple and Strawberries

1 qt. strawberries
¹/₄ cup Cointreau
1 medium very ripe pineapple
¹/₄ cup sugar

Wash and hull strawberries. Set 8 perfect berries aside for garnish and put remainder in glass of blender and buzz to make a purée (you should have about 2 cups). Add Cointreau and chill.

Cut pineapple into small cubes and put in a bowl. Add sugar and let stand at room temperature until sugar is dissolved, stirring often. Chill.

Spoon pineapple into sherbet glasses at serving time and spoon strawberry sauce over. Garnish with whole berries. (Serves 8.)

### Grapefruit à la Mode

3 large grapefruit
2 medium oranges
¹/₄ cup maraschino cherry
    halves
3 tbsp. liquid honey
lime or lemon sherbet

Cut each grapefruit into halves. Cut around sections with a serrated knife and lift out pieces. Carefully remove any membranes from shells, making sure not to tear shells. Peel and section oranges and cut sections into bite-size pieces.

Combine grapefruit sections, orange pieces and cherries and pile mixture in prepared grapefruit shells. Drizzle fruit with honey. Chill very well.

Set each grapefruit half in a dish at serving time. Top each with a scoop of sherbet. Serve immediately. (Serves 6.)

### Peaches with Citrus Freeze

1¹/₃ cups cold water
1 envelope (1 tbsp.)
    unflavored gelatin
1 cup sugar
¹/₂ cup strained lime juice
¹/₂ cup strained lemon juice
6 large peach halves or
    6 small peaches, sliced

Measure cold water into a small saucepan. Add gelatin and let stand 5 minutes. Set over low heat and stir until gelatin is dissolved. Add sugar and continue stirring until sugar is dissolved. Remove from heat. Stir in lime and lemon juices. Cool.

Pour into a metal pan and freeze until just firm, stirring several times during freezing.

At serving time, put peaches in serving dishes and top each with a large spoonful of the frozen mixture. Serve immediately. (Serves 6.)

## Pears and Blueberries

Combine sugar, 1 cup water and cloves and bring to a boil. Boil hard 5 minutes. Turn down heat.

Wash pears and core from bottom ends, leaving pears whole and stems in place. Peel pears, peeling carefully around stems so as not to loosen them. (I find a vegetable peeler does the smoothest job of peeling.)

Put whole pears into simmering syrup, cover and simmer until just beginning to get tender, about 5 minutes. Remove from heat and stir in vanilla.

Let pears cool in syrup, then lift out to a plate and chill well.

Remove cloves from syrup when pears are chilled and boil syrup hard until about the thickness of corn syrup. Remove from heat and stir in blueberries.

Put chilled pears in individual serving dishes and spoon blueberry syrup over (syrup should be thick enough to form a light glaze when it hits the cold pears). Chill again until serving time. (Serves 6.)

*Note:* If desired, the pears can be peeled, quartered and cored, then poached in the syrup and chilled as above. If you do it this way, put poached pears in a serving bowl and pour warm blueberry sauce over. Chill and serve at table.

*2 cups sugar*
*1 cup water*
*4 whole cloves*
*6 ripe pears*
*1/2 tsp. vanilla extract*
*2 cups fresh blueberries*

## Pears with Sabayon

Boil 2 cups water, 1/2 cup sugar, 1 tbsp. lemon juice and vanilla bean in a large saucepan 5 minutes. Peel pears, cut into halves and core. Drop pears into boiling syrup and simmer, uncovered, until just tender, about 10 minutes. Cool in syrup.

Combine egg yolks, 1/3 cup sugar, sherry, 1 tbsp. lemon juice and lemon rind in the top of a double boiler. Set over simmering (not boiling) water and beat with a whip or rotary beater until quite thick, about 15 minutes.

Beat egg whites until stiff but not dry and fold into hot mixture. Cool.

Put a poached pear half in each of 6 sherbet glasses, cut side up. Fill hollow in each pear with a small spoonful of red currant jelly. Spoon sauce over all. (Serves 6.)

*2 cups water*
*1/2 cup sugar*
*1 tbsp. lemon juice*
*2-inch piece vanilla bean*
*  (optional)*
*3 large pears*
*2 egg yolks*
*1/3 cup sugar*
*1/4 cup sweet sherry*
*1 tbsp. lemon juice*
*1 tsp. grated lemon rind*
*2 egg whites*
*red currant jelly*

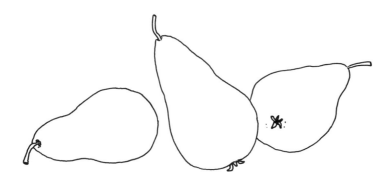

## Strawberry Shortcakes

1 qt. strawberries
1/2 cup sugar
Rich Shortcake Biscuits
  (recipe follows)
soft butter or margarine
sweetened whipped cream
  (optional)

Wash and hull strawberries and cut a few of them into halves. Put in a bowl and add sugar. Let stand at room temperature at least 30 minutes, stirring often. (The sugar should be dissolved and there should be quite a lot of juice on the berries.)

Split hot Rich Shortcake Biscuits and spread generously with butter or margarine. Spoon some of the berries on each bottom half. Add top halves of biscuits, split side up, and top with remaining berries. Add a dab of whipped cream, if desired, and serve immediately. (Makes 6.)

Advance preparation: Biscuits can be baked, wrapped in foil and reheated in a 400°F oven 10 minutes.

## Rich Shortcake Biscuits

2 cups sifted all-purpose flour
4 tsp. baking powder
1 tsp. salt
1/2 tsp. cream of tartar
1 tbsp. sugar
1/2 cup shortening
3/4 cup milk
1 egg

Heat oven to 450°F.

Sift flour, baking powder, salt, cream of tartar and sugar into a mixing bowl. Add shortening and cut in finely. Beat milk and egg together with a fork and add to first mixture. Mix with a fork until just blended. Dough should be soft and puffy.

Round up dough and knead gently on a floured board about 6 times.

Roll out 1/2 inch thick and cut into six 4-inch biscuits. Put on an ungreased cookie sheet and bake until golden, 12 to 15 minutes. (Makes 6.)

## Lemon Baked Apples

4 medium baking apples
1 egg
1/3 cup sugar
1/4 cup milk
pinch salt
grated rind of 1 lemon
1 tbsp. lemon juice
3 tbsp. melted butter or
  margarine

Heat oven to 375°F. Butter a 1 1/2-qt. casserole.

Wash and core apples and peel them 1/3 of the way down from the top. Set in prepared casserole. Cover and bake until apples are just tender, 30 to 45 minutes.

Beat remaining ingredients together and pour over apples. Bake, uncovered, 10 minutes. Serve immediately. (Serves 4.)

## Apple Cream

1/4 medium lemon
19-oz. can applesauce
250 g pkg. cream cheese
  (room temperature)
1/2 cup sugar
1 tsp. vanilla extract
1 cup whipping cream

Cut lemon into 3 pieces. Put in glass of blender and buzz 30 seconds. Add 1 cup of the applesauce, cheese, sugar and vanilla and buzz 1 minute. Add remaining applesauce and buzz until smooth, about 30 seconds. Stir in cream.

Pour into a metal pan and put in freezer until frozen to about 1 inch from the outside edge. Scrape back into glass of blender and buzz again until smooth. Return to pan and freeze until solid.

Remove from freezer about 15 minutes before serving time. Spoon into sherbet glasses to serve. (Serves 8.)

## Frozen Eggnog with Rum-Fruit Sauce

1 cup sugar
1/3 cup water
4 egg whites
1/4 tsp. salt
1 1/2 cups whipping cream
4 egg yolks
1/2 tsp. ground nutmeg
1 tsp. vanilla extract
Rum-Fruit Sauce (recipe
  follows)

Chill a 2-qt. mold. (Choose a mold with a simple design for easiest unmolding.)

Combine sugar and 1/3 cup water in a small saucepan. Stir over low heat until sugar is dissolved. Turn heat to high and boil hard, uncovered, until candy thermometer registers 236°F or a drop of syrup falls from the tines of a fork in a short thread.

While sugar syrup is cooking, beat egg whites and salt in a large bowl until stiff peaks form. Pour hot syrup in a thin stream into beaten egg whites, beating constantly. Continue beating until mixture is cool and soft peaks form when beaters are raised. Cover and chill 30 minutes.

Beat cream until stiff. Beat egg yolks in another bowl until thick and lemon colored, about 5 minutes at high speed on the mixer. Beat in nutmeg and vanilla.

Add cream and egg yolk mixture to egg whites and fold just until blended. Spoon into chilled mold. Cover with transparent wrap or foil and freeze until serving time.

Invert on a serving plate and wrap a towel that has been wrung out in warm water around the mold just until dessert drops out. Return to freezer if you unmold before serving time.

Spoon a little of the Rum–Fruit Sauce over dessert before bringing it to the table. Cut in large wedges and pass the rest of the sauce. (Serves 12.)

## Rum-Fruit Sauce

1/2 cup sugar
1/2 cup water
1 cup quartered maraschino
  cherries
1/2 cup chopped mixed
  candied fruit
1 cup orange marmalade
1/4 cup chopped candied
  ginger
1/4 cup maraschino cherry
  juice
1/2 cup golden rum

Boil sugar and 1/2 cup water together in a medium saucepan 5 minutes. Add all remaining ingredients except rum and stir to blend well. Cool. Stir in rum. Chill. (Makes about 3 cups.)

Note: This sauce is delicious over vanilla ice cream. It keeps well in the refrigerator.

## Raspberry Parfait

1 envelope (1 tbsp.)
 unflavored gelatin
¹/₄ cup cold water
14-oz. pkg. frozen raspberries,
 thawed
¹/₂ cup sugar
1 cup champagne or
 champagne-type wine
1 cup whipping cream
sweetened whipped cream
candied violets or partly
 thawed frozen raspberries
 (see note)

Soak gelatin in ¹/₄ cup cold water in a medium saucepan 5 minutes.

Force raspberries through a sieve. Discard seeds. Add purée to gelatin and heat, stirring, until gelatin is dissolved. Add sugar and stir until it dissolves. Cool but do not chill. Stir in champagne. Chill by setting in a bowl of ice water until purée begins to thicken. Beat with a rotary beater until fluffy.

Whip cream. Fold into raspberry mixture. Spoon into parfait glasses and chill.

Garnish with a dab of sweetened whipped cream and a candied violet or a raspberry. (Serves 4.)

*Note:* Candied violets are usually imported from France and are available in some food specialty stores. I have suggested partly thawing frozen raspberries because ice crystals in the berries make them look almost like fresh berries.

## Coconut Bavarian Cream with Melon

¹/₂ cup sugar
2 envelopes (2 tbsp.)
 unflavored gelatin
¹/₄ tsp. salt
2¹/₄ cups milk
2 egg yolks, lightly beaten
1 cup whipping cream
1 cup flaked coconut
1 tsp. vanilla extract
¹/₂ tsp. almond extract
4 cups mixed melon balls
 (see note)

Blend sugar, gelatin, salt, milk and egg yolks in a medium saucepan. Set over moderate heat and stir until mixture comes to a boil. Chill by setting in ice water until mixture mounds when dropped from a spoon.

Whip cream and fold in along with coconut, vanilla and almond extracts. Pour mixture into a 5-cup ring mold. Chill until set. Unmold on a serving plate and fill centre with melon balls. (Serves 8.)

*Note:* Choose melons of contrasting color such as watermelon, casaba and Persian or cantaloupe.

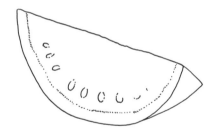

## Rich Chocolate Custard

¹/₂ cup water
4 squares (4 oz.) sweet baking
 chocolate, cut up
2 cups milk, scalded
4 eggs
4 egg yolks
¹/₂ cup sugar
1 tsp. vanilla extract

Heat oven to 325°F. Butter a 1¹/₂-qt. casserole.

Combine ¹/₂ cup water and chocolate in a small saucepan. Cook over very low heat, stirring constantly, until smooth. Combine with scalded milk.

Beat eggs, egg yolks, sugar and vanilla together very well. Stir in hot milk mixture gradually.

Strain into prepared casserole. Set in a pan of hot water and bake until a knife inserted near the centre comes out clean, about 50 minutes. Chill. (Serves 6 to 8.)

## Ginger-Orange Bavarian Cream

*1/2 cup orange juice*
*2 tbsp. grated orange rind*
*1 tsp. grated lemon rind*
*1/2 cup sugar*
*1 envelope (1 tbsp.) unflavored gelatin*
*1/4 tsp. salt*
*1 1/2 cups milk*
*4 egg yolks*
*yellow food coloring*
*2 tbsp. ginger syrup (from preserved ginger)*
*1/4 cup light cream*
*2 tbsp. finely chopped preserved ginger*
*1 cup whipping cream*

Bring orange juice to a boil in a small saucepan. Remove from heat. Add grated orange and lemon rinds and let stand 30 minutes.

Combine sugar, gelatin and salt in a medium saucepan. Stir in milk gradually. Set over moderate heat and cook, stirring constantly, just until mixture comes to a boil.

Beat egg yolks lightly. Add about half of hot mixture to yolks gradually, stirring well after each addition. Pour back into saucepan and bring back to a boil, stirring constantly. Boil 1 minute. Set in ice water and chill until beginning to thicken. Divide mixture into 2 equal parts (about 1 cup each).

Add orange juice-rind mixture to one part. Add a few drops of yellow food coloring. Chill until mixture mounds when dropped from a spoon.

Add ginger syrup, light cream and chopped ginger to second part of mixture. Chill until mixture mounds when dropped from a spoon.

Beat whipping cream until stiff and fold half into each mixture.

Spoon mixtures alternately into a 1-qt. mold to give a marbled effect. Chill several hours or overnight. Unmold onto a serving plate. (Serves 6.)

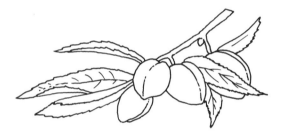

## Praline Fromage

*1/3 cup sugar*
*1/2 cup blanched almonds*
*1 envelope (1 tbsp.) unflavored gelatin*
*3 tbsp. water*
*3 eggs*
*1/2 cup sugar*
*1 tsp. instant coffee*
*1 cup whipping cream*
*1/2 tsp. almond extract*
*sweetened whipped cream (optional)*
*slivered toasted almonds (optional)*

Put 1/3 cup sugar and almonds in a heavy iron skillet. Heat over moderate heat until sugar melts and both sugar and almonds are dark golden brown.

Turn out onto a buttered cookie sheet immediately and spread as thinly as possible by pulling with 2 forks. Cool. Break up and put through the fine blade of the food chopper. Set aside.

Add gelatin to 3 tbsp. water and let stand 5 minutes. Set in a pan of boiling water to melt. Cool slightly.

Beat eggs until frothy. Gradually beat in 1/2 cup sugar and instant coffee and continue beating until very thick, about 5 minutes at high speed on the mixer. Add slightly cooled gelatin in a thin stream, beating constantly.

Beat 1 cup whipping cream until it begins to thicken. Add almond extract and continue beating until stiff. Fold into egg mixture. Fold in almond mixture.

Pour into a 1-qt. mold and chill several hours or overnight. Unmold and, if desired, garnish with whipped cream and slivered toasted almonds. (Serves 4 to 6.)

162

## Café au Lait Cheescake

Combine vanilla wafer crumbs, 1/4 cup sugar and melted butter or margarine, blending well. Turn into a 9-inch springform pan and pack down firmly. Set aside.

Press cottage cheese through a sieve with the back of a spoon.

Combine 3/4 cup sugar, gelatin and salt thoroughly in a large saucepan. Stir in milk gradually. Stir in egg yolks. Set over low heat and heat until gelatin is dissolved, stirring constantly. Remove from heat.

Stir in instant coffee and vanilla. Cool by setting in ice water until mixture begins to thicken slightly. Stir in cottage cheese and chill again until mixture mounds when dropped from a spoon.

Beat egg whites until foamy. Beat in 1/4 cup sugar gradually. Beat until stiff peaks form. Beat cream until stiff. Fold cream into coffee mixture. Fold egg whites into coffee mixture. Pour on top of crumb crust in springform pan. Chill until set. Remove sides of pan and set cheesecake on a serving plate. Garnish top with chocolate curls. (Serves 12.)

*Note:* To make chocolate curls, warm a square or bar of chocolate slightly, then take off thin shavings from back or sides with a vegetable peeler.

1 cup crushed vanilla wafer
 crumbs
1/4 cup sugar
1/4 cup butter or margarine,
 melted
3 cups cream-style cottage
 cheese
3/4 cup sugar
2 envelopes (2 tbsp.)
 unflavored gelatin
1/4 tsp. salt
1 cup milk
2 egg yolks, lightly beaten
1 tbsp. instant coffee
1 tsp. vanilla extract
2 egg whites
1/4 cup sugar
1 cup whipping cream
chocolate curls (see note)

## Egg White Custard

Heat oven to 325°F. Have ready six 6-oz. custard cups. Add hot water 1/2 inch deep to a pan large enough to hold custard cups. Put in oven.

Beat egg whites, vanilla and salt with an electric mixer until foamy. Add sugar, a little at a time, beating well after each addition. Continue beating until stiff.

Scald cream. Add cream slowly to beaten egg whites, beating at low speed until blended. Pour into custard cups and set in pan of hot water in oven.

Bake until a knife inserted near centres comes out clean, about 45 minutes. Cool, then cover with transparent wrap and chill well.

Unmold at serving time. Spoon Rum-Raspberry Sauce over. (Serves 6.)

3 egg whites
1 tsp. vanilla extract
pinch salt
1/4 cup sugar
2 cups light cream
**Rum-Raspberry Sauce**
 *(recipe follows)*

## Rum-Raspberry Sauce

Heat raspberries in a small saucepan just until boiling. Combine 1/4 cup cold water and cornstarch and stir into boiling raspberries. Cook, stirring constantly, until boiling, thickened and clear. Remove from heat. Stir in rum to taste, then chill. (Makes about 1 cup.)

9-oz. pkg. frozen raspberries,
 thawed
1/4 cup cold water
1 tbsp. cornstarch
1 to 2 tbsp. golden rum

## Queen of Puddings

Heat oven to 350°F. Generously butter a 2-qt. casserole. Put a pan of hot water large enough to hold casserole dish in oven.

Scald milk in a large saucepan. Add butter or margarine, stir until melted, then add bread cubes. Beat egg yolks. Stir in $^1/_2$ cup sugar, $^1/_2$ tsp. salt, 1 tsp. vanilla and nutmeg. Combine with bread mixture.

Pour into prepared casserole and set in pan of hot water in oven. Bake until a knife inserted near the centre comes out clean, about 1 hour.

Beat egg whites until foamy. Add pinch of salt and $^1/_2$ tsp. vanilla, then gradually beat in $^1/_3$ cup sugar, beating until stiff and glossy.

Dot pudding with jelly and spread meringue mixture over all. Bake until meringue is lightly browned, about 15 minutes.

Beat cream and 2 tbsp. sugar just until cream is beginning to thicken but still of pouring consistency. Serve pudding hot with some of cream mixture poured over each serving. (Serves 6.)

4 cups milk
$^1/_4$ cup soft butter or margarine
4 cups $^1/_2$-inch cubes stale bread (about 8 slices)
3 egg yolks
$^1/_2$ cup sugar
$^1/_2$ tsp. salt
1 tsp. vanilla extract
pinch ground nutmeg
3 egg whites
pinch salt
$^1/_2$ tsp. vanilla extract
$^1/_3$ cup sugar
$^1/_4$ cup tart jelly (red currant is good)
1 cup whipping cream
2 tbsp. sugar

## Raisin Rice Pudding

Heat oven to 325°F. Butter a $1^1/_2$-qt. casserole.

Add butter or margarine to hot milk and stir until butter or margarine melts.

Combine eggs, sugar, salt, vanilla and nutmeg in a medium bowl and beat together lightly to blend. Stir in milk gradually. Stir in rice and raisins. Pour into prepared casserole.

Bake 20 minutes. Stir with a fork and continue baking until set, 20 to 30 minutes more.

Serve warm with cream. (Serves 6.)

1 tbsp. soft butter or margarine
$1^1/_3$ cups whole milk, scalded
3 eggs
$^1/_3$ cup sugar
pinch salt
$1^1/_2$ tsp. vanilla extract
$^1/_4$ tsp. ground nutmeg
$1^1/_2$ cups cooked regular long-grain rice
$^1/_2$ cup seeded raisins
pouring cream

## Honey-Apple Crisp

Heat oven to 375°F. Butter an 8-inch square glass baking dish.

Peel, core and slice apples thinly. Spread evenly over bottom of prepared pan. Sprinkle with walnuts. Combine lemon juice and honey and drizzle over all.

Mix flour, 3 tbsp. brown sugar, salt and butter or margarine first with a fork, then with fingers to make a crumbly mixture. Sprinkle over apples.

Bake until apples are very tender, about 30 minutes.

Whip cream, 1 tbsp. brown sugar and cardamom or cinnamon just until cream begins to thicken but can still be poured. Serve pudding warm with some of cream mixture poured over each serving. (Serves 4.)

6 medium baking apples
$^1/_4$ cup chopped walnuts
1 tbsp. lemon juice
$^1/_2$ cup liquid honey
$^1/_2$ cup all-purpose flour
3 tbsp. brown sugar
$^1/_4$ tsp. salt
$^1/_4$ cup butter or margarine
$^1/_2$ cup whipping cream
1 tbsp. brown sugar
$^1/_4$ tsp. ground cardamom or cinnamon

## Rhubarb Pudding

6 cups cut-up rhubarb
2 tbsp. quick-cooking tapioca
1 tbsp. grated orange rind
1/4 tsp. salt
1 tsp. lemon juice
1 1/2 cups sugar
1/3 cup butter or margarine, melted
2 1/2 cups 1/4-inch cubes soft bread
pouring cream or sweetened whipped cream

Heat oven to 400°F. Butter a 2-qt. casserole.

Combine rhubarb, tapioca, orange rind, salt, lemon juice and sugar, tossing to mix well.

Combine melted butter or margarine and bread cubes, tossing to coat bread with butter or margarine.

Alternate layers of rhubarb mixture and bread cubes in prepared casserole, ending with a layer of bread cubes. Cover casserole and bake 25 minutes. Uncover and continue baking until rhubarb is tender and crumbs are brown, about 10 minutes more.

Serve warm with pouring cream or sweetened whipped cream. (Serves 6.)

Advance preparation: Make but do not bake. Refrigerate until shortly before time to bake.

## Cherry Cups

19-oz. can red pitted cherries
2 tbsp. butter or margarine
1/3 cup all-purpose flour
1/3 cup quick-cooking rolled oats
3 tbsp. brown sugar
1/4 tsp. ground cinnamon
pinch salt
3 tbsp. melted butter or margarine
ice cream
Cherry Sauce (recipe follows)

Heat oven to 375°F.

Drain cherries well, setting juice aside for sauce.

Put cherries in six 6-oz. custard cups, dividing them evenly. Dot with 2 tbsp. butter or margarine.

Combine flour, rolled oats, brown sugar, cinnamon, salt and 3 tbsp. melted butter or margarine, mixing with a fork to make a crumbly mixture. Sprinkle mixture over cherries.

Bake until topping is well browned, about 30 minutes.

Serve warm, topped with a small scoop of ice cream and a spoonful of Cherry Sauce. (Serves 6.)

Advance preparation: Make but do not bake. Refrigerate until shortly before time to bake.

## Cherry Sauce

1/4 cup sugar
1 1/2 tbsp. cornstarch
1 1/2 cups liquid

Measure cherry juice and add enough water to make the 1 1/2 cups liquid called for. Combine sugar and cornstarch thoroughly in a small saucepan. Stir in liquid gradually, blending until smooth. Bring to a boil over high heat, stirring constantly. Turn down heat and cook, stirring, 1 minute. Serve warm. (Makes about 1 cup.)

## Colonial Pudding

Heat oven to 350°F. Grease a 9-inch pie pan.

Combine brown sugar, sugar, flour, cinnamon and salt, mixing well with a fork. Add egg yolk, vanilla, apple and nuts and blend well. Beat egg white until stiff and fold in.

Spoon into prepared pan and bake until a toothpick stuck in the centre comes out clean. Serve warm, cut in wedges and topped with ice cream. (Serves 4 to 6.)

*1/2 cup packed brown sugar*
*1/2 cup sugar*
*1/2 cup sifted all-purpose flour*
*1/2 tsp. ground cinnamon*
*1/4 tsp. salt*
*1 egg yolk, lightly beaten*
*1 tsp. vanilla extract*
*2 cups coarsely grated apple*
*1/2 cup chopped nuts*
*1 egg white*
*vanilla ice cream*

## Cranberry Pudding

Heat oven to 375°F. Grease a 9-inch square cake pan.

Wash and look over cranberries. Cut each berry into halves.

Sift flour, sugar, baking powder, salt and cinnamon together into a mixing bowl. Add milk and melted butter or margarine and stir just until smooth. Fold in cranberries and orange rind.

Spoon into prepared pan and bake until a toothpick stuck in the centre comes out clean, about 30 minutes.

Cut into squares and serve warm, topped with Cinnamon-Orange Sauce. (Serves 9.)

*2 cups fresh cranberries*
*2 cups sifted all-purpose flour*
*1 cup sugar*
*2 tsp. baking powder*
*1/4 tsp. salt*
*1/2 tsp. ground cinnamon*
*1 cup milk*
*1 tbsp. melted butter or*
  *margarine*
*1 tbsp. grated orange rind*
*Cinnamon-Orange Sauce*
  *(recipe follows)*

## Cinnamon-Orange Sauce

Combine sugar, cornstarch and salt in a saucepan, blending well. Stir in 2 cups boiling water gradually. Bring to a boil over high heat, stirring constantly. Turn down heat and continue stirring 3 minutes.

Remove from heat. Stir in butter or margarine, cinnamon, orange rind and orange juice.

Serve hot with Cranberry Pudding. (Makes about 2 cups.)

*1 cup sugar*
*2 tbsp. cornstarch*
*pinch salt*
*2 cups boiling water*
*1/4 cup butter or margarine*
*1 1/2 tsp. ground cinnamon*
*1 tsp. grated orange rind*
*1 tbsp. orange juice*

## Pineapple Upside-Down Cake

1/4 cup butter or margarine
1/2 cup packed brown sugar
14-oz. can unsweetened
  sliced pineapple
8 maraschino cherries
pecan halves
1 1/3 cups sifted all-purpose
  flour
1 cup sugar
2 tsp. baking powder
1/2 tsp. salt
1/3 cup soft shortening
2/3 cup milk
1 tsp. vanilla extract
1 egg
whipped cream (optional)

Heat oven to 350°F.

Melt butter or margarine in a 10-inch heavy iron skillet that can go in the oven, or in a 9-inch square cake pan. Sprinkle brown sugar over melted butter.

Drain pineapple slices thoroughly and dry on paper toweling. Dry maraschino cherries on paper toweling. Arrange pineapple slices in pan (you should have 8 slices). Put a cherry in the centre of each pineapple slice. Add pecan halves to fill in spaces around pineapple.

Sift flour, sugar, baking powder and salt into a mixing bowl. Add shortening, milk and vanilla. Beat 2 minutes at medium speed on the mixer or 300 hard strokes by hand. Add egg and beat 2 minutes. Pour over fruit in pan.

Bake until cake springs back when touched lightly, about 45 minutes.

Invert pan carefully on a serving plate and let pan stand over cake for 2 minutes so all fruit and nuts drop out. Remove pan.

Serve warm, cut in wedges or squares. Add whipped cream to each serving if desired. (Serves 8.)

## Marmalade Pudding

4 tsp. baking soda
1/2 cup boiling water
1/4 cup soft butter or margarine
1/4 cup sugar
1/2 cup thick orange marmalade
4 egg yolks, beaten
1 1/2 cups sifted all-purpose
  flour
4 egg whites
Caramel Sauce (recipe follows)

Grease a 1 1/2-qt. mold with a tube in the centre. Sprinkle in granulated sugar and shake it around to coat the bottom and sides of the mold.

Measure soda into a mixing bowl. Add 1/2 cup boiling water and stir until soda is dissolved. Add butter or margarine and stir until melted. Add sugar, marmalade, egg yolks and flour and beat until blended. Beat egg whites until stiff but not dry and fold into batter.

Pour batter into prepared mold. Cover tightly with aluminum foil. Set mold on a rack in a large kettle. Add boiling water to the kettle until it comes about halfway up the sides of the mold. Cover kettle tightly and steam (have water boiling gently) until a toothpick stuck in the centre of the pudding comes out dry, about 1 3/4 hours.

Serve, cut in large wedges and topped with warm Caramel Sauce. (Serves 8 to 12.)

Advance preparation: Make completely and store in the refrigerator, wrapped in foil. Steam about 30 minutes to reheat.

## Caramel Sauce

4 egg yolks, lightly beaten
2 cups packed brown sugar
1 cup water
1/2 cup butter or margarine
2 tsp. vanilla extract

Combine egg yolks, sugar, 1 cup water and butter or margarine in a heavy saucepan. Set over moderate heat and bring to a boil, stirring constantly. Boil 1 minute. Remove from heat and stir in vanilla. Serve warm. (Makes about 1 1/2 cups.)

## Cheese and Pear Dumplings

pastry for 2-crust 9-inch pie
  (recipe p. 172)
1/2 cup grated Gouda cheese
6 ripe pears
1/2 cup chopped walnuts
1/2 cup seedless raisins
1/2 cup liquid honey
2 tbsp. flour
1/4 tsp. ground ginger
1/4 cup water
1 tbsp. butter or margarine
1/2 cup light cream
1/2 tsp. vanilla extract
Gouda cheese

Heat oven to 400°F. Have ready a large shallow baking pan (a jelly roll pan is fine).

Mix pastry as usual except add grated cheese to dry ingredients before adding the liquid. Roll pastry very thinly into a 21 × 14-inch oblong. Cut into 7-inch squares.

Peel and core pears, keeping them whole. Set each pear in the centre of a pastry square. Combine walnuts, raisins, honey, flour and ginger and use about half of this mixture to stuff pears. Moisten edges of pastry and wrap completely around pears, sealing well. Set on baking pan.

Bake until pastry is very well browned, 30 to 35 minutes.

Combine remaining nut-raisin mixture with 1/4 cup water and butter or margarine in a small saucepan. Bring to a boil over moderate heat, stirring constantly. Remove from heat when thick and smooth. Stir in cream and vanilla. Return to moderate heat and heat until just blended and hot.

Spoon over warm dumplings as sauce. Serve with slices of Gouda cheese. (Serves 6.)

Advance preparation: Make but do not bake until 35 minutes before serving time. Make sauce except for adding cream and vanilla.

## English Apple Pie

6 medium baking apples
3/4 cup brown sugar
1/2 tsp. ground nutmeg
2 whole cloves
1 tbsp. butter or margarine
pastry for 1-crust 9-inch pie
  (recipe p. 172)
1 tbsp. sugar
Custard Sauce (recipe follows)

Heat oven to 400°F.

Peel, core and slice apples very thinly. Pile in a 9-inch pie pan. Sprinkle with brown sugar and nutmeg. Add cloves and dot with butter or margarine. Cover with foil and bake 20 minutes. Cool to lukewarm.

Roll pastry thinly and lay over apples. Turn pastry edge under and press down with a fork to seal well to edge of pan. Brush pastry with cold water and sprinkle with 1 tbsp. sugar. Cut slashes in pastry to allow steam to escape.

Bake until apples are tender, about 40 minutes. Serve warm with Custard Sauce. (Serves 6.)

Advance preparation: Make completely and reheat in 400°F oven until just warmed through, about 10 minutes. Make sauce and refrigerate until serving time.

## Custard Sauce

1 1/2 cups milk
4 egg yolks
1/4 cup sugar
1/4 tsp. salt
1 1/2 tsp. vanilla extract

Scald milk in the top of a double boiler over direct heat. Beat egg yolks. Blend in sugar and salt. Gradually stir in milk. Pour back into top of double boiler and set over simmering water. Cook, stirring constantly, until mixture coats a metal spoon, about 10 minutes. Cool quickly. Blend in vanilla. (Makes 2 cups.)

## Deep Plum Pie

two 15-oz. cans prune plums
3 tbsp. butter or margarine
2/3 cup packed brown sugar
1 tbsp. flour
1/2 tsp. ground cinnamon
pinch salt
1 tbsp. lemon juice
pastry for 1-crust 9-inch pie
    (recipe p. 172)
light cream
sugar
Plum Sauce (recipe follows)

Heat oven to 425°F. Have ready an 8-inch square glass baking dish.

Drain plums, saving juice for sauce. Cut plums into halves, pit and put in dish, cut sides up. Measure out 1/4 cup of the plum juice and drizzle over fruit. Save remaining juice for Plum Sauce. Cream butter or margarine, brown sugar, flour, cinnamon, salt and lemon juice together. Drop mixture by small spoonfuls over plums.

Roll pastry into a square slightly larger than the pan and lay it on top of fruit. Turn edges of pastry under and press firmly to sides of pan to seal well. Brush pastry with light cream and sprinkle generously with sugar. Cut large slashes in pastry to allow steam to escape.

Bake until pastry is well browned, 25 to 30 minutes. Serve warm with hot Plum Sauce. (Serves 6.)

Advance preparation: Make completely and reheat in 400°F oven until just warmed through, about 10 minutes. Make sauce, store, covered, then reheat at serving time.

## Plum Sauce

1/4 cup sugar
2 tbsp. cornstarch
pinch salt
plum juice

Combine sugar, cornstarch and salt thoroughly in a saucepan. Measure plum juice and add water to make 2 cups liquid. Stir in liquid gradually, blending until smooth. Bring to a boil over high heat, stirring constantly. Turn down heat and boil gently 1 minute. Keep hot to serve over Deep Plum Pie. (Makes about 2 cups.)

## Rhubarb-Raisin Pie

pastry for 2-crust 9-inch pie
    (recipe p. 172)
1 cup sugar
1/4 cup flour
4 cups cut-up rhubarb
1/2 cup golden raisins
1 tbsp. grated orange rind
1 tbsp. butter or margarine

Heat oven to 425°F.

Line a 9-inch pie pan with half the pastry. Mix sugar and flour and sprinkle about 1 tbsp. of mixture evenly over bottom of pastry-lined pan.

Combine remaining sugar mixture, rhubarb, raisins and orange rind. Turn into pastry-lined pan and dot with butter or margarine. Cover with remaining pastry, sealing edge well. Cover edge with a narrow strip of aluminum foil to keep it from browning too much. Cut slashes in top crust to allow steam to escape.

Bake until pastry is well browned and rhubarb juice is bubbling well, about 45 minutes. Serve warm or cold. (Serves 6.)

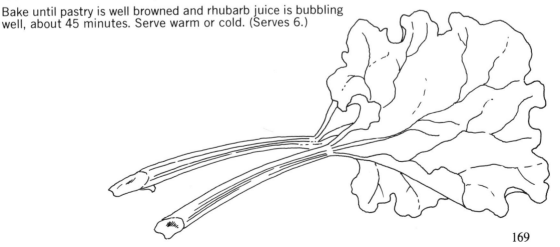

## Presidential Pumpkin Pie

pastry for 2-crust 9-inch pie
  (recipe p. 172)
5 eggs
28-oz. can pumpkin
1½ cups packed brown sugar
½ cup sugar
¼ cup molasses
1½ cups light cream
1 tsp. salt
3 tsp. ground cinnamon
1½ tsp. ground nutmeg
½ tsp. ground ginger
¼ tsp. ground cloves
125 g pkg. cream cheese
  (room temperature)
1 tbsp. light cream
1 tbsp. molasses

Divide pastry into 2 equal pieces and use to line two 9-inch pie pans, building high fluted edges to hold filling. Do not prick pastry.

Heat oven to 425°F.

Beat eggs lightly in a large bowl. Stir in pumpkin, brown sugar, sugar, ¼ cup molasses, 1½ cups cream, salt and spices. Beat until well blended.

Pour pumpkin mixture into unbaked pie shells (about 4 cups per pie). Cover edges of crusts with narrow strips of aluminum foil to keep them from browning too much.

Bake 20 minutes. Reduce oven temperature to 325°F and continue baking until a knife inserted about 1 inch from edges comes out clean, about 35 minutes (centres will be a little soft but will set as pies stand). Remove foil about 10 minutes before end of baking. Cool.

Blend cream cheese, 1 tbsp. cream and 1 tbsp. molasses until fluffy. Put through an icing tube to form a lattice on top of each pie. Chill until shortly before serving time. (Makes 2 pies, serves 12.)

## Pumpkin-Pecan Pie

pastry for 1-crust 9-inch pie
  (recipe p. 172)
3 eggs
1 cup canned pumpkin
1 cup sugar
½ cup liquid honey
1 tsp. vanilla extract
½ tsp. ground cinnamon
¼ tsp. ground allspice
⅛ tsp. ground cloves
½ tsp. salt
1 cup coarsely chopped
  pecans

Heat oven to 350°F.

Line a 9-inch pie pan with pastry, building up a high fluted edge to hold filling. Do not prick pastry.

Beat eggs lightly with a rotary beater. Add pumpkin, sugar, honey, vanilla, spices and salt. Beat to blend well. Pour into unbaked pie shell. Sprinkle top of pie with pecans.

Bake until a knife inserted about 1 inch from edge of pie comes out clean, about 40 minutes. Cool before serving. (Serves 6.)

## Whipped Orange Pie

1 cup evaporated milk
$^2/_3$ cup water
$^1/_3$ cup orange juice
3-oz. pkg. orange jelly powder
$^1/_2$ cup sugar
1 tbsp. grated orange rind
2 tbsp. lemon juice
Chocolate Wafer Crumb Crust
    (recipe follows)
orange wedges (optional)

Pour evaporated milk into a metal pan and freeze until ice crystals form around edges.

Heat $^2/_3$ cup water and orange juice to boiling. Combine jelly powder and sugar in a bowl. Add hot liquid and stir until gelatin is dissolved. Stir in orange rind. Set in a bowl of ice water to chill until mixture begins to thicken.

Beat evaporated milk until stiff, about 2 minutes. Add lemon juice and beat until very stiff, about 2 minutes. Fold into chilled orange mixture. Pile into crumb crust. Chill until set. Garnish with orange wedges if desired. (Serves 6.)

## Chocolate Wafer Crumb Crust

$1^1/_2$ cups fine chocolate wafer
    crumbs
$^1/_4$ cup sugar
$^1/_3$ cup melted butter or
    margarine

Heat oven to 400°F.

Combine crumbs, sugar and butter or margarine, blending with a fork until crumbs are completely coated with butter or margarine. Press firmly into a 9-inch pie pan, building up as high an edge as possible.

Bake 8 minutes. Cool and fill.

## Pink Grapefruit Chiffon Pie

4 medium pink grapefruit
1 envelope (1 tbsp.)
    unflavored gelatin
3 egg yolks
$^1/_2$ cup sugar
$^1/_4$ tsp. salt
$^1/_2$ tsp. grated lemon rind
$^1/_4$ cup lemon juice
red food coloring
3 egg whites
$^1/_4$ tsp. cream of tartar
$^1/_4$ cup sugar
9-inch baked pie shell
    (recipe p. 172)

Grate enough of the rind from one of the grapefruit to make 1 tsp. Set aside. Section 2 grapefruit and put sections in a sieve over a bowl and drain well.

Squeeze other 2 grapefruit, strain juice, add juice drained from grapefruit sections and measure. Add water, if necessary, to make $1^1/_2$ cups liquid. Add gelatin to $^1/_2$ cup of this liquid and let stand.

Beat egg yolks in a small saucepan. Add remaining 1 cup liquid, $^1/_2$ cup sugar, salt, lemon rind, lemon juice and the 1 tsp. grapefruit rind you set aside. Set over moderate heat and cook, stirring constantly, until mixture comes to a boil.

Remove from heat, add gelatin mixture and stir until gelatin is dissolved. Add enough red food coloring to tint to a delicate pink. Set in ice water to chill until mixture begins to mound when dropped from a spoon.

Beat egg whites and cream of tartar until frothy. Add $^1/_4$ cup sugar gradually, beating constantly, and continue beating until stiff and glossy.

Beat thickened gelatin mixture until fluffy. Cut all but 6 of the grapefruit sections into 3 pieces and add these pieces to gelatin mixture. Add egg whites and fold in carefully. Chill again for a few minutes if mixture is not holding shape.

Pile into cooled baked pie shell and chill several hours until firm. Garnish with saved grapefruit sections. (Serves 6.)

### Standard Pastry
#### (For 2-crust 9-inch pie)

2 cups sifted all-purpose flour
1 tsp. salt
$2/3$ cup lard or $3/4$ cup
   shortening
$1/4$ cup ice water

Measure flour into a bowl. Mix in salt with a fork. Add lard or shortening and cut in coarsely with a pastry blender. Sprinkle in $1/4$ cup water a tablespoonful at a time, mixing lightly with a fork just until all flour is dampened. Gather into a ball with fingers and press firmly.

Divide into halves and shape each half into a round. Flatten slightly with hand. Roll one half thinly (slightly less than $1/8$ inch) on a floured board or pastry cloth, using as little extra flour as possible on board and rolling pin. Roll gently from centre rather than back and forth. Keep rounding up edges with hands. Roll to 1 inch larger than inverted pie pan.

Lift on rolling pin to pan and ease pastry loosely into pan. Do not stretch. Add filling, then trim off pastry even with edge of pie pan.

Roll remaining dough 1 inch larger than top of pie pan. Fold in quarters and cut several slashes to allow steam to escape.

Dampen edge of bottom pastry with water and put folded top crust in place. Unfold, press to bottom crust to seal and trim evenly to $1/2$ inch. Roll edge of top crust under edge of bottom crust. Flute.

Cover edge of pie with a narrow strip of aluminum foil to keep it from browning too much during baking. Bake as directed in recipe.

#### (For 1-crust 9-inch pie)

Use half of preceding ingredients. Roll out and put in pan as for lower crust of 2-crust pie. Trim to $1/2$ inch, roll edge under and flute.

Do not prick if filling goes in unbaked crust. Fill and bake as directed in recipes.

Prick all over with the tines of a fork if baked pie shell is called for. Bake at 475°F until browned, 8 to 10 minutes. Cool and fill.

172

## After-School Snacks

Eighteen good-tasting, nutritious ways to fill up hungry children.

## Coffee Break

Eight treats, each suitable for a coffee-time pickup. Cinnamon Toast Deluxe, Tiny Buttermilk Muffins and other delights to please guests or just for yourself.

## Afternoon Tea

Nineteen to choose from — dainty sandwiches, party cookies and very special cakes.

## Cocktail Snacks

Eighteen delicious ways to please party guests — from simple Health Crackers to exotic Stuffed Mushrooms.

## Drinks

Nineteen different and delicious liquid refreshments. Try Minty Apple Cooler, Toe Warmer, Hot Chocolate Nog, Wine Julep or a punch for a crowd.

## Picnic and Barbecue

Twenty-six ways to make eating outdoors everyone's pleasure. Here are appetizers, cold meats for picnics, hot meats and fish on the grill or spit and the salads and vegetables to accent them all.

# 4
# Specials

Each cookbook I have done has presented the same problem. I always end up with a group of recipes that simply must be included but which don't really fit in any of the neat categories I've so carefully worked out. In each case I've ended up with a kind of miscellaneous section that usually turns out to be a favorite part of the book. This book is no exception. I must give suggestions for appetizing and healthful after-school snacks; for special treats to serve with coffee, afternoon tea or cocktails; for hot and cold drinks; for good food for barbecues and picnics. None of these recipes are really regular breakfast, lunch or dinner suggestions, so here they are — in their own Specials section.

"What's to eat?" is a familiar cry occurring in the late afternoon in homes all across the country. What is it about getting home from school that makes all kids hungry? I have a friend who tells me that no matter what time her children arrive home they want their dinner, so she either has to give them some sustaining snacks or the whole family ends up eating in relays.

We're all concerned that children learn to eat healthful snacks rather than junk food. But it's no use making something that's good for them but doesn't taste good, so we've suggested fruit and vegetable snacks that can be left in the refrigerator or made by starving children in a hurry, hot snacks that can be made by teenagers, plus cookies, wafers and bars that are full of good things and taste superspecial, too.

### Cheese Stuffed Celery

Wash celery thoroughly and strip off any coarse strings on the outside with a vegetable peeler. Cut stalks into pieces 1 to 2 inches long.

Beat cream cheese, onion, salt and Tabasco together until fluffy. Stir in Brazil nuts. Fill pieces of celery with mixture. Chill until shortly before serving time. (Makes about 20.)

4 large stalks celery (approx.)
125 g pkg. cream cheese
 (room temperature)
1 1/2 tsp. finely grated onion
dash salt
1 drop Tabasco (optional)
1/4 cup finely chopped Brazil
 nuts

### Apple Snacks

Cut large, cored but unpeeled apples into rings 1/4 inch thick and spread some of any of these mixtures between 2 of them to make a sandwich.

*Cheese:* Combine 1/4 cup finely grated old Cheddar cheese with 1 tbsp. mayonnaise. (Makes enough for 2 snacks.)

*Jam and Cheese:* Combine a 125 g pkg. softened cream cheese with 3 tbsp. thick strawberry jam. (Makes enough for 4 snacks.)

*Ham and Pickle:* Combine 1/4 cup finely ground cooked ham, 1 tbsp. well-drained pickle relish and enough mayonnaise to hold mixture together, about 1 1/2 tsp.(Makes enough for 3 snacks.)

## Apple Wedges

Combine cheese, onions and pimento. Cut unpeeled apples into 8 wedges each. Cut out core and spread cut sides of each wedge with some of cheese mixture. Roll in walnuts. (Makes 16.)

125 g pkg. cream cheese
 (room temperature)
2 tbsp. finely chopped green
 onions
2 tsp. finely chopped pimento
2 large apples
1/2 cup finely chopped walnuts

## Fruit Dip

Blend yogurt, honey and orange juice concentrate. Chill, then use as a dip for fruit pieces. (Makes about 3/4 cup.)

2/3 cup plain yogurt
 (one 175 g carton)
2 tsp. liquid honey
2 tbsp. thawed orange juice
 concentrate
apple and pear sections,
 banana strips, melon chunks

## Little Pizzas

Stir soup, garlic and oregano together. Cut each muffin into 3 round slices and toast lightly. Spread with soup mixture and top with cheese. Put on a cookie sheet and broil until cheese melts, about 3 minutes. (Makes 12.)

10-oz. can tomato soup
1 small clove garlic, crushed
1/2 tsp. dried leaf oregano
4 English muffins
1/4 lb. Mozzarella cheese,
 thinly sliced

## Pickle Strips

Heat oven to 375°F.

Fry bacon until crisp and drain well on paper toweling, then crumble and mix with cheese spread. Spread on bread and cut each slice into 3 narrow strips. Put on a cookie sheet. Spread each strip with 1/2 tsp. relish. Heat in oven until bubbly, 5 to 8 minutes. (Makes 12.)

4 slices bacon
1/3 cup process cheese spread
4 slices buttered whole wheat
 bread
well-drained sweet pickle
 relish

## Cabbage-Orange Sandwiches

Combine all ingredients except bread and mix well. Spread on bread to make open-face sandwiches. Cut into quarters to serve. (Makes 32.)

2 medium oranges, peeled,
 sectioned, diced and
 well drained
1/2 cup finely grated cabbage
1/4 cup smooth peanut butter
1/4 cup chopped salted
 peanuts
1/4 cup chopped raisins
1 tbsp. grated orange rind
2 tbsp. mayonnaise
8 slices buttered whole wheat
 bread

## Rusks

Heat oven to 400°F. Have ready ungreased cookie sheets.

Cream butter or margarine and sugar together. Beat in eggs one at a time.

Sift flour, baking powder, cardamom and salt together. Add whole wheat flour and blend with a fork. Add dry ingredients to first mixture alternately with milk. Stir just until blended after each addition.

Gather dough into a ball and knead lightly on a floured board 6 times to smooth. Roll out to $^1/_2$ inch thick. Cut dough into $2^1/_2$-inch rounds. Put on cookie sheets. Bake 10 minutes.

Remove sheets from oven and split each round into 2 rounds by prying it apart with 2 forks. Return rounds to cookie sheets.

Bake until lightly browned and dry to the touch, about 20 minutes more. (Makes about 48.)

$^1/_2$ cup soft butter or margarine
2 tbsp. sugar
2 eggs
$4^1/_2$ cups sifted all-purpose flour
4 tsp. baking powder
$^1/_2$ tsp. ground cardamom
$^1/_2$ tsp. salt
$^1/_2$ cup whole wheat flour
$1^1/_2$ cups milk

## Whole Wheat Sweet Wafers

Put flour in a bowl and add salt, baking powder and sugar. Mix with a fork. Add butter or margarine and cut in finely with a pastry blender. Stir in $^3/_4$ cup water with a fork. Chill 30 minutes.

Heat oven to 325°F. Grease 2 large cookie sheets.

Divide dough into halves, shape half into a flattened rectangle with hands and roll it out on cookie sheet into a large rectangle about 12 × 10 inches. Cut rectangle into 2-inch squares with a pastry wheel or knife. Prick each square in several places. Repeat with second half of dough.

Bake until lightly browned, about 35 minutes. (Makes about 5 dozen.)

*Note:* If desired, replace sugar with $^1/_2$ cup liquid honey, adding the honey at the same time as water. Reduce water to $^1/_2$ cup.

$3^1/_2$ cups whole wheat flour
$^1/_2$ tsp. salt
$^1/_2$ tsp. baking powder
$^1/_2$ cup packed brown sugar (see note)
$^3/_4$ cup butter or margarine
$^3/_4$ cup cold water

## Health Bars

Heat oven to 350°F. Grease a 15 × 10 × 1-inch jelly roll pan.

Beat eggs with butter or margarine, oil, honey and vanilla. Mix remaining ingredients well with a fork. Add to first mixture and mix well. Turn into prepared pan and pack down firmly.

Bake until set and lightly browned, about 25 minutes. Cool 5 minutes, then cut into $2^1/_2$ × $1^1/_2$ - inch bars. Finish cooling in pan. (Makes 3 dozen.)

3 eggs
$^1/_4$ cup butter or margarine, melted
$^1/_4$ cup cooking oil
$^1/_2$ cup liquid honey
1 tsp. vanilla extract
2 cups quick-cooking rolled oats
1 cup whole wheat flour
$^1/_2$ cup flaked coconut
$^1/_2$ cup wheat germ
$^1/_2$ cup sesame seeds
$^1/_2$ cup chopped walnuts
$^1/_2$ cup skim milk powder
$^1/_4$ tsp. salt
$^1/_2$ tsp. ground nutmeg

## Jam Bars

Heat oven to 400°F. Grease an 8-inch square cake pan.

Cream butter or margarine with corn syrup and extracts until fluffy. Mix flour, baking powder, salt, cloves and cinnamon with a fork and add to creamed mixture. Blend well.

Spread half of mixture in prepared pan. Top with jam, spreading it to within 1/2 inch of edge. Drop remaining dough by small spoonfuls on top of jam. Spread as much as possible, but don't worry if jam shows through.

Bake 25 minutes. Cool and cut into large bars. (Makes 8 to 12.)

1/2 cup soft butter or margarine
1/3 cup corn syrup
1/2 tsp. almond extract
1/2 tsp. vanilla extract
1 1/4 cups whole wheat flour or sifted all-purpose flour
1 tsp. baking powder
1/4 tsp. salt
1/4 tsp. ground cloves
1/2 tsp. ground cinnamon
1/2 cup thick raspberry jam

## Applesauce Cookies

Heat oven to 375°F. Grease cookie sheets.

Cream shortening with honey and stir in applesauce. Mix flour, soda, salt, cinnamon and cloves with a fork and add to first mixture. Stir to blend. Stir in raisins and nuts.

Drop by rounded tablespoonfuls onto prepared sheets. Bake until lightly browned, 12 to 14 minutes. (Makes about 2 1/2 dozen large.)

1/2 cup soft shortening
1/2 cup liquid honey
1 cup canned applesauce
2 cups whole wheat flour
1 tsp. baking soda
1/4 tsp. salt
1 tsp. ground cinnamon
1/2 tsp. ground cloves
1/2 cup raisins
1/2 cup chopped nuts

## Honey-Peanut Butter Cookies

Heat oven to 350°F. Have ready ungreased cookie sheets.

Beat shortening, honey, sugar and egg together until light and fluffy. Beat in peanut butter. Stir flour, soda and salt together with a fork and add to peanut butter mixture, blending well.

Shape dough into small balls, about 1-inch in diameter, and put on cookie sheets. Flatten with the tines of a fork. Bake until set, 12 to 15 minutes. (Makes about 3 dozen.)

1/2 cup soft shortening
1/2 cup liquid honey
1/2 cup packed brown sugar
1 egg
1/2 cup smooth peanut butter
1 1/4 cups whole wheat flour
1/2 tsp. baking soda
1/2 tsp. salt

## English Currant Cookies

Beat shortening, butter or margarine, brown sugar, egg and egg yolk together until fluffy. Stir in lemon juice and rind. Stir flour, soda and salt together with a fork and add to creamed mixture, blending well. Blend in currants. Chill several hours.

Heat oven to 350°F. Grease cookie sheets.

Roll dough out to about 1/8 inch thick. Cut into 3-inch rounds with a cookie cutter and put on prepared cookie sheets, leaving about 2 inches between cookies.

Beat egg white and 1 tbsp. water together with a fork. Brush some of this mixture on top of each cookie and sprinkle generously with sugar.

Bake until nicely browned and set, 12 to 15 minutes. (Makes about 3 dozen large.)

1/2 cup soft shortening
1/2 cup soft butter or margarine
1 1/2 cups packed brown sugar
1 egg
1 egg yolk
2 tbsp. lemon juice
1 tsp. grated lemon rind
3 cups whole wheat flour
1 tsp. baking soda
1 tsp. salt
1 cup currants
1 egg white
1 tbsp. water
sugar

## School Day Cookies

1 cup soft shortening
1 cup sugar
2 eggs
1/4 cup orange juice
2 tbsp. grated orange rind
1 tsp. vanilla extract
2 cups sifted all-purpose flour
1 tsp. baking soda
1/2 tsp. salt
2 cups quick-cooking
   rolled oats
1/2 cup chopped dates
1/2 cup chopped walnuts

Heat oven to 375°F. Grease cookie sheets.

Beat shortening, sugar and eggs together until fluffy. Add orange juice, orange rind and vanilla. Sift flour, soda and salt together and stir into first mixture. Blend in rolled oats, dates and walnuts.

Drop dough by rounded teaspoonfuls onto prepared cookie sheets and bake about 12 minutes. (Makes about 5 dozen.)

## Blender Banana Cookies

1/2 cup walnuts
1/2 cup liquid honey
1/2 cup cooking oil
1 egg
2 large very ripe bananas
1 3/4 cups rolled oats
1 1/2 cups whole wheat flour
1 tsp. salt
3/4 tsp. ground cinnamon
1/4 tsp. ground nutmeg

Heat oven to 350°F. Grease cookie sheets.

Grind nuts finely in glass of blender. Empty blender glass into a bowl. Put honey, oil, egg and bananas in blender glass and buzz until smooth and blended. Add to nuts. Add all remaining ingredients and mix well (batter should be stiff).

Drop by rounded teaspoonfuls onto cookie sheets. Flatten slightly with the tines of a fork. Bake about 15 minutes. (Makes about 4 dozen.)

## Fruit Squares

1/2 cup cooking oil
1/2 cup liquid honey
2 eggs
3/4 cup whole wheat flour
1/4 cup wheat germ
1/2 cup chopped nuts
1/4 cup cut-up dates
2 tbsp. chopped raisins
2 tbsp. flaked coconut

Heat oven to 350°F. Grease an 8-inch square cake pan.

Beat oil, honey and eggs together well. Stir in all remaining ingredients.

Spread in prepared pan and bake until top springs back when touched lightly, 25 to 30 minutes. Cut into 2-inch squares to serve. (Makes 16.)

## Raisin-Lemon Drops

1 cup golden raisins
1/2 cup soft shortening
1/2 cup liquid honey
2 eggs
2 tsp. grated lemon rind
3 tbsp. lemon juice
2 cups whole wheat flour
1 tsp. salt
1 tsp. baking powder
1/2 tsp. baking soda

Cover raisins with boiling water and let stand 5 minutes. Drain.

Heat oven to 375°F. Grease cookie sheets.

Beat shortening, honey and eggs together until fluffy. Blend in lemon rind and juice. Stir flour, salt, baking powder and soda together with a fork. Blend into creamed mixture. Stir in raisins.

Drop by rounded teaspoonfuls onto prepared cookie sheets. Bake until lightly browned and set, about 15 minutes. (Makes about 3 1/2 dozen.)

# Coffee Break

A lifesaver I always keep in my freezer is a loaf or two of fruit or nut bread already sliced. Then when I have unexpected company and want to offer coffee I can take out a few slices and toast them if I am in a hurry or let them thaw a few minutes if no one is rushing. A planned coffee party can include many nice things — in fact, the choice is nearly unlimited. Here are a few suggestions, with emphasis on quick breads.

## Cinnamon Toast Deluxe

½ cup sugar
1½ tsp. ground cinnamon
8 thick slices fresh white bread
½ cup butter or margarine (approx.)

Combine sugar and cinnamon in a clean paper or plastic bag.

Cut crusts from bread and cut each slice into 2 pieces diagonally. Heat about 2 tbsp. of the butter or margarine in a large heavy skillet. Add a few pieces of bread and fry quickly until golden brown on both sides. Shake bread while hot and buttery in bag to coat well with sugar-cinnamon mixture. Keep warm in low oven.

Continue frying bread pieces, adding a little butter or margarine as needed, and shaking them in sugar mixture until all are done. Cut pieces into halves again to make small triangles and serve warm. (Serves 4 to 6.)

## Potato Scones

¾ cup sour cream
2 tbsp. sugar
1½ tsp. salt
large pinch ground mace
¼ cup butter or margarine
½ tsp. baking soda
½ cup mashed potatoes (you can use prepared instant if desired)
½ cup warm water
1 tsp. sugar
1 pkg. dry yeast
3 cups all-purpose flour (approx.)
butter or margarine

Combine sour cream, 2 tbsp. sugar, salt, mace and butter or margarine in the top of a double boiler. Set over simmering water and heat just until well blended and warm to the touch. Remove from heat and stir in soda and potatoes.

While cream mixture is heating, measure warm water into a large mixing bowl. Add 1 tsp. sugar and stir until sugar is dissolved. Sprinkle yeast over and let stand 10 minutes. Stir well. Add warm (not hot) sour cream mixture and 1½ cups of the flour. Beat until smooth. Stir in enough of remaining flour to make a soft dough that is easy to handle.

Turn out onto a floured board and knead until smooth and elastic, about 5 minutes. Round up dough. Grease a medium bowl and put dough in it, turning it over once so top is greased. Cover with a damp cloth and let rise in a warm place until double, about 1¼ hours.

Punch dough down and divide into 4 equal parts. Roll each part out on a well-floured board into a thin round about 8 inches in diameter. Turn round over once during rolling to flour both sides. Cut each round into 4 triangles and put them well apart on greased cookie sheets. Let rise until double, about 45 minutes.

Heat oven to 375°F. Bake scones until nicely browned, about 15 minutes. Serve warm with butter or margarine. (Makes 16.)

## Tiny Buttermilk Muffins

1/4 cup cooking oil
1 egg, beaten
1 1/4 cups buttermilk
2 cups sifted all-purpose flour
1/2 tsp. baking soda
1/2 tsp. salt
1 tbsp. cornmeal
1 tbsp. sugar
butter or margarine
jam

Heat oven to 400°F. Grease 18 tiny muffin cups, 1 1/2 to 2 inches in diameter.

Combine oil, egg and buttermilk in a bowl. Sift dry ingredients together into mixture and stir just to blend. Spoon into prepared muffin cups, filling about 2/3 full.

Bake until tops spring back when touched lightly, about 10 minutes. Serve hot with butter or margarine and jam. (Makes 18 small.)


## Whole Wheat Banana Bread

1/2 cup butter or margarine
1 cup sugar
2 eggs
1 cup mashed ripe bananas (about 3)
1 cup sifted all-purpose flour
1 tsp. salt
1 tsp. baking soda
1/2 tsp. ground nutmeg
1 cup whole wheat flour
1/3 cup hot water
1/2 cup chopped pecans

Heat oven to 325°F. Grease a 9 × 5 × 3-inch loaf pan.

Beat butter or margarine, sugar and eggs together until light and fluffy. Stir in bananas.

Sift all-purpose flour, salt, soda and nutmeg together. Mix in whole wheat flour with a fork. Add this mixture to first mixture alternately with 1/3 cup hot water, stirring just to blend. Stir in pecans.

Spoon into prepared pan and bake until a toothpick stuck in the centre comes out clean, about 60 minutes. Turn out onto a cake rack to cool. Wrap in heavy aluminum foil to store. (Makes 1 loaf.)


## Raisin-Bran Bread

1 egg
1/4 cup molasses
2 tbsp. cooking oil
1 cup All-Bran
1 cup sugar
1 cup milk
2 cups sifted all-purpose flour
4 tsp. baking powder
1 tsp. salt
1/2 cup raisins

Heat oven to 350°F. Grease a 9 × 5 × 3-inch loaf pan.

Beat egg. Stir in molasses and oil. Add bran, sugar and milk and beat to blend.

Sift dry ingredients together into first mixture. Add raisins and stir just to blend.

Spoon into prepared pan. Bake until a toothpick stuck in the centre comes out clean, about 45 minutes. Wrap in heavy aluminum foil to store. (Makes 1 loaf.)

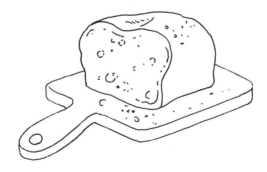

## Zucchini Loaf

Heat oven to 375°F. Grease a 9 × 5 × 3-inch loaf pan.

Beat eggs. Gradually beat in honey and oil. Stir in zucchini, lemon rind, raisins and nuts. Sift flour, baking powder, soda, salt, ginger and nutmeg together into mixture and stir to blend.

Spoon into prepared pan and bake 5 minutes. Reduce heat to 350°F and bake until a toothpick stuck in the centre comes out clean, about 35 minutes more. Let stand 10 minutes, then turn out onto a rack to cool. Wrap in heavy aluminum foil to store. (Makes 1 loaf.)

2 eggs
1/4 cup liquid honey
1/2 cup cooking oil
1 cup coarsely grated unpeeled zucchini
1 tsp. lemon rind
1/2 cup seedless raisins
1/2 cup chopped walnuts
1 1/2 cups sifted all-purpose flour
2 tsp. baking powder
1/2 tsp. baking soda
1/2 tsp. salt
1/2 tsp. ground ginger
1/8 tsp. ground nutmeg

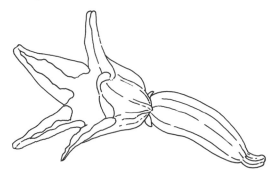

## Marmalade Loaf

Heat oven to 350°F. Grease an 11 × 5 × 3-inch loaf pan.

Beat eggs. Stir in 3 tbsp. butter or margarine, marmalade and nuts. Sift flour, sugar, baking powder and salt together and stir into first mixture alternately with orange juice.

Spoon into prepared pan and bake until a toothpick stuck in the centre comes out clean, about 70 minutes.

Wrap in heavy aluminum foil when cold and let mellow for a day, then slice very thinly and spread with butter or margarine. (Makes 1 loaf.)

2 eggs
3 tbsp. butter or margarine, melted
1/2 cup orange marmalade
1 cup chopped nuts
2 3/4 cups sifted all-purpose flour
1 cup sugar
4 tsp. baking powder
1 tsp. salt
3/4 cup orange juice
butter or margarine

## Cranberry Bread

Cover raisins with boiling water and let stand 5 minutes. Drain and dry well on paper toweling.

Heat oven to 350°F. Grease a 9 × 5 × 3-inch loaf pan.

Sift flour, sugar, baking powder, soda and salt into a mixing bowl. Add shortening and cut in finely.

Beat orange juice and egg together lightly with a fork. Add to dry ingredients along with orange rind, cranberry sauce and raisins. Stir just to blend.

Spoon into prepared pan and bake until a toothpick stuck in the centre comes out clean, 60 to 70 minutes. Turn out onto a rack to cool. Wrap in heavy aluminum foil to store. (Makes 1 loaf.)

1 cup seedless raisins
2 cups sifted all-purpose flour
1/2 cup sugar
1 1/2 tsp. baking powder
1/2 tsp. baking soda
1 tsp. salt
1/4 cup shortening
1/4 cup orange juice
1 egg
1 tbsp. grated orange rind
15-oz. can whole cranberry sauce

# Afternoon Tea

There was a time, not so long ago, when the ladies of the household collected unmatched and beautiful teacups. A tea tray set with them, the best silver and tiny embroidered linen napkins was a joy to behold. I still have some of my mother's English teacups, and though I don't want to iron all those tiny napkins, I do like to occasionally prepare a proper tea tray and to make dainty sandwiches and a special cookie or cake like the ones suggested here.

### Chutney Sandwiches

Combine cheese, dates, fruit from chutney and chutney liquid. Cut crusts from bread and discard. Butter bread lightly and spread half of slices thinly with cheese mixture. Top with remaining slices. Wrap in transparent wrap and chill until shortly before serving time. Cut each sandwich into 3 fingers to serve. (Makes 18 fingers.)

125 g pkg. cream cheese (room temperature)
1/4 cup chopped dates
1 tbsp. fruit from chutney, chopped
1 tbsp. liquid from chutney
12 slices whole wheat bread
butter or margarine

### Cheese and Salted Almond Sandwiches

Blend cream cheese and mayonnaise. Stir in process cheese and almonds. Cut crusts from bread and discard. Butter bread lightly and spread half of slices with cheese mixture. Top with remaining slices. Wrap in transparent wrap and chill until serving time. Cut into quarters to serve. (Makes 24.)

1/4 cup cream cheese (room temperature)
2 tbsp. mayonnaise
1 cup grated process cheese
1/4 cup chopped, toasted salted almonds
12 slices bread
butter or margarine

### Ham and Raisin Sandwiches

Combine ham, raisins and capers and enough of the mayonnaise to make a mixture that is easy to spread but not wet.

Cut crusts from bread and discard. Butter bread and spread half of the slices with ham mixture. Top with remaining slices. Wrap in transparent wrap and chill until shortly before serving time. Cut into quarters to serve. (Makes 32.)

1 cup finely ground cooked ham
1/2 cup seedless raisins, ground
1 tsp. drained capers, chopped
4 tbsp. mayonnaise (approx.)
16 slices bread
butter or margarine

### Watercress Spread

Blend cheese and butter or margarine. Stir in watercress leaves and pepper. Use between slices of whole wheat bread and cut into small sandwiches. (Makes 1¼ cups.)

250 g pkg. cream cheese
   (room temperature)
¼ cup soft butter or
   margarine
¼ cup finely chopped
   watercress leaves
¼ tsp. black pepper
thin slices whole wheat bread

### Cheese-Olive Spread

Blend cream cheese, blue cheese and mayonnaise well with a fork. Stir in olives and celery and use to fill dainty sandwiches made from thin slices of rye or whole wheat bread. (Makes about 1 cup.)

125 g pkg. cream cheese
   (room temperature)
¼ cup crumbled blue cheese
2 tbsp. mayonnaise
¾ cup chopped ripe olives
¼ cup finely chopped celery
rye or whole wheat bread

### Cheese-Nut Spread

Cream cheeses together until smooth. Blend in remaining ingredients except bread, adding only enough mayonnaise to make filling a good spreading consistency. Spread on rye bread to make open-face sandwiches. (Makes about 1 cup.)

125 g pkg. cream cheese
   (room temperature)
¼ cup crumbled blue cheese
¼ cup very finely chopped
   walnuts
¼ tsp. grated onion
½ tsp. Worcestershire sauce
¼ tsp. salt
¼ cup mayonnaise (approx.)
small thin slices rye bread

### Old-Fashioned Sugar Cookies

Cream butter or margarine, 1½ cups sugar, eggs and vanilla until fluffy. Sift flour, soda, baking powder, salt and nutmeg together and add to creamed mixture alternately with sour cream. Blend well. Wrap dough in waxed paper and chill several hours or overnight.

Heat oven to 375°F. Grease cookie sheets lightly.

Roll dough out on a floured board to ¼ inch thick. Cut into rounds with a cookie cutter, put on prepared cookie sheets and sprinkle with sugar. Bake until lightly browned, about 12 minutes. (Makes 7 to 8 dozen.)

1 cup soft butter or margarine
1½ cups sugar
2 eggs
1½ tsp. vanilla extract
4½ cups sifted all-purpose
   flour
1 tsp. baking soda
1 tsp. baking powder
1 tsp. salt
½ tsp. ground nutmeg
1 cup sour cream
sugar

## Coconut Macaroons

3 cups ground coconut
(use fine blade of food
chopper)
$^1/_3$ cup sugar
1 egg white
6 tbsp. sifted cake flour
$^1/_2$ tsp. baking powder
$^1/_2$ tsp. almond extract
$^1/_2$ tsp. vanilla extract
1 egg white
$^1/_4$ tsp. salt
$^1/_3$ cup sugar

Heat oven to 325°F. Cover cookie sheets with aluminum foil.

Combine coconut (use desiccated if you prefer, but I find the ground shredded coconut gives better flavor), $^1/_3$ cup sugar and 1 egg white in the top of a double boiler. Set over boiling water and heat, stirring occasionally, until mixture is warmed through, about 15 minutes. Remove from heat.

Sift flour and baking powder together into mixture. Add almond and vanilla extracts and blend all thoroughly.

Beat remaining 1 egg white and salt until frothy. Add $^1/_3$ cup sugar gradually, beating well after each addition. Continue beating until stiff and glossy. Fold into coconut mixture.

Drop on foil-covered cookie sheets by rounded teaspoonfuls. Bake until lightly browned and set but still chewy, about 15 minutes. Remove from foil when cool. (Makes about 3 dozen.)

## Rum Balls

5 cups dried and crumbled
yellow cake (see note)
2 cups sifted icing sugar
$^1/_4$ cup sifted cocoa
2 cups finely chopped walnuts
$^1/_3$ cup corn syrup
$^1/_2$ cup golden rum
icing sugar
chocolate decorating candies
(chocolate shot)

Combine cake crumbs, 2 cups icing sugar, cocoa, walnuts, corn syrup and rum, blending very well. Shape into small balls about 1 inch in diameter. Run hands under cold water occasionally and leave them damp so mixture doesn't stick to them. Roll half of balls in icing sugar, the other half in chocolate decorating candies.

Store in a tightly covered container in a cool place. For long storage it is best to refrigerate or freeze. (Makes about 6 dozen.)

*Note:* Any yellow cake (butter type) is fine for this recipe. One thick 8- or 9-inch layer or about half of a 13 × 9-inch oblong cake should give enough crumbs. Be sure the cake is quite dry before crumbling and crumble finely but not to powder. I usually cut the cake into strips and put them in a very slow oven for about 30 minutes to be sure it is dry enough.

## Crunchy Oatmeal Cookies

$^1/_3$ cup bacon drippings
$^2/_3$ cup packed brown sugar
1 egg
1 tsp. vanilla extract
$^1/_2$ cup sifted all-purpose flour
$^1/_2$ tsp. baking powder
$^1/_4$ tsp. salt
$^1/_2$ tsp. ground cinnamon
$1^1/_2$ cups quick-cooking
rolled oats
$^1/_2$ cup finely chopped walnuts

Beat bacon drippings, brown sugar, egg and vanilla together until fluffy. Sift flour, baking powder, salt and cinnamon together into first mixture. Blend well. Stir in rolled oats and nuts. Chill.

Heat oven to 375°F. Grease cookie sheets.

Shape dough into small balls about 1 inch in diameter. Put on prepared cookie sheets and flatten with a fork. Bake until lightly browned, about 10 minutes. (Makes about 3 dozen.)

## Hermits

3/4 cup butter or margarine
1 1/2 cups packed brown sugar
2 eggs
1 tsp. vanilla extract
2 tbsp. milk
1 cup chopped raisins
1 cup chopped walnuts
1 cup chopped dates
2 cups sifted all-purpose flour
1/2 tsp. baking powder
1/2 tsp. baking soda
1/2 tsp. salt
1 tsp. ground cinnamon
1/2 tsp. ground nutmeg

Heat oven to 350°F. Grease cookie sheets.

Beat butter or margarine, sugar and eggs together until fluffy. Stir in vanilla, milk, raisins, walnuts and dates. Sift dry ingredients together and add to mixture, blending well with a wooden spoon.

Drop by rounded teaspoonfuls onto prepared cookie sheets. Bake until tops spring back when touched lightly, 15 to 18 minutes. (Makes about 6 1/2 dozen.)

## Lemon Crisps

1/2 cup soft butter or margarine
1 cup sugar
2 egg yolks
1 tsp. lemon juice
2 tsp. water
1 1/4 cups sifted all-purpose flour
1 tsp. baking powder
1/2 tsp. salt
1 tbsp. grated lemon rind
1 egg white
sugar

Beat butter or margarine and 1 cup sugar together until creamy. Beat in egg yolks, lemon juice and 2 tsp. water.

Sift flour, baking powder and salt and blend into creamed mixture along with lemon rind. Chill dough.

Heat oven to 375°F. Grease cookie sheets lightly.

Work dough with hands until pliable and roll out on a floured board to 1/16 inch thick. Cut into rounds and put on prepared cookie sheets. Brush lightly with unbeaten egg white and sprinkle with sugar. (Be careful not to let egg white run over sides of cookies or they will stick to cookie sheet.)

Bake until very lightly browned, about 8 minutes. Let stand a minute or so, then loosen cookies carefully and lift off to cool on racks. (Makes about 4 1/2 dozen.)

## Cheese Pastry Bars

1 3/4 cups sifted all-purpose flour
1/2 cup sugar
1/2 tsp. salt
2 tsp. baking powder
1 cup butter or margarine
1 cup grated old Cheddar cheese
1/4 cup milk
1 egg
1 cup orange marmalade

Sift flour, sugar, salt and baking powder together into a bowl. Add butter or margarine and cut in finely with a pastry blender or 2 knives. Stir in cheese with a fork. Beat milk and egg together with a fork. Add to dry mixture and blend in lightly with fork. Chill several hours.

Heat oven to 350°F. Lightly grease a 13 × 9 × 2-inch pan.

Keep 1/4 of the dough chilled. Roll out remaining 3/4 of the dough on a floured board until slightly smaller than the bottom of the pan. Lift into pan and press with hand into corners of pan and slightly up sides.

Spread dough with marmalade. Roll remaining dough thinly, cut into strips and lay strips on top of marmalade, lattice style. (Don't worry if the rich dough breaks — just patch strips and they will bake together.)

Bake until nicely browned, about 25 minutes. Cool in pan and cut into squares or bars. (Makes about 4 dozen.)

## Seed Cake

1 1/2 cups soft butter or
    margarine
1 3/4 cups sugar
1/2 tsp. ground nutmeg
1/2 tsp. ground mace
6 eggs
4 cups sifted all-purpose flour
2 tsp. caraway seeds

Heat oven to 325°F. Grease and line with greased heavy brown paper a 10-inch tube pan.

Cream butter or margarine until fluffy. Add sugar and spices and beat very well. Add eggs one at a time, beating well after each addition. Stir in flour and caraway seeds, blending well.

Spoon into prepared pan. Bake until a toothpick stuck in the centre comes out clean, about 1 hour and 40 minutes. Turn out of pan to cool on a rack. Wrap in heavy aluminum foil and let mellow a few days before cutting.

## Lemon Cake

2/3 cup soft butter
2 cups sugar
4 eggs
3 cups sifted all-purpose flour
2 tsp. baking powder
2 tsp. salt
1 cup milk
3 tbsp. grated lemon rind
1 cup finely ground blanched
    almonds
2 tbsp. lemon juice
1/4 cup sugar
icing sugar

Heat oven to 350°F. Grease a 10-inch tube pan.

Beat butter and 2 cups sugar together until light and fluffy (medium speed on the mixer). Add eggs one at a time, beating well after each addition.

Sift flour, baking powder and salt together. Add to first mixture alternately with milk, stirring just to blend after each addition. Fold in lemon rind and almonds.

Spoon into pan and bake until a toothpick stuck in the centre comes out clean, about 1 1/4 hours.

While cake bakes, combine lemon juice and 1/4 cup sugar. Let mixture sit in a warm place and stir occasionally.

Leave cake in pan 10 minutes when it comes out of oven, then prick top in several places with fork tines. Drizzle lemon mixture over top slowly, letting it soak in. Cool cake in pan, then invert on plate. Sift icing sugar over cake before serving.

## Fresh Coconut Cake

1 cup soft butter or margarine
1 cup sugar
3$^1$/$_3$ cups sifted cake flour
4 tsp. baking powder
1 tsp. salt
1$^1$/$_4$ cups milk
2 tsp. vanilla extract
1 cup egg whites (about 8)
$^3$/$_4$ cup sugar
Lemon Filling (recipe follows)
Fluffy White Icing
   (recipe follows)
1 cup finely grated fresh
   coconut

Heat oven to 350°F. Grease and flour three 9-inch round layer cake pans.

Cream butter or margarine until fluffy. Add 1 cup sugar gradually, creaming well after each addition.

Sift flour, baking powder and salt together and add to creamed mixture alternately with milk and vanilla, beating well after each addition.

Beat egg whites until foamy. Add $^3$/$_4$ cup sugar gradually, beating well after each addition. Beat until stiff and glossy. Fold into first mixture using a rubber scraper.

Pour batter into prepared pans and bake until tops spring back when touched lightly in the centre, 25 to 30 minutes. Let cool in pans 5 minutes, then turn out onto cake racks to cool.

Spread Lemon Filling thickly between layers and ice outside of cake with Fluffy White Icing. Sprinkle top and sides with fresh grated coconut.

## Lemon Filling

1 cup sugar
$^1$/$_4$ cup cornstarch
$^1$/$_4$ tsp. salt
1 cup water
1$^1$/$_2$ tbsp. butter or margarine
3 tbsp. grated lemon rind
$^1$/$_2$ cup lemon juice
3 egg yolks, lightly beaten

Blend sugar, cornstarch and salt very well in a saucepan. Stir in 1 cup water gradually. Set over high heat and bring to a boil, stirring constantly. Turn down heat and cook, stirring, 1 minute. Remove from heat and stir in butter or margarine, lemon rind and lemon juice.

Blend hot mixture gradually into egg yolks and return all to saucepan. Bring back to a boil, stirring constantly, and boil 1 minute. Cool.

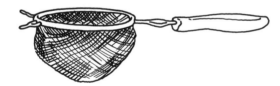

## Fluffy White Icing

$^1$/$_2$ cup sugar
2 tbsp. water
$^1$/$_4$ cup corn syrup
2 egg whites
1 tsp. vanilla extract

Combine sugar, 2 tbsp. water and corn syrup in a small saucepan. Set over high heat and stir until sugar is dissolved. Boil, without stirring, until syrup reaches a temperature of 242°F on the candy thermometer (syrup spins a 6- to 8-inch thread when dropped from the tines of a fork).

Beat egg whites until stiff. Pour hot syrup in a thin stream into egg whites, beating constantly with a rotary beater. Continue beating until stiff peaks form. Beat in vanilla.

## Strawberry Cream Cakes

Cupcakes (recipe follows)
¹/₂ cup apricot jam
¹/₂ cup finely chopped toasted
  almonds
2 tbsp. apricot jam
1 tbsp. rum
¹/₂ cup whipping cream
Cream Filling (recipe follows)
¹/₂ cup small slices
  strawberries
12 small whole strawberries

Remove paper cups and cut large cones from tops of Cupcakes shortly before serving time. Leave cones in place during next step.

Heat ¹/₂ cup apricot jam in a small saucepan. (Cut up any large pieces of apricot with kitchen shears if necessary.) Brush outsides of Cupcakes (not tops and bottoms) lightly with this jam, using a pastry brush. Roll jam-coated area of each cake in almonds to coat completely. Set on a cookie sheet as they are completed.

Lift cones out of cakes. Combine 2 tbsp. apricot jam and rum, blending well. Spread a small amount of mixture in the centre of each cake, where the cone was cut out.

Whip cream until stiff. Add about ¹/₄ of the whipped cream to Cream Filling and fold together carefully. Fold in cut strawberries. Spoon mixture into the hollow in each cake, piling it quite high. Set cones back on tops of cakes, pressing them lightly into place.

Put remaining whipped cream in a pastry bag or tube and press it through a rosette tip on top of each cone. Add a whole strawberry to the top of each cake. Chill until serving time. (Makes 12.)

## Cupcakes

1 egg white
¹/₄ cup sugar
1 cup plus 2 tbsp. sifted cake
  flour
¹/₂ cup sugar
1¹/₂ tsp. baking powder
¹/₂ tsp. salt
3 tbsp. cooking oil
¹/₂ cup milk
¹/₂ tsp. almond extract
1 egg yolk

Heat oven to 375°F. Line 12 large muffin cups with paper baking cups.

Beat egg white until foamy in a small bowl. Add ¹/₄ cup sugar gradually, beating after each addition. Continue beating until stiff and glossy.

Sift flour, ¹/₂ cup sugar, baking powder and salt together into another small bowl. Add oil, a little more than half of the milk and almond extract. Beat 1 minute (medium speed on the mixer). Add remaining milk and egg yolk. Beat 1 minute more. Fold in egg white mixture.

Spoon batter into paper baking cups. Bake until tops spring back when touched lightly, about 15 minutes. Cool on racks. (Makes 12.)

## Cream Filling

3 tbsp. sugar
2¹/₂ tsp. cornstarch
pinch salt
³/₄ cup milk
1 egg yolk
2 tsp. butter or margarine
³/₄ tsp. vanilla extract

Combine sugar, cornstarch and salt in a small saucepan. Stir in milk gradually. Bring to a boil quickly, stirring constantly. Turn down heat and boil 1 minute, stirring.

Stir some of hot mixture gradually into egg yolk. Return to saucepan and bring back to a boil, stirring constantly. Remove from heat and stir in butter or margarine and vanilla. Cover with waxed paper and cool quickly by setting in ice water. Stir occasionally.

## Spanish Cake Roll

1 cup sifted all-purpose flour
1 tsp. baking powder
$1/4$ tsp. salt
3 large eggs
1 cup sugar
$1/3$ cup orange juice
1 tsp. grated lemon rind
icing sugar
Sherry Filling (recipe follows)
$1/4$ cup apricot jam
$1/4$ cup sherry
2 tsp. grated orange rind

Heat oven to 375°F. Grease a 15 × 10 × 1-inch jelly roll pan and line bottom with greased heavy brown paper.

Sift flour, baking powder and salt together onto waxed paper.

Beat eggs in a small mixer bowl until they are very light colored and fluffy, about 5 minutes at high speed on the mixer.

Beat in sugar gradually, beating well after each addition. Stir in orange juice and lemon rind. Add sifted dry ingredients and stir to blend.

Pour into prepared pan and spread evenly. Bake until top springs back when touched lightly in the centre, 12 to 15 minutes.

Sift icing sugar over top of cake, loosen edges and turn it out onto a clean towel. Strip off paper. Spread thinly with half of Sherry Filling immediately and roll up tightly. Set on a rack to cool.

Mash apricot jam until smooth. Combine with sherry and orange rind. Stir into remaining filling. Spoon over thick slices of cake at serving time. (Serves 8.)

## Sherry Filling

$1/2$ cup sugar
1 tbsp. cornstarch
$1/4$ tsp. ground cinnamon
$1/8$ tsp. ground cloves
$1/2$ cup orange juice
$1/2$ cup sherry
2 egg yolks, beaten

Blend sugar, cornstarch, cinnamon and cloves in a saucepan. Stir in orange juice and sherry gradually. Put over moderately high heat and bring to a boil, stirring constantly. Turn down heat and boil 1 minute.

Stir about half of hot mixture gradually into egg yolks. Return to saucepan and bring back to boil. Cook until thickened and smooth.

## Sweet Cheese with Strawberries

2 cups sour cream
3 egg yolks
125 g pkg. cream cheese
  (room temperature)
$1/2$ cup sugar
2 strips lemon rind (cut full
  length of lemon with
  vegetable peeler)
saltines
fresh unhulled strawberries
fruit sugar

Put sour cream in the top of a double boiler and set over simmering water. Heat until cream is very hot.

Beat egg yolks, cheese and sugar together until smooth. Stir about half of sour cream into cheese mixture gradually, then return it to double boiler. Add lemon rind.

Cook, stirring constantly, over simmering water until thickened, about 10 minutes. Remove from heat and cover top of double boiler and let stand over hot water 15 minutes.

Line a sieve about 5 inches in diameter with 4 thicknesses of cheesecloth and set over a small bowl. Pour in cheese mixture. Let stand at room temperature 2 hours to drain. Turn cheesecloth in over cheese mixture and set bowl and sieve in refrigerator to chill and drain several hours or overnight.

Turn cheese out onto a large serving plate a few minutes before serving to let it warm up a little. Surround cheese with saltines and unhulled berries and provide a little bowl of fruit sugar for dipping the berries. (Serves 6 to 8.)

# Cocktail Snacks

It's not reasonable to expect all the snacks served at a cocktail party to be good for you, but it would be nice to think that at least some of the tasty bits offer some food value. For example, it's fun to make crackers, and when you do you can add good things such as whole wheat flour, soy flour, sesame seeds, wheat germ, sunflower seeds and cheese. Or you can make exceptionally good dips for those familiar raw vegetables. If you want hot hors d'oeuvres, I think the ones that reheat the best and are tastiest are little tarts such as the various cheese tarts and the spicy Empañadas in this section.

## Health Crackers

2 cups whole wheat flour
1/2 cup soy flour
1/2 cup unhulled sesame seeds (see note)
1/4 cup wheat germ
1/4 cup chopped sunflower seeds
1 tsp. salt
1/4 cup vegetable oil
3/4 to 1 cup cold water

Mix whole wheat flour, soy flour, sesame seeds, wheat germ, sunflower seeds and salt together in a medium bowl. Add oil and blend well with a fork. Add 1/2 cup of the water, mixing well, then add more water, 1 tbsp. at a time, to make a firm dough that sticks together and rolls easily. Knead on a floured board 10 minutes.

Heat oven to 400°F.

Pull off small chunks of dough and roll each very thinly on a lightly floured board (dough should be so thin you can nearly see through it). Cut into small squares or diamonds with a pastry wheel or knife. Don't bother to reroll scraps of dough — just cut and bake them in odd shapes.

Set oven rack just at or slightly above middle of oven. Put crackers on ungreased cookie sheets and bake until golden brown, 7 to 8 minutes. Watch carefully — they burn easily. Cool and store in a tightly sealed tin. (Makes about 300.)

*Note:* Unhulled sesame seeds are available in health food stores. Hulled seeds can be used instead.

## Sesame Cheese Strips

1/4 cup sesame seeds
1 cup sifted all-purpose flour
1/2 tsp. salt
1/2 tsp. sugar
1/2 tsp. ground ginger
1 cup grated old Cheddar cheese
1 egg yolk, lightly beaten
1/3 cup melted butter or margarine
1 tbsp. water
1/2 tsp. Worcestershire sauce

Heat oven to 300°F.

Put sesame seeds in a shallow pan and toast in oven until golden, stirring often, about 10 minutes. Remove from oven. Cool. Increase oven temperature to 350°F.

Sift flour, salt, sugar and ginger together into a bowl. Add cheese and sesame seeds and mix lightly with a fork.

Combine egg yolk, melted butter or margarine, 1 tbsp. water and Worcestershire. Add to flour mixture and stir lightly with a fork to blend. Shape into a ball and roll out on a lightly floured board into a rectangle 1/8 inch thick. Cut into strips 1 inch wide and cut strips into pieces 3 inches long.

Put on ungreased cookie sheets and bake until nicely browned, about 10 minutes. Cool on racks. (Makes about 4 dozen.)

## Potato Wafers

1 cup riced boiled potatoes
1/2 cup soft butter or
    margarine
1 cup sifted all-purpose flour
1 egg, lightly beaten
1 egg yolk
2 tsp. milk
salt
caraway seeds

Blend potatoes, butter or margarine, flour and egg together with a fork to make a smooth dough. Chill 30 minutes

Heat oven to 400°F. Grease cookie sheets.

Roll dough out on a floured board to about 1/16 inch thick. Cut into 3 × 1-inch strips and put on prepared cookie sheets.

Beat egg yolk and milk together lightly with a fork. Brush tops of strips of dough with this mixture. Sprinkle lightly with salt and generously with caraway seeds.

Bake until lightly browned, about 12 minutes. (Makes about 3 dozen.)

## Seeded Rye Crackers

2 cups rye flour
3/4 cup sifted all-purpose flour
1 tsp. salt
1 tsp. baking powder
1/2 cup wheat germ
2 tsp. caraway seeds
1/4 cup chopped sunflower
    seeds
1/3 cup shortening
3/4 cup milk
1 egg
coarse salt (optional)

Combine rye flour, all-purpose flour, salt and baking powder in a bowl, mixing well with a fork. Mix in wheat germ and caraway and sunflower seeds. Add shortening and cut in finely with a pastry blender. Beat milk and egg together lightly with a fork and stir into mixture until blended. Gather dough into a ball and divide into halves.

Heat oven to 325°F.

Put half of dough on a large ungreased cookie sheet. Pat into a rectangle, then roll into a 15 × 12-inch oblong. Cut with a knife or pastry wheel into small crackers roughly 2 inches square. (Do not separate crackers.) Prick each cracker in 3 places and, if desired, sprinkle lightly with coarse salt.

Bake until set and lightly browned on the bottom, about 30 minutes. Cool on racks. Repeat with other half of dough. Store in a tight tin. (Makes about 7 dozen.)

## Camembert in Wine

1/2 lb. Camembert cheese
    (in a round)
dry white wine
1/3 cup soft unsalted butter
1 tbsp. butter
1/4 tsp. chili powder
1/2 cup pecans, finely chopped
crackers

Put cheese in a bowl that is just large enough to hold it flat on the bottom. Pour wine over cheese to cover. Weigh cheese down with another bowl or plate and let stand at room temperature overnight.

Lift cheese out of wine and scrape any crusty or dark bits off outside. Put cheese in a bowl, add 1 tbsp. of the wine the cheese was soaked in and unsalted butter. Cream together until completely smooth. Chill until mixture can be handled.

Heat oven to 300°F.

Put butter in a small baking pan. Sprinkle in chili powder and set in oven until butter is melted. Add chopped pecans, stir to blend and heat until pecans are lightly browned, about 15 minutes. Cool.

Shape cheese mixture back into a round cake about the same size as the original cheese and cover all over with the toasted pecans. Chill until about 1 hour before serving time, then remove from refrigerator and let stand at room temperature. Serve with crackers.

## Three Cheese Spread

Press cottage and blue cheeses through a sieve or use the steel blade of a processor. Mix with Cheddar cheese, cream, sherry and salt. Pack into a small bowl and refrigerate until about 1 hour before serving time. Surround with crackers and apple slices. (Makes about 1²/₃ cups.)

1 cup cream-style cottage
   cheese (one 250 g carton)
¹/₄ cup crumbled blue cheese
1 cup grated old Cheddar
   cheese
1 tbsp. light cream
2 tbsp. dry sherry
¹/₂ tsp. salt
crackers
apple slices

## Mushroom-Ham Dip

Heat butter or margarine in a small skillet over high heat. Add mushrooms and stir 2 minutes. Cool.

Whip cream until soft peaks form. Stir in mushrooms along with yogurt, ham and onions. Put in a small bowl and sprinkle lightly with cayenne. Chill at least 2 hours. Especially good with raw vegetables. (Makes 2 cups.)

2 tbsp. butter or margarine
1 cup finely chopped fresh
   mushrooms
¹/₂ cup whipping cream
²/₃ cup plain yogurt
   (one 175 g carton)
¹/₂ cup very finely chopped
   cooked ham
2 tbsp. finely chopped green
   onions
cayenne

## Vegetable Dip

Heat oil in the top of a double boiler over direct heat. Add onion and cook gently 3 minutes, stirring. Add tomatoes, hot peppers, basil, salt and a good grating of pepper. Cover and simmer 15 minutes, stirring occasionally.

Set top of double boiler over simmering water. Add cheese and heat, stirring often, until cheese is half melted. Gradually stir in cream and continue cooking over simmering water until cheese is completely melted and mixture is blended.

Serve hot (use a chafing dish if you have one) surrounded by raw vegetables for dipping. (Makes about 2¹/₂ cups.)

1 tbsp. cooking oil
1 small onion, finely chopped
1 cup chopped, well-drained
   canned tomatoes
1 tbsp. very finely chopped
   pickled hot peppers
¹/₂ tsp. dried leaf basil
¹/₄ tsp. salt
grating fresh black pepper
¹/₂ lb. mild Cheddar cheese,
   cut in small cubes (about
   2 cups)
1 cup light cream
raw vegetable pieces

## Dill Dip

Combine all ingredients except raw vegetables and chill well. Serve as a dip with raw vegetables. (Makes 1½ cups.)

1 cup mayonnaise
½ cup plain yogurt
1 tbsp. finely chopped parsley
1 tbsp. snipped chives
1 tsp. snipped fresh dill or
  ½ tsp. dried dill weed
¼ tsp. salt
⅛ tsp. curry powder
1½ tsp. lemon juice
½ tsp. Worcestershire sauce
2 tsp. capers, drained and
  chopped
raw vegetable pieces

## Mushroom Caviar

Heat butter or margarine in a skillet. Add onions and cook quickly, stirring, 1 minute. Add mushrooms and stir until mixture is golden and quite dry. Remove from heat, turn into a bowl and cool.

Add lemon juice, ¼ tsp. salt, grating of pepper, Worcestershire, Tabasco and mayonnaise. Blend well and taste, adjusting seasoning if necessary. Chill well. Serve as a spread with melba toast or crackers. (Makes about 1 cup.)

2 tbsp. butter or margarine
½ cup very finely chopped
  green onions with tops
½ lb. (1 pt.) fresh mushrooms,
  very finely chopped
2 tbsp. lemon juice
¼ tsp. salt
grating fresh black pepper
½ tsp. Worcestershire sauce
dash Tabasco
⅓ cup mayonnaise
melba toast or crackers

## Brandied Cheese in Celery

Combine blue cheese, butter, brandy and Worcestershire and fill celery pieces. Chill until shortly before serving time. (Makes about 4 dozen.)

¼ lb. blue cheese
¼ lb. unsalted butter
2 tbsp. brandy
¼ tsp. Worcestershire sauce
1-inch pieces celery
  (about 4 dozen)

## Blue Cheese Tarts

Beat cheeses, beer and soya sauce together. Stir in pecans. Refrigerate until about 30 minutes before serving time, then spoon about 1 tbsp. into each tart shell. Garnish with parsley. (Makes 48.)

½ lb. blue cheese (room
  temperature)
250 g pkg. cream cheese
  (room temperature)
½ cup flat beer
2 tsp. soya sauce
1 cup lightly toasted chopped
  pecans
48 baked 2-inch tart shells
48 small sprigs parsley

### Tiny Cheddar Tarts

2 tbsp. butter or margarine
2 tbsp. flour
1/4 tsp. salt
1/4 tsp. dry mustard
dash garlic salt
pinch ground nutmeg
dash cayenne
1 cup light cream
1 cup grated old Cheddar
  cheese
24 baked 2-inch tart shells
paprika

Heat butter or margarine in a medium saucepan. Sprinkle in flour, salt, mustard, garlic salt, nutmeg and cayenne and stir to blend. Remove from heat and stir in cream all at once. Return to heat and stir constantly until boiling, thickened and smooth. Remove from heat and stir in cheese.

Heat broiler and put oven rack just above middle of oven.

Fill tart shells right to top with cheese mixture and sprinkle with paprika. Broil until filling is lightly browned and bubbling. Serve hot. (Makes 24.)

### Empañadas

2 tbsp. butter or margarine
1/4 lb. ground beef
1 medium onion, chopped
1/2 tsp. crushed dried red
  pepper
1 green pepper, chopped
1 large tomato, peeled,
  seeded and chopped
6 ripe olives, chopped
2 tbsp. seedless raisins
1 hard-cooked egg, chopped
1/2 tsp. sugar
1/2 tsp. salt
double recipe of pastry
  for 2-crust 9-inch pie
  (recipe p. 172)
1 egg, beaten
coarse salt

Heat butter or margarine in a skillet over moderate heat. Add beef, onion, red pepper and green pepper and stir until meat loses its pink color. Add tomato and simmer gently 5 minutes. Remove from heat, stir in olives, raisins, egg, sugar and salt and cool.

Roll pastry thinly and cut into 3-inch rounds. (You should have about 60.) Put a generous teaspoonful of meat mixture on one half of each round. Moisten edge of pastry, fold over and seal to make a tiny turnover. Prick top with a fork. Put on ungreased cookie sheets and chill.

Heat oven to 425°F shortly before serving time. Beat egg lightly and brush over pastries. Sprinkle lightly with salt. Bake until well browned, about 15 minutes. Serve hot. (Makes about 5 dozen.)

### Stuffed Mushrooms

1 1/2 oz. Chinese black
  mushrooms (15 to 18)
1/2 lb. ground pork or beef
4 oz. cooked or raw shrimp,
  finely chopped
1 tbsp. cornstarch
1/4 tsp. salt
dash black pepper
1 small sweet red pepper, cut
  in small strips

Soak mushrooms in warm water 15 minutes. Lift out of water and squeeze dry. Remove stems.

Combine pork or beef, shrimp, cornstarch, salt and pepper. Put mushroom caps top sides down on a plate and fill them with meat mixture. Top each one with a strip of red pepper.

Set plate in a steamer or on a rack in a large saucepan over boiling water. Cover tightly and steam until meat is cooked through, about 20 minutes. (Makes 15 to 18.)

### Quick Sausage Roll Bites

8 sausages (about $1/2$ lb.)
8 slices white bread
1 cup finely grated old
    Cheddar cheese
$1/4$ cup soft butter or
    margarine
sesame seeds

Fry sausages until completely cooked through and browned. Drain well.

Heat oven to 400°F. Grease a cookie sheet lightly.

Cut and discard crusts from bread slices and roll slices with a rolling pin until as thin as possible. Combine Cheddar cheese and butter or margarine and spread about $2/3$ of mixture on one side of bread slices. Roll a sausage in each slice of bread and press firmly to seal.

Put rolls on prepared cookie sheet, sealed sides down. Spread top of each roll with some of remaining cheese mixture. Sprinkle with sesame seeds.

Bake until nicely browned, about 20 minutes. Cut each roll into 3 pieces and serve hot. (Makes 24.)

### Turkey Balls

3 tbsp. butter or margarine
$2/3$ cup finely chopped onion
1 clove garlic, crushed
$1/2$ cup mashed potatoes
4 cups finely ground cooked
    turkey
2 eggs, beaten
$1 1/2$ tsp. salt
$1/4$ tsp. black pepper
$1/4$ tsp. ground nutmeg
$1/2$ cup fine dry bread crumbs
2 tbsp. ketchup
$1/2$ cup well-drained sweet
    pickle relish
1 tbsp. finely chopped parsley
$1/4$ cup butter or margarine
    (approx.)

Heat 3 tbsp. butter or margarine in a small skillet. Add onion, garlic and mashed potatoes. Cook gently, stirring constantly, until potatoes are lightly browned. Remove from heat.

Combine turkey, eggs, seasonings, bread crumbs, ketchup, relish and parsley. Blend in mashed potato mixture. Shape into small balls about 1 inch in diameter.

Heat $1/4$ cup butter or margarine in a large heavy skillet and brown turkey balls slowly on all sides, adding more butter or margarine if necessary. Keep hot in a chafing dish. (Makes about 5 dozen small.)

### Bacon Roll-ups

12 slices bacon
1 small unsliced sandwich
    loaf
soft butter or margarine
$3/4$ cup grated Parmesan
    cheese
$1/3$ cup chopped parsley
paprika

Fry bacon until crisp. Drain and cool on paper toweling and crumble.

Cut crusts from sandwich loaf and cut bread into 6 slices lengthwise. Butter bread generously. Sprinkle each slice with some of the bacon bits, 2 tbsp. of the Parmesan and a scant 1 tbsp. of the parsley. Sprinkle lightly with paprika. Roll up each slice of bread into a pinwheel. Wrap in transparent wrap and chill until just before serving time.

Cut each roll into 4 slices and lay on a cookie sheet. Put low under the broiler and toast until golden on both sides. Serve hot. (Makes 24.)

# Drinks

Here are beverages for all seasons. Some are coolly refreshing, made with fruit juices, milk, yogurt and ice cream, and suitable for all ages. Others are hot and warming — a fine welcome on a cold night. Beautiful, elegant and good-tasting wine-based drinks and some pleasant punches round out the list.

### Minty Apple Cooler

2 cups apple juice
2 tsp. chopped fresh mint
1 tbsp. lemon juice
ice
soda water

Heat apple juice to boiling point. Add mint, stir and remove from heat. Let stand until cool. Strain and stir in lemon juice.

Pour over ice in 8-oz. glasses. Fill with soda water and serve immediately. (Serves 3.)

### Orange Fresh-up

Put ¹/₂ cup orange juice, a scoop of orange sherbet and a scoop of vanilla ice cream in a tall glass for each serving. Fill with chilled soda water. Serve with a long spoon and straws.

### Orange Milk

2 cups cold milk
2 tbsp. liquid honey
3 tbsp. thawed undiluted
frozen orange juice

Combine ingredients in glass of blender. Buzz until well blended. Pour into 4-oz. glasses and serve with straws. (Serves 4.)

### Yogurt and Fruit Juice

³/₄ cup undiluted frozen grape
juice (one 6-oz. can)
2 cups plain yogurt
(three 175 g cartons)
¹/₂ cup powdered skim milk
¹/₂ cup cold water

Put all ingredients in glass of blender and buzz until blended. Pour into glasses and serve with straws. (Serves 6.)

### Grape-Banana Cooler

2 large very ripe bananas
1 cup bottled grape juice
1 cup cold milk
4 tsp. sugar
chilled ginger ale

Beat peeled bananas with mixer to make a smooth purée. Beat in grape juice, milk and sugar. Divide mixture evenly among 4 tall glasses (about ³/₄ cup of mixture per glass). Add chilled ginger ale to fill glasses. (Serves 4.)

## Pink Banana Whip

Combine ingredients in glass of blender and buzz until well mixed. Pour into tall glasses and serve immediately. (Serves 4.)

2 cups chilled cranberry-apple drink
2 cups chilled fresh orange juice
1 ripe banana
6 ice cubes

## Icy Chocolate

Combine coffee and 1 tbsp. sugar. Cool, then pour into an ice cube tray and freeze.

Combine chocolate, 1/4 cup sugar, 1 cup boiling water and salt and bring to a boil, stirring constantly. Remove from heat and stir into hot milk. Add vanilla and chill.

Put 2 or 3 coffee ice cubes in each of six 8-oz. glasses and divide chocolate among them. Top floating ice cubes with a dab of whipped cream if desired. (Serves 6.)

2 cups strong coffee
1 tbsp. sugar
2 squares (2 oz.) unsweetened chocolate
1/4 cup sugar
1 cup boiling water
pinch salt
3 cups milk, scalded
1/2 tsp. vanilla extract
sweetened whipped cream (optional)

## Toe Warmer

Combine all ingredients except orange slices in a large saucepan. Bring to simmering, turn down heat and continue heating, without boiling, 20 minutes.

Put a half slice of orange in each of 6 mugs. Strain in apple juice. (Serves 6.)

48-oz. can apple juice
1/3 cup packed brown sugar
8 whole cloves
1 large stick cinnamon, broken
3 thin slices orange, cut in half

## Quick Vienna Mocha

Heat milk to scalding. Stir in chocolate drink mix, coffee and vanilla. Whip cream and sugar until stiff. Pour hot mixture into mugs and top with a dab of whipped cream. Add cinnamon sticks for muddlers. (Serves 6.)

6 cups milk
1/4 cup instant chocolate drink mix
2 tbsp. instant coffee
1/4 tsp. vanilla extract
1/3 cup whipping cream
1 1/2 tbsp. sugar
6 whole sticks cinnamon

### Hot Chocolate Nog

5 cups eggnog
1 cup chocolate syrup
$^1/_2$ tsp. ground cinnamon
$^1/_4$ tsp. ground nutmeg
pinch ground cloves
6 oz. golden rum (optional)
cinnamon sticks
whipped cream

Combine eggnog, chocolate syrup and spices in the top of a double boiler. Set over simmering water, cover and heat very well, stirring occasionally. Beat with a rotary beater until foamy.

If desired, put 1 oz. of rum into each of 6 mugs. Add a cinnamon stick to each. Pour in hot eggnog mixture and top with a dab of whipped cream. (Serves 6.)

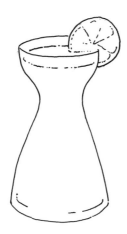

### Spritzer

For each drink, combine half chilled dry white wine and half chilled soda water in a tall glass. Add some ice cubes and a twist of lemon.

### Kir

For each drink, combine 3 or 4 oz. chilled dry white wine with 1 oz. chilled crème de cassis (or make the combination to your taste) in a large wine glass or goblet. Add an ice cube if desired. This is a beautiful, elegant and refreshing drink for a hot summer day.

### Grapefruit Cassis

two 19-oz. cans grapefruit juice
$^1/_2$ cup cassis syrup (see note)
chilled soda water
mint sprigs

Freeze contents of 1 can of grapefruit juice in an ice cube tray. Chill other can.

For each serving, fill a tall glass with grapefruit ice cubes. Combine cassis syrup with chilled juice and pour about $^2/_3$ cup into each glass. Fill with soda water and garnish with a mint sprig. (Serves 4.)

*Note:* You can find cassis syrup, which is nonalcoholic, in supermarkets and food specialty stores.

### Wine Julep

Combine orange juice, lemonade and wine in a pitcher and chill well. For each serving, put about 6 oz. in a 10-oz. glass. Add 3 ice cubes and fill with soda water. Hang an orange slice on the rim for garnish. (Serves 6.)

6-oz. can frozen orange juice, thawed
6-oz. can frozen lemonade, thawed
750 mL bottle dry white wine
ice cubes
chilled soda water
orange slices

### Raspberry Punch

Thaw raspberries and press through a sieve to remove seeds. Discard seeds and combine raspberry purée with sugar. Stir until sugar is dissolved.

Put 2 or 3 trays of ice cubes in a punch bowl and pour raspberry purée over. Add orange juice and lemonade. Pour in ginger ale slowly. (Makes about twenty 4-oz. servings.)

two 15-oz. pkg. frozen raspberries
$2/3$ cup sugar
ice cubes
2 cups orange juice, chilled
6-oz. can frozen lemonade, thawed
750 mL bottle ginger ale, chilled

### Spicy Wassail Bowl

Heat oven to 350°F.

Prick apples in several places with a fork and put them in a shallow baking pan. Heat in oven 10 minutes. Boil 2 cups water, sugar, spices and 1 cup of the dry sherry 5 minutes. Strain.

Combine egg whites and yolks and beat at high speed with an electric mixer 5 minutes. Gradually beat in hot sherry mixture and pour into a large kettle. Add remaining dry sherry and all of sweet sherry and heat but do not boil.

At serving time, pour into a hot, heatproof bowl and float apples on top. (Makes about twenty 4-oz. servings.)

6 small apples, cored but not peeled
2 cups water
$1/2$ cup sugar
2 tsp. ground nutmeg
1 tsp. ground ginger
6 whole cloves
2 sticks cinnamon, broken
750 mL bottle dry sherry
3 egg whites
6 egg yolks
750 mL bottle sweet sherry

## Tea and Wine Punch

Bring 2 cups water to a boil in a saucepan. Remove from heat. Add tea immediately. Cover and brew 5 minutes. Stir and strain into a large jug or other container. Add 2 cups water, undiluted lemonade and fruit punch. Chill.

Pour over ice in a punch bowl at serving time. Add wine and stir to blend. Garnish with orange and lemon slices. (Makes about thirty-five 4-oz. servings.)

*2 cups cold water*
*8 tsp. tea or 4 tea bags*
*2 cups cold water*
*6-oz. can frozen lemonade*
*48-oz. can mixed fruit punch*
*ice cubes*
*two 750 mL bottles rosé wine, chilled*
*orange and lemon slices*

## Gin Punch

Put a large block of ice in a punch bowl. Add juices, grenadine and gin and stir to mix. Add soda water and stir gently. Garnish with fruit. (Makes forty to fifty 4-oz. servings.)

*ice*
*2 cups lemon juice*
*6 cups orange juice*
*1 tbsp. grenadine*
*two 25-oz. bottles dry gin*
*two 750 mL bottles soda water*
*orange slices*
*lemon slices*
*maraschino cherries*

## Wedding Punch

Combine sugar, lemon juice and pineapple juice and stir until sugar is dissolved.

Put a block of ice in a punch bowl at serving time. Pour pineapple juice mixture over. Add white wine and stir well. Pour in champagne-type wine. Garnish with mint sprigs. (Makes about forty 4-oz. servings.)

*³/4 cup sugar*
*¹/2 cup lemon juice*
*48-oz. can pineapple juice*
*ice*
*two 750 mL bottles sweet white wine, chilled*
*two 750 mL bottles champagne-type wine, chilled*
*fresh mint sprigs*

# Picnic and Barbecue

A picnic is no longer just packages of cold sandwiches. Since many people carry small barbecues or hibachis with them everywhere and almost everyone has a cooler, picnics often include cooked food and can be quite sophisticated — starting with appetizers and including roast or other hot meat or very special cold meats, great salads and even hot vegetables. Of course, most of these things can also be added to the backyard barbecue, since it too has changed. No longer is it just a steak or hamburger. Everything, including dessert, can be cooked over the coals.

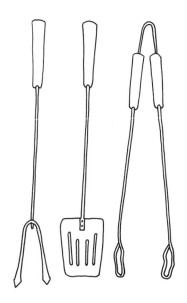

## Appetizer Rolls

Spread half the meat slices with the pimento cream cheese and the other half with the pineapple cream cheese, rolling each slice up like a jelly roll. Press lightly to seal rolls. Chill. Carry to picnic in the cooler.

Cut each roll into 5 pieces at serving time. (Makes 80 to 90).

two 6-oz. pkg. cooked ham or other square luncheon meat
125 g pkg. pimento cream cheese (room temperature)
125 g pkg. pineapple cream cheese (room temperature)

## Melon and Salami Appetizers

Cut cantaloupe into quarters lengthwise, seed and peel. Cut each piece of melon into 9 strips lengthwise. Wrap a slice of salami around each strip of melon and fasten with a cocktail pick. Pack in a plastic container and chill. Carry to picnic in the cooler. (Makes about 36.)

1 small cantaloupe
1/2 lb. thin slices skinned salami

## Spicy Pickled Eggs

Put eggs in a large saucepan. Add enough cold water to cover eggs by 1 inch. Set uncovered pan over high heat and bring water just to a boil. Remove from heat. Cover tightly. Let stand 20 minutes. Drain and run cold water over eggs until they are chilled. Peel eggs and pack into hot sterilized jars.

Tie allspice, ginger, cloves, red peppers and garlic loosely in a cheesecloth bag. Combine vinegar, 1 cup water, sugar and salt in a saucepan. Add spice bag. Bring to a boil, turn down heat and simmer 10 minutes. Discard spice bag. Pour boiling liquid over eggs in jars and seal. Refrigerate 2 days. Carry to picnic in the cooler. (Makes 12.)

12 eggs
1 tbsp. whole allspice
1 tbsp. finely chopped fresh ginger
1 tsp. whole cloves
2 whole dried red peppers
1 clove garlic, crushed
3 cups cider vinegar
1 cup water
1 tbsp. sugar
1 tsp. salt

## Cold Pork with Barbecue Sauce

5 lb. loin of pork
$1/2$ cup water
1 cup ketchup
$1/2$ cup packed brown sugar
2 tbsp. prepared mustard
2 tbsp. lemon juice
1 tbsp. Worcestershire sauce
$1/4$ tsp. chili powder
$1/2$ tsp. salt
1 tbsp. finely chopped
  pimento
$1/4$ cup finely chopped celery
1 tbsp. white vinegar

Heat oven to 325°F.

Put pork on bones in a small roasting pan. Add $1/2$ cup water, cover loosely with aluminum foil and roast $1^1/2$ hours.

Combine ketchup, sugar, mustard, lemon juice, Worcestershire, chili powder and salt in a small saucepan and bring to a boil. Turn down heat and simmer 5 minutes.

Remove roast from oven. Discard foil. Slash fat on roast as you would slash the fat on a ham, making shallow cuts. Spread with $1/2$ cup of the ketchup mixture. Continue roasting about $1^1/2$ hours more (35 to 40 minutes a pound total cooking time or 170°F on meat thermometer for medium, 185°F for well-done), basting often with sauce in bottom of pan. Cool, wrap in aluminum foil and chill.

Add pimento, celery and vinegar to remaining barbecue sauce, put in a small jar and chill.

Carry roast and sauce to picnic in the cooler (slice roast at home if you wish). Serve slices of meat, topped with a little of the spicy sauce. (Serves 8.)

*Note:* If desired, take along buttered buns, fill buns with meat and spread with a little of the sauce for very good sandwiches.

## Ham Loaf

2 lb. uncooked ham
1 lb. ground veal
2 cups soft bread crumbs
2 eggs, lightly beaten
1 cup milk
$1/2$ cup finely chopped onion
$1/4$ cup chopped parsley
1 tsp. dry mustard
$1/4$ tsp. black pepper
$1/4$ cup red currant jelly
2 tsp. orange juice
whole cloves

Heat oven to 325°F. Grease a large oval area in the centre of a large baking sheet with sides (a jelly roll pan is good.)

Combine all ingredients except red currant jelly, orange juice and cloves in a large bowl, blending well. Turn out onto baking sheet and shape into a large oval loaf about $2^1/2$ inches thick. Press firmly into shape with hands. Bake 2 hours.

Shortly before ham loaf is done, combine red currant jelly and orange juice in a small saucepan and heat until jelly melts.

Remove loaf from oven and score it shallowly on top. Put a whole clove in each square of scoring and spread jelly mixture over evenly to glaze top completely. Return to oven and continue baking 15 minutes.

Remove from oven, loosen from pan and cool. Cover a piece of heavy cardboard with aluminum foil and lift Ham Loaf onto it. Cover with foil or transparent wrap and chill well. Carry to picnic in the cooler. (Serves 8.)

## Crown Meat Loaf

4 lb. ground chuck
4 cups soft bread crumbs
1¹/₂ cups finely chopped onion
¹/₂ cup finely chopped green
 pepper
2 eggs, lightly beaten
2 tbsp. prepared horseradish
2 tsp. Worcestershire sauce
5 tsp. salt
¹/₂ tsp. black pepper
2 tsp. dry mustard
¹/₂ cup milk
¹/₂ cup ketchup
1 cup finely chopped parsley
1¹/₂ tbsp. cooking oil
3 tbsp. finely chopped onion
¹/₂ cup ketchup
2 tbsp. white vinegar
1 tbsp. brown sugar
1 tsp. prepared mustard
1 tbsp. Worcestershire sauce
pinch salt
radishes and green onions

Heat oven to 375°F. Grease an 11-cup ring mold well.

Combine meat, bread crumbs, 1¹/₂ cups onion, green pepper, eggs, horseradish, 2 tsp. Worcestershire, 5 tsp. salt, pepper, dry mustard, milk, ¹/₂ cup ketchup and parsley in a large bowl. Mix lightly with a fork. Pack lightly into prepared ring mold. Bake 30 minutes.

While meat loaf is cooking, heat oil in a small saucepan. Add 3 tbsp. onion and cook gently 3 minutes, stirring. Add all remaining ingredients except radishes and green onions. Bring to a boil, turn down heat and simmer 10 minutes. Remove meat loaf from oven and spread top with mixture. Continue baking 1 hour.

Cool in pan, cover with aluminum foil and chill well. Carry to picnic in the cooler. Turn out onto a large round plate. Fill centre of loaf with radishes and green onions. Cut into large wedges to serve. (Serves 12.)

## Wieners and Sauerkraut

1 lb. wieners
1 cup drained canned
 sauerkraut
¹/₄ cup bottled chili sauce
1 tsp. caraway seeds
bacon slices (about 12)

Slit wieners lengthwise almost through. Combine sauerkraut, chili sauce and caraway seeds and use a spoonful of this mixture to stuff each wiener. Wrap each wiener with a strip of bacon. Fasten bacon in place with small metal skewers or toothpicks.

Cook over hot coals, turning often until bacon is crisp. Serve hot. (Makes about 12.)

## Wieners with Barbados Sauce

¹/₂ cup molasses
¹/₃ cup prepared mustard
¹/₂ cup white vinegar
2 tbsp. Worcestershire sauce
¹/₂ tsp. Tabasco
1 cup ketchup
2 lb. wieners

Combine all ingredients except wieners in a saucepan and heat on the barbecue.

Put wieners on barbecue and brown well over hot coals, brushing often with the sauce. Serve very hot, topped with more sauce. (Serves 6 to 8.)

## Cheese-Filled Burgers

Combine cheese, Worcestershire and chili sauce. Blend beef, salt, pepper and garlic salt together with a fork. Shape into 12 thin patties about 3 inches in diameter. Spoon some of the cheese mixture onto the centre of 6 of the patties. Top with remaining 6 patties and press edges together.

Put patties on barbecue and broil over hot coals about 5 minutes a side. Put between buns or slices of bread to serve. (Makes 6.)

*1 cup finely grated old Cheddar cheese*
*1 tbsp. Worcestershire sauce*
*1/4 cup bottled chili sauce*
*1 1/2 lb. ground beef*
*1 1/2 tsp. salt*
*1/4 tsp. black pepper*
*1/8 tsp. garlic salt*
*6 heated and buttered hamburger buns or 12 slices crusty buttered French bread*

## Eye of the Round on the Rotisserie

Combine all ingredients except meat and blend well.

Put roast on spit, being sure to centre it well. Fasten it with holding forks. Insert meat thermometer if you are using one. Push moderately hot coals to back of fire box and put a foil drip pan under the spit area. Attach spit and start rotisserie.

Roast 1 1/2 to 2 hours (140°F for rare or 160°F for medium on the meat thermometer). Brush often with oil mixture. (Don't have fire too hot — the meat should cook rather slowly. This cut is likely to be tough if cooked too much so check it often.) Slice thinly to serve.

*1/2 cup cooking oil*
*1 1/2 tsp. seasoned salt*
*4 large cloves garlic, crushed*
*1/2 tsp. coarsely cracked black pepper*
*1 large bay leaf, crumbled*
*1 tsp. dried leaf marjoram*
*4-lb. eye of the round roast*

## Marinated Steak with Barbecue Sauce

Sprinkle steak on both sides with meat tenderizer as the label directs. Put meat in a shallow glass baking dish. Combine onion, garlic, salt, celery salt, mustard, chili powder, Worcestershire, oil and vinegar in a small jar with a tight lid. Shake to blend well. Pour over meat. Cover dish and refrigerate at least 2 hours, turning occasionally.

Lift meat out of marinade shortly before cooking time. Combine marinade and all remaining ingredients in a small saucepan. Set on grill to heat while meat is cooking.

Broil steak about 6 inches from hot coals about 10 minutes a side for medium rare. Cut into thin slices across the grain to serve and pass the hot sauce. (Serves 4 or 5.)

*2 lb. top round steak, 1 1/2 inches thick*
*meat tenderizer*
*1/2 cup chopped onion*
*1 clove garlic, crushed*
*1 tsp. salt*
*1/2 tsp. celery salt*
*1/2 tsp. dry mustard*
*1/8 tsp. chili powder*
*1 tbsp. Worcestershire sauce*
*1/4 cup cooking oil*
*1/4 cup cider vinegar*
*1/4 cup packed brown sugar*
*7 1/2-oz. can tomato sauce*
*5 1/2-oz. can tomato paste*
*4 thin slices lemon*
*dash Tabasco*
*1/4 cup water*

## Duckling on the Spit

5-lb. duckling
salt and pepper
1 stalk celery with leaves,
  cut up
3 sprigs parsley
1 small onion, quartered
1/2 small orange with skin,
  quartered
Orange Sauce (recipe follows)

Sprinkle inside of duckling generously with salt and pepper. Fasten neck skin to body with a small skewer. Put celery, parsley, onion and 1/2 orange inside body cavity, close opening with small skewers and lace opening closed. Tie wings and legs close to duckling with string. Put duckling on spit.

Put spit in place over moderately hot coals. Start the spit and roast slowly, brushing with Orange Sauce every 15 minutes, until duckling is very tender, about 2 hours.

Simmer remaining Orange Sauce for a few minutes on back of barbecue and serve with slices of duckling. (Serves 4.)

## Orange Sauce

3 oranges
1/2 cup white vinegar
1/4 cup brown sugar
1 tbsp. prepared mustard
1/4 tsp. dried leaf rosemary
1/8 tsp. dried leaf tarragon

Grate rind of one of the oranges and set orange aside to use later. Put orange rind in a small saucepan. Squeeze other 2 oranges. (You should have about 3/4 cup orange juice.) Add to orange rind along with remaining ingredients. Simmer 20 minutes. Strain and use as directed to baste duckling as it cooks.

Peel and section the orange you set aside. Add sections to any remaining orange mixture before serving it as a sauce for the cooked duckling.

## Barbecued Salmon Steaks

1/2 cup ketchup
1/4 cup cooking oil
3 tbsp. lemon juice
2 tbsp. white vinegar
1 tsp. Worcestershire sauce
1 tsp. salt
1/2 tsp. grated onion
1/2 tsp. dry mustard
1/4 tsp. paprika
1 clove garlic, crushed
dash Tabasco
4 or 6 salmon steaks, 1 to
  1 1/2 inches thick

Combine all ingredients except salmon steaks. Pour mixture into a shallow glass or pottery baking dish.

Put salmon steaks in dish and turn them over so they are coated with mixture on both sides. Cover dish and let stand 30 minutes, turning after 15 minutes.

Lift salmon steaks out of marinade, saving marinade. Put salmon on a greased grill or in a basket grill and cook about 4 inches from moderately hot coals 10 to 15 minutes on first side. Baste well with sauce. Turn and cook on second side about same length of time or until fish is cooked through. Check around backbone to be sure meat is opaque. (Serves 4 to 6.)

## Picnic Vegetable Salad

Cook vegetables according to package directions, being sure not to overcook. Drain and put in a large bowl.

Combine all remaining ingredients except cheese in a small jar with a tight lid and shake to blend well. Pour over vegetables while they are hot. Let stand until cool. Cover tightly and chill. Toss in cheese cubes at serving time. (Serves 8.)

three 11-oz. pkg. frozen mixed
  vegetables
1/2 cup salad oil
1/3 cup red wine vinegar
2 tbsp. sugar
2 tsp. salt
1/4 tsp. black pepper
1 tsp. dried parsley
1 tsp. prepared mustard
1 tsp. grated onion
1 small clove garlic, crushed
1 tsp. celery seeds
pinch dried leaf tarragon
1 1/2 cups tiny cubes process
  cheese

## Summer Coleslaw

Toss cabbage, onions, celery, green pepper, carrot and radishes and store in a plastic bag. Chill.

Combine sour cream, celery seeds, vinegar, sugar and salt in a small jar with a tight lid and shake to blend well. Chill.

Toss together at picnic. (Serves 4 to 6.)

4 cups finely shredded
  cabbage
2 tbsp. minced green onions
1/2 cup chopped celery
1/2 cup chopped green pepper
1 medium carrot, finely grated
1/4 cup thinly sliced radishes
1/2 cup sour cream
1/2 tsp. celery seeds
1 tbsp. tarragon vinegar
1/4 tsp. sugar
1/2 tsp. salt

## Three Bean Salad

Add 1/2 tsp. salt to the boiling water in a medium saucepan. Add green and yellow beans and cook until just tender, 5 to 10 minutes. Drain, saving cooking water.

Put hot beans in a large bowl. Add kidney beans, onion, sweet pickle, green pepper and celery.

Put bean cooking water in a saucepan. Add vinegar, sugar, celery seeds, mustard, 1 tsp. salt and pepper. Bring to a boil. Pour over bean mixture. Cover and chill well.

Drain bean mixture at serving time, discarding liquid. Toss bean mixture with rice, eggs and mayonnaise. Serve salad in lettuce-lined bowl. (Serves 6.)

1/2 tsp. salt
1 cup boiling water
1 lb. green beans, cut in
  1-inch pieces on the
  diagonal
1 lb. yellow beans, cut in
  1-inch pieces on the
  diagonal
14-oz. can kidney beans,
  drained
1 medium onion, sliced
  paper thin and separated
  into rings
1/2 cup chopped sweet pickle
1/4 cup chopped green pepper
1/4 cup chopped celery
1/2 cup cider vinegar
1/4 cup sugar
1 tsp. celery seeds
1/4 tsp. dry mustard
1 tsp. salt
1/4 tsp. black pepper
1 cup cold cooked rice
2 hard-cooked eggs, chopped
1/3 cup mayonnaise
lettuce

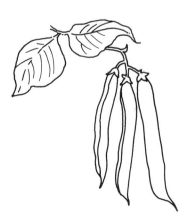

## Butter-Steamed Cabbage

1 small cabbage
butter
water
sugar
salt and pepper
ground mace

Remove and discard coarse outer leaves of the cabbage and cut it into 6 wedges. Trim away most of the core. Put each wedge of cabbage on a piece of doubled heavy aluminum foil. Turn up edges of foil a little.

Add to each piece of cabbage 1 tbsp. butter, 1 tbsp. water, 1/8 tsp. sugar, a sprinkling of salt and pepper and a dash of mace.

Wrap each piece of cabbage loosely in foil, making double folds to seal well. Cook about 4 inches from hot coals until tender, about 30 minutes. Turn package halfway through cooking. (Serves 6.)

## Carrots and Celery

6 medium carrots
2 large stalks celery
2 green onions, chopped
1 tbsp. chopped parsley
1/2 tsp. salt
1/4 tsp. black pepper
1/2 tsp. dried dill weed or
  snipped fresh dill
2 tbsp. butter or margarine
1 tsp. lemon juice

Cut carrots into slender sticks and celery into thin slices on the diagonal. Put carrots and celery on a large piece of doubled heavy aluminum foil. Add onions, parsley, salt, pepper and dill and toss together lightly. Add butter or margarine and lemon juice.

Wrap vegetables loosely in foil, making double folds to seal well. Cook about 3 inches from hot coals until tender, about 45 minutes. Turn package halfway through cooking. (Serves 6.)

## California Corn

6 medium cobs corn
1/4 cup soft butter or
  margarine
1/4 cup smooth peanut butter

Husk corn and put each cob on a square of doubled heavy aluminum foil. Cream butter or margarine and peanut butter together and spread some of mixture on each cob.

Wrap tightly in foil and put about 3 inches from hot coals. Cook about 20 minutes, turning often. (Serves 3 to 6.)

## Baked Cucumbers

2 medium cucumbers
1 medium onion, chopped
2 tbsp. chopped parsley
1/4 cup butter or margarine
1 tsp. salt
1/4 tsp. black pepper
1/2 tsp. dried leaf marjoram

Peel cucumbers, cut into quarters lengthwise and remove seeds. Cut into pieces about 2 inches long. Put on a large piece of doubled heavy aluminum foil. Add remaining ingredients.

Wrap foil loosely around cucumber, making double folds to seal well. Cook about 4 inches from hot coals until tender, about 15 minutes. Turn package halfway through cooking. (Serves 4.)

## Eggplant Italian Style

1 large eggplant
2 tbsp. tomato paste
3 tbsp. water
2 tbsp. olive oil
1/4 cup grated Parmesan
   cheese
1 tsp. salt
1/4 tsp. black pepper
1/4 tsp. dried leaf oregano

Peel eggplant and cut into fingers about 1/2 inch thick by 2 inches long. Put eggplant on a large piece of doubled heavy aluminum foil. Combine all remaining ingredients and pour over eggplant. Stir mixture through eggplant pieces carefully to coat as much as possible. (Do the stirring with a wooden spoon or a rubber scraper so foil isn't punctured and eggplant isn't broken up.)

Wrap foil loosely around vegetable, making double folds to seal well. Cook about 4 inches from hot coals until tender, about 30 minutes. Turn package halfway through cooking. (Serves 4.)

## Savory Onions

3 large onions
2 tbsp. cooking oil
2 tbsp. white vinegar
1 tsp. brown sugar
1/2 tsp. salt
1/8 tsp. black pepper
1/4 tsp. dried leaf savory

Peel and slice onions and put on a large piece of doubled heavy aluminum foil. Turn up edges of foil a little. Combine remaining ingredients and pour over.

Wrap foil loosely around onions, making double folds to seal well. Cook about 4 inches from hot coals until tender, about 1 hour. Turn package halfway through cooking. (Serves 2.)

## Peas Amandine

two 10-oz. pkg. frozen peas
1/2 tsp. dried leaf chervil
1/2 tsp. sugar
1/4 tsp. black pepper
1/4 cup toasted slivered
   almonds
2 tbsp. butter or margarine
salt

Put peas on a large piece of doubled heavy aluminum foil. Sprinkle with chervil, sugar, pepper and almonds. Dot with butter or margarine.

Wrap foil loosely around peas, making double folds to seal well. Cook about 3 inches from hot coals until tender, about 30 minutes. Turn package halfway through cooking. Open foil and sprinkle peas lightly with salt at serving time. (Serves 6.)

## Baked Potatoes with Cheese

baking potatoes
salt and pepper
grated old Cheddar cheese
chopped parsley

Scrub as many potatoes as you need and prick all over with the tines of a fork. Cut each potato into halves lengthwise. Scoop out a heaping tablespoonful of raw potato from each half. Sprinkle each half with salt and pepper.

Combine grated Cheddar cheese and parsley, using 2 tbsp. cheese and 1 tsp. parsley per potato. Divide mixture evenly among potatoes.

Put the 2 halves of each potato together again and wrap each potato in heavy aluminum foil. Cook over hot coals, turning often, until tender, about 1 hour.

## Mixed Vegetables

Put vegetables on a large sheet of doubled heavy aluminum foil and toss together lightly. Cream butter or margarine, mustard, sugar, salt and pepper together and dot over vegetables.

Wrap foil loosely around vegetables, making double folds to seal well. Cook until vegetables are just tender, directly on hot coals for 30 to 40 minutes or 3 inches from coals for 1 hour. Turn package halfway through cooking. (Serves 4.)

$1/2$ lb. fresh green beans, cut
  in 1-inch pieces
1 medium onion, thinly sliced
  and separated into rings
$1/2$ green pepper, cut in strips
$1/4$ lb. fresh mushrooms,
  sliced
2 medium tomatoes, sliced
$1/3$ cup butter or margarine
2 tsp. horseradish mustard
1 tbsp. brown sugar
$1 1/2$ tsp. salt
$1/4$ tsp. black pepper

## Grill-Baked Apples

Wash apples and core to within $1/2$ inch of bottom. Put each apple on a square of doubled heavy aluminum foil. Mix sugar, raisins, lemon rind, cinnamon, nutmeg and salt and pile mixture into centres of apples. Dot with butter or margarine.

Wrap foil loosely around apples and twist at top to seal. Cook about 4 inches from hot coals until tender, about 30 minutes. Serve warm with cream. (Serves 6.)

6 large baking apples
$1/2$ cup packed brown sugar
$1/2$ cup seedless raisins
1 tbsp. grated lemon rind
1 tsp. ground cinnamon
$1/2$ tsp. ground nutmeg
dash salt
2 tbsp. butter or margarine
whipped cream, pouring
  cream or ice cream

## Guide for Reheating Cooked Foods in a Microwave Oven

(This is intended only as a guide for food prepared in advance to be used within a day or two. Remember, each unit added increases heating time. For thawing and reheating frozen foods see the book that came with your oven.)

| Food | Number of Units | Heating Utensil | Time | Comments |
|---|---|---|---|---|
| **Breads** | | | | |
| roll, muffin, Danish, square of coffee cake, scone, biscuit, pita, doughnut | 1 | paper plate or napkin | 10 sec. | Paper keeps bread from getting soggy on bottom. Four of any of these breads take about 50 sec. |
| French bread | 1 loaf | paper towel | 30 sec. | |
| pancakes | 3 | serving plate | 50 sec. | Uncovered. |
| waffles | 2 squares | serving plate | 25 sec. | Uncovered. |
| **Cereal** | | | | |
| long-cooking | 1 cooked portion | serving bowl | 1 to 2 min. | Uncovered. |
| **Hors d'oeuvres** (cooked ingredients) | 12 small | shallow glass baking dish | 1 to $1\frac{1}{2}$ min. | Do not spread topping on pastry, toast or cracker bases until just before heating. |
| **Sandwiches** | | | | |
| submarine or 2 pieces bread with several layers of filling | 1 | paper plate | 2 min. | Uncovered. |
| hamburger (cooked patty) | 1 | paper towel or napkin | 1 to $1\frac{1}{2}$ min. | Put patty in buttered bun and wrap in towel or napkin. Add ketchup if desired. |
| hot dog | 1 | paper towel or napkin | 30 to 35 sec. | Put wiener in buttered bun, wrap in paper towel or napkin. Add mustard if desired. |
| **Pasta** | | | | |
| spaghetti in sauce macaroni & cheese meat & noodles in sauce | 2 servings | 1-quart glass casserole | 4 to 6 min. | Cover with glass lid or transparent wrap. Stir halfway through heating. |
| cold cooked rice or pasta | 2 cups | 1-quart glass casserole | 3 to $3\frac{1}{2}$ min. | Cover with glass lid or transparent wrap. Stir halfway through heating. |
| **Main Dishes** | 2 or 3 servings | 1-quart glass casserole | 5 to 7 min. | Fill casserole $\frac{2}{3}$ full, cover with glass lid or transparent wrap. Stir halfway through heating. Let stand 5 minutes before serving. |
| | 3 to 6 servings | $1\frac{1}{2}$-quart glass casserole | 8 to 10 min. | |

| Food | Number of Units | Heating Utensil | Time | Comments |
|---|---|---|---|---|
| Stews, Curries | 2 servings | 1-quart glass casserole | 4 to 6 min. | Cover with glass lid or transparent wrap. Stir halfway through heating. Let stand 5 minutes before serving. |
| **Poultry and Meat** | | | | |
| whole cooked turkey | 8 to 10 lb. | shallow baking dish or platter | 15 to 18 min. | Remove stuffing and heat separately (7 min.). Do not cover turkey. Invert half-way through heating. |
| slices cooked turkey | whole bird 8 to 10 lb. | platter | 5 to 7 min. | Cover with waxed paper. Time depends on number of slices on platter. |
| cooked roast, chicken, or turkey | 1 serving | serving plate | 1 to 1$^1$/2 min. | Cover with waxed paper. |
| cooked sausages | 4 | paper towel on plate | 1 to 1$^1$/2 min. | Cover with transparent wrap. |
| Quiche | one 9-inch | glass pie plate | 2 to 4 min. | Allow slightly more time if very cold or very thick. |
| **Vegetables** | | | | |
| cooked vegetables | 2 servings | glass casserole | 1 to 2 min. | Cover with glass lid or transparent wrap. Do not add liquid. |
| mashed potatoes | 2 servings | glass casserole | 1 min. | Cover with glass lid or transparent wrap. Do not add liquid. |
| stuffed baked potatoes | 4 medium | serving plate | 5 min. | Time allowed for reheating from cold. |
| **Pies and Tarts** | | | | |
| pie | 9-inch 2-crust whole | glass pie plate | 4$^1$/2 to 5 min. | |
| | 1 piece of pie or 1 tart | glass or china dessert plate | 30 to 35 sec. | |

## Metric Memo

Many cooks are worried about how the metric system will affect their cooking. They tell me they don't mind new recipes being given in metric measures, but they do want to keep using their old favorite recipes and wonder how to relate ingredients that are sold in metric sizes to the old ounce and cup measures. I'm sure you've noticed that it's usually quite easy to choose a size almost identical to the size you're used to because, while more and more packages and cans are marked only in grams or milliliters, the packages and cans look very much as they always did. However, here are some hints I have found useful when buying ingredients packaged in metric sizes for use in recipes given in imperial measures.

**Relating millilitres (mL) to cups:** Since 250 mL is very close to 1 cup, you'll need to buy a 250 mL size if your old recipe calls for 1 cup, or a 500 mL size for a 2-cup recipe.

**Relating grams (g) to pounds or ounces:** Since 1 kilogram (kg) is 1000 g and a little more than 2 pounds, it's simple to calculate that you'll need 500 g if your meat loaf recipe calls for 1 lb. ground beef. If it also calls for $1/4$ lb. ground pork, you'll need to buy 125 g.

To relate grams to ounces, a useful number to remember is 28. For a rough estimate, divide the number of grams by 28 to get ounces, or multiply the number of ounces by 28 to get grams.

Of course, you'll want to continue using new recipes, and more and more you'll see metric recipes you'll be anxious to make. For these you'll need an inexpensive set of metric measuring utensils. You quite likely already have a glass measuring cup marked in milliliters. Nested dry measures in 50, 125 and 250 mL sizes and small measures in 1, 2, 5, 15 and 25 mL sizes are the other utensils you'll need.

When it comes to using recipes written in the metric way, you'll put your new measures to work, but you won't need to change such things as your appliance thermostats and utensils if you keep these things in mind.

**Relating Celsius to Fahrenheit:** If you remember that 200° C is about 400° F and 150° C is about 300° F you can easily judge the temperatures between.

**Relating metric and imperial pan sizes:** Metric pan and casserole sizes are given in liters (L) but your quart-size utensils are so close to the new sizes that you can use ones marked in the same amount — either quarts or liters — interchangeably. For example, a $1^1/2$-qt. casserole is fine when a $1^1/2$ L casserole is called for.

For baking pans, a metric ruler will be your best help. You'll find almost all your old pans are within just a fraction of the metric sizes and are perfectly usable. Since 2 inches is very close to 5 centimeters (cm), it's easy to see that a 20 cm square cake pan is about the same size as your old friend the 8-inch square.

Although this book is still in imperial measures, many ingredients are listed in metric sizes because producers are rapidly changing over to metric packaging. Before all new recipes are completely changed over, try to gradually start thinking in the metric way.

# Index

Margo Oliver, *Today Magazine's* food editor, has considerable experience in writing for Canadian cooks. From 1959 to 1979 she wrote the food column for *Weekend Magazine* and *Canadian Weekend* and in March, 1980, moved to her present position with *Today*.

During these years she has compiled many of her own and her readers' favorite recipes into five cookbooks, this being the most recent.

Margo was born in Winnipeg and took a home economics degree at the University of Manitoba, continuing her study of foods and nutrition at the University of Minnesota. From there she went to work in the Betty Crocker home service department of General Mills in Minneapolis, then moved back to Canada as the Betty Crocker representative when the company began its Canadian operation. Finally she found the work that has given her pleasure ever since — writing about food and recipes for readers across the country.

She has traveled extensively in Canada and the United States and has visited a number of countries in Europe in connection with her work. She and her husband presently live in Toronto.